MW00533861

Antony Cummins is an author and a historical researcher, as well as leading the 'resurrection' of the *samurai* school of war Natori-Ryū. He concentrates on investigating and disseminating the history of the Japanese *shinobi*. As project manager with the Historical Ninjutsu Research Team, Antony has overseen the translation and publication of multiple *shinobi* and *samurai* manuals, including: *The Book of Ninja, The Book of Samurai: Fundamental Samurai Teachings, Iga and Koka Ninja Skills, The Secret Traditions of the Shinobi, True Path of the Ninja, The Lost Samurai School* and *Samurai War Stories*. Antony has also published his own writing: two books on the *samurai* and *shinobi, In Search of the Ninja* and *Samurai and Ninja*; and a look at the darker side of Japanese folklore called *The Dark Side of Japan*. He has appeared in the TV documentaries *Samurai Headhunters, Ninja Shadow Warriors, Samurai Warrior Queens, The 47 Ronin* and *Ninja*. For more information about Antony and his team, see his website: www.natori.co.uk.

Yoshie Minami was born in Tokyo and currently lives in Saitama, Japan. She has a BA degree in Linguistics from the International Christian University. As a translator, she has worked alongside Antony Cummins to publish the following books: *True Path of the Ninja, The Secret Traditions of the Shinobi, Iga and Koka Ninja Skills, Samurai War Stories, The Book of Ninja* and *The Book of Samurai* series.

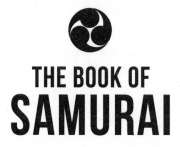

THE BOOK OF
SAMURAI

SAMURAI ARMS, ARMOUR & THE TACTICS OF WARFARE

The Collected Scrolls of
NATORI-RYŪ

ANTONY CUMMINS
& YOSHIE MINAMI

WATKINS
Sharing Wisdom Since 1893

This edition first published in the UK and USA 2018 by
Watkins, an imprint of Watkins Media Limited
Unit 11, Shepperton House, 89 Shepperton Road
London N1 3DF

enquiries@watkinspublishing.com

Design and typography copyright © Watkins Media Limited 2018

10 9 8 7 6 5 4 3 2

Designed and typeset by JCS Publishing Services Ltd
Illustrations by Jay Kane, Vangelis Drosos and Andrija Dreznjak
Calligraphy by Yamamoto Jyuho
Special thanks to Taiji Mizushima for his assistance with historical
Japanese castles

Printed and bound in the United Kingdom by TJ International Ltd

A CIP record for this book is available from the British Library

ISBN: 978-1-78678-173-4

www.watkinspublishing.com

CONTENTS

Heigu Yōhō
Important Ways On Military Tools 269

AN INTRODUCTION TO NATORI-RYŪ

LISTENING TO THE *SAMURAI*

This book was written by the seventeenth-century *samurai* tactician Natori Sanjūrō Masazumi, also known as Issui-sensei, who was to become the most influential grandmaster of the Natori-Ryū school of war. It gives us an unprecedented insight into what the *samurai* knew about their own specialization – armour and warfare. By listening to a genuine *samurai*, we can discover a huge amount about the thoughts, ideals, codes and even the feelings of this much admired, but often misunderstood, warrior class.

In 1654 Issui-sensei began his service under the Kishū-Tokugawa clan. This was a time when Japan had just come out of a long period of wars. Being born into the generation of children and grandchildren of experienced *samurai* from the age of wars, he was surrounded by peers of a much older age who had seen the great wars at first hand. Although these veterans would have passed on their knowledge directly to their sons, a lack of wars in which to put this learning into practice led to a decline in tactical and military prowess. This was the context in which Issui-sensei set about collecting a vast array of *samurai* arts, expanding his family traditions to create one of the most comprehensive warfare schools of his time.

The result of his tireless efforts is an outstanding record of *samurai* ways, from the earliest *samurai* times to his day. It allows us to trace the considerable evolution in armour, weapons and tactics over that period. We also discover that some of the misconceptions that are prevalent today had their origins in mistakes already being made by the *samurai* of the seventeenth century in interpreting earlier teachings. Through Issui-sensei's hard work, we are now able to correct these misunderstandings.

This book will show you the evolution of the first sets of 'great armour' from the days of mounted combat and horse archery all the way through to the middle period of the *samurai*. By this time armour had become more compact to adapt to the new way of grand armies of soldiers on foot on the field of battle. Although their armour may have changed, the *samurai* still revered the armour and exploits of the warriors of old, as we discover from numerous references in Issui-sensei's writings. He also tells us how *samurai* armour related to the timeless truths of Japanese mythology and cosmology. Armour carried representations of sacred boundaries, which connected the wearer to the pantheon of deities, and was designed and assembled with consideration for the wonderful interplay between *yin* and *yang* and the Five Elements. As such, a *samurai*'s armour was a map of his spiritual power and an item of prestige to be gazed upon.

ABOUT *THE BOOK OF SAMURAI* SERIES
Each book in *The Book of Samurai* series focuses on a specific aspect of historical *samurai* warfare. This volume deals with arms, armour and the tactics of warfare.

The first book in the series, *The Book of Samurai: Fundamental Samurai Teachings*, contained a translation of two scrolls:
1. *Heika Jōdan* – Discussions on *samurai* families
2. *Ippei Yōkō* – Important points for the independent soldier

This volume, the second book in the series, continues with another two scrolls:
1. *Heieki Yōhō* – Important ways on military duties
2. *Heigu Yōhō* – Important ways on military tools

The full multi-volume collection represents the whole curriculum of the *samurai* school of war known as Natori-Ryū (also known as Shin-Kusunoki-

Ryū or Kusunoki-Ryū). The school is officially and historically listed as a *gungaku* school. Meaning 'military studies', *gungaku* represents the collation of various structured teachings under one system with the aim of preserving and continuing historically accurate *samurai* ways. This makes Natori-Ryū an important cultural asset for understanding traditional Japanese ways and gives a reliable insight into the complex world of the *samurai*.

THE SCROLLS USED IN THIS VOLUME

Heieki Yōhō, the first scroll translated in this book, is divided into two parts: *Ken* and *Kon*. The first part (*Ken*) establishes the military command structure of a *samurai* army and the role that the leader plays. It goes on to give advice for a commander on a battlefield, including tactics to be used and lessons for specific scenarios. The second part (*Kon*) deals with the various positions within a *samurai* army and explains each role and its associated teachings, thereby painting a clear picture of the Japanese military machine at war.

Heigu Yōhō, the second scroll, is an extremely technical account of *samurai* arms and armour. It gives us a rare and precious glimpse into historical *samurai* equipment, allowing us to understand how *samurai* armour and weapons were constructed, their typology, the mythology connected to them, regulations relating to social status and equipment, and the designation of tools for specific tasks. From mythical legends to Buddhist doctrine, lacing manufacture to ceremonial and battle swords, this scroll holds a treasure trove of information for anyone interested in *samurai* arms and armour, which when digested and studied gives a depth of insight few people can claim.

It is our hope that the teachings in this scroll will bring to life any trip to a museum or online collection of Japanese armour. For those who wish to study the art of armour in more depth, we recommend Trevor Absolon's two volumes on the subject: *Samurai Armour (Volume I): The Japanese Cuirass* and *Samurai Armour (Volume II): Helmets, Masks and Other Armour*.

A NOTE ON TRANSLATION

As we have discussed, Issui-sensei studies ways that would have been ancient even for the *samurai* of his day during the mid-seventeenth century. Some of the military roles and positions he describes date from the heyday of the *samurai*, several centuries earlier, and some of these appear to be identical or nearly identical to other titles when they are translated into English. For example, the terms *shu* and *kun* carry different connotations but are both translated into English as 'overall commander' or 'lord' and are often interchangeable depending on the situation. Also, the role of *shō* ('general') is very similar to that of *shin* ('minister'); and *bugyō* ('commander' or 'magistrate') corresponds closely to *kashira* ('captain').

It can be difficult for a modern reader to appreciate the subtle differences between similar roles, but it would not be practical to give a fully nuanced English translation of each term every time; doing so would make for a very jarring read. Where appropriate, we give the original Japanese term as well as the English translation, so that readers can consult the glossary (see page 477) to explore the particular connotations of each position in greater detail. For the more avid student of Japanese history and warfare, the original ideograms have also been given in parenthesis whenever we think they might be useful. They may mean little to a casual reader but are invaluable to a serious student.

The text sometimes refers to Japanese positions that contain words known in English: for example, '*shōgun* of the right', '*shōgun* of the left', 'upper *shōgun*' and 'lower *shōgun*'. However, be careful not to assume that these positions correspond to our normal understanding of these terms, as they date to an earlier era than that which informs our general knowledge of Japanese history. Even for the *samurai* of the seventeenth century, much of the information contained within the text would have been ancient and complex.

Lastly, be aware that the text features a vast array of names of people, books, court titles, etc. We have often qualified these names with brief descriptions such as 'the warrior...', 'the manual...', 'the book...' and so on. These descriptions do not appear in the original text, but we have added them for clarity.

THE VOICES OF FOUR MASTERS

Although the historical texts contained within this volume were both written by Issui-sensei, as in all *samurai* schools some teachings were left to oral tradition, which is known as *kuden*. Teachings were passed down orally and then subsequent students of the school wrote and recorded them and annotated the various points, which is what has happened in these documents. This book actually has four separate authors: Issui-sensei himself and three later commentators, recorded here as commentators one, two and three, each of whom annotated a separate transcription of the texts.

The three transcriptions are now held in Tōkyō, Koga and Odawara. By comparing the different versions, we gain a much better understanding of the text and we can also see where the school branches started to diverge. The names of the commentators are unknown and the original place of writing has now been lost. However, the Odawara text appears to be the oldest; the Tōkyō script may have originally been written in Kishū domain, the home of Natori-Ryū; and the Koga transcription appears to be the most recent.

STORIES AND EPISODES

Both the main text and the commentaries often refer to well-known exploits of famous Chinese and Japanese heroes to support certain teachings. The warriors of Issui-sensei's time would have instantly understood the meaning and connotations of each story, and so these historical analogies would have helped students to digest particularly difficult concepts. Of course, the effect is not the same for modern readers, as the stories are unknown or are not found in Western culture. Therefore, understand that these stories had a purpose and view them as an opportunity for further study into Chinese and Japanese history and legend.

IMAGES WITHIN THE TEXT

All the original scrolls contain illustrations, although the quality varies between commentators. These images have been digitally recreated by replicating the best example from the three transcriptions and have been placed at the correct points in the text. However, modern illustrations have been added to clarify particularly complex teachings. These modern illustrations can be identified by the box line around them, which the digital recreations of the original images do not have (see comparison images below).

THE ORIGINAL ORDER OF THE SCROLLS

The original order of the scrolls differs slightly from the order in which they have been published in this book and in the preceding volume, *The Book of Samurai: Fundamental Samurai Teachings*.

Original order:

1. *Heika Jōdan* – Discussions on *samurai* families
2. *Heigu Yōhō* – Important ways on military tools
3. *Ippei Yōkō* – Important points for the independent soldier
4. *Heieki Yōhō* – Important ways on military duties

Published order:

1. *Heika Jōdan* – Discussions on *samurai* families
2. *Ippei Yōkō* – Important points for the independent soldier
3. *Heieki Yōhō* – Important ways on military duties
4. *Heigu Yōhō* – Important ways on military tools

The manual *Heigu Yōhō* (Important ways on military tools) seemed too technical to belong in the first volume. We have decided to move it to the second part of the second volume so that it appears after the more general information to be found in the other three scrolls.

The list of the school's main scrolls can be found at the beginning of *The Book of Samurai: Fundamental Samurai Teachings*.

DIFFICULT CHAPTERS

Any text written by a *samurai* of the seventeenth century will inevitably be somewhat intellectual in nature. However, Issui-sensei was particularly well educated, cultured and investigative, making his writing extremely well written and researched. While it is rewarding to study such a deep and complex work, it can make for difficult reading for a person in the modern era – particularly one from another culture. Many of the areas Issui-sensei covered, such as archaic army positions and the history of armour, would have been considered 'high brow' even by *samurai* readers of the time and many of them required further explanation. This was provided by the commentators and can be found in the commentary sections below each part of the main text.

Particularly difficult chapters include chapter 20 (pages 242–51) and chapter 28 (pages 353–71). To aid the flow of reading, chapters 20 and 21 have been moved from the beginning to the end of the first scroll, *Heieki Yōhō*. Because of their archaic complexity and focus on episodes of Chinese wisdom, they make for a confusing start. However, by the time that the reader reaches them at the end of *Heieki Yōhō*, he or she will be well accustomed to the terms used in the text. All of the chapters have been renumbered and some start and finish points have been changed.

The key to dealing with these difficult chapters, as with the text as a whole, is to remember at all times that teachings should not be *read* in the conventional manner, but instead should be *studied*. Students of *samurai* ways should have their notebook to hand and their mind engaged in deconstructing the text and understanding the ancient ways of the warrior.

UNDERSTANDING ARMOUR

Japanese armour is a highly specialized subject. What makes the information on armour in this book particularly valuable is that it comes not only from an actual *samurai*, but from a war-master of one of the greatest *samurai* families in history – the Tokugawa. Furthermore, Issui-sensei realized that even in his day understanding of armour was dying out and so he included as much information as he could find about archaic forms. This means that he gives us not only the correct terminology, but also the legends, styles and meanings behind armour, many of which were unknown in the Western world and some even in Japan. However, because the subject of armour is so specialized a modern reader can become lost. The following sections give you an overview of the subject, to which you can refer for clarification if you become confused.

The parts of armour

The English terms used in this book have purposely been simplified to make this complex subject as accessible as possible. Western armour is just as esoteric a subject as Japanese armour and the use of the historically correct English terms here would only have alienated the general reader. So, for example, instead of 'pauldron' we have used 'shoulder guard'; instead of 'besagew' we have used 'armpit protectors'; and instead of 'bevor' we have used 'throat protector'. Also note that we have used the widely recognized term 'chain mail' despite it being considered improper by purists.

The following diagram serves as a key to the Japanese terms used in the text.

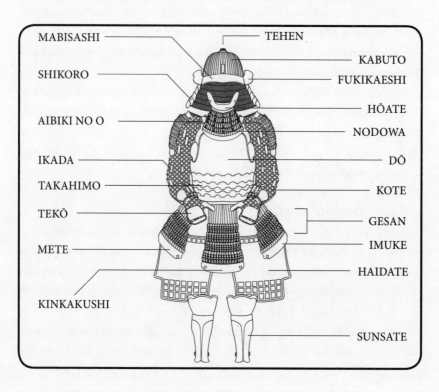

MABISASHI — TEHEN

KABUTO

SHIKORO — FUKIKAESHI

HŌATE

AIBIKI NO O — NODOWA

IKADA — DŌ

TAKAHIMO — KOTE

TEKŌ — GESAN

METE — IMUKE

HAIDATE

KINKAKUSHI

SUNSATE

The only exception to this principle is our use of the specialist term 'tasset', which we have retained to avoid confusion with *haidate* ('thigh protectors'). As shown in the image below, the tasset is a form of lower-body and upper-leg protection, which is always attached to the main body armour and is distinct from the thigh protectors below, which are a form of armoured apron.

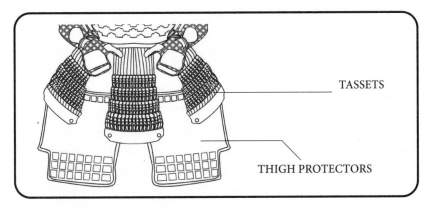

TASSETS

THIGH PROTECTORS

Archaic and compact armour

Japanese armour can be divided into two very basic categories, *ōyoroi* and *gusoku*, the former referring to armour of the early *samurai* period and the latter to armour of the middle ages. The term *ōyoroi* has been rendered as 'archaic armour', but *gusoku* is translated as 'compact armour' to highlight the

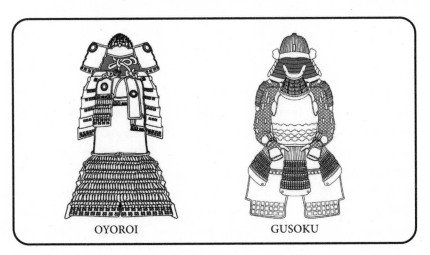

OYOROI   GUSOKU

teaching that this armour was invented for a new period in warfare in which more soldiers fought on foot rather than on horseback and so needed armour that was lighter and allowed a greater range of movement. However, the distinction between ōyoroi and gusoku is quite loose and the terms are at times interchangeable.

Plates

Traditional Japanese armour consisted of plates (*sane*), which were small lacquered slats laced together to form bands, which in turn formed the armour. At first, these small plates were made from leather, but later they were made from iron. To simplify the construction process, the small iron plates were replaced by larger single plates, but notches were cut into the tops to retain the impression of many plates laced together. After this, full plate body armour was developed, often based on European models, which were considered to be superior – even by the Japanese. Within the translation there are multiple references to *sane*, so be aware of this term.

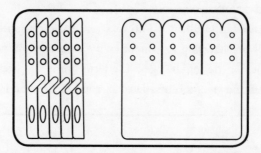

Lacing

In ancient times the colour, style and combination of colours in the lacing used to tie together plates of armour was of paramount importance to a *samurai* and often reflected a deeper meaning beyond simple decoration. Like medals and military badges do today, the colours used for lacing could inform others of a *samurai's* intent, position and affiliation.

The combination of colours used for the lacing and the plates themselves could also relate to the Five Elements from the Taoist origin-of-creation myth. For example, black represents the element of water, which nourishes the earth (represented by yellow). Therefore, armour that had black plates and yellow lacing was in a state of generation and positivity, just as water generates the 'soil' of earth. In contrast, warriors would avoid a colour combination that reflected the Cycle of Destruction.

Furthermore, lacing could graduate in colour upwards or downwards across the bands of armour, being either darker at the top or the bottom. The image below shows an example of this along with the Japanese terms.

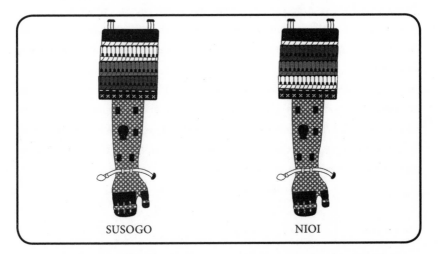

SUSOGO   NIOI

While technical in terminology, steeped in mythology and full of symbolic meaning, the subject of armour is in itself not difficult. Whenever you find a complex passage about armour, remember that the only aspects that matter are shape, colour and construction; the rest is just jargon that can always be simplified to allow for a better understanding.

JOINING NATORI-RYŪ

Natori-Ryū was formed at some point before 1570 when the Natori family served the Takeda clan during Japan's Warring Period (c1467–c1603). After the demise of the Takeda clan, the school was expanded between the 1650s and 1681 by the third grandmaster, Natori Sanjūrō Masazumi, using a branch of Kusunoki-Ryū and the collected knowledge of various other schools to supplement the teachings. The official branch serving the ruling Tokugawa clan in Kii province closed its doors in the late nineteenth century with the collapse of the *samurai* class.

In 2013 the Natori family gave their blessing to Antony Cummins to reopen the school's vast scroll collection and the annotated oral traditions from Natori-Ryū masters from ages past, which are collected here and in the first *Book of Samurai* volume. Therefore, Natori-Ryū now exists in its 'reincarnated' form with the blessing of the original Natori family and under the guidance of Monk Yamamoto, the grave-keeper of the Natori family. Monk Yamamoto and the three treasures of Natori-Ryū (the grave of Natori Sanjūrō Masazumi, his death tablet and his death record) can be found in Eunji Temple in the Japanese city of Wakayama.

This new line of the school now lives on through its current members, who are all active in bringing the teachings of the school back to life and who help to preserve historically accurate *samurai* ways. Antony Cummins, as project leader, invites you to become a fully fledged member of the school and to join others from around the world in dedicating their time to the cultural preservation of ancient Japanese ways.

For more information visit www.natori.co.uk

THE SECRETS OF
NATORI-RYŪ

The Collected Teachings of
NATORI SANJŪRŌ MASAZUMI

Heieki Yōhō

**IMPORTANT WAYS ON
MILITARY DUTIES**

KEN

THE SCROLL OF HEAVEN

CHAPTER ONE

CONCERNING THE IDEOGRAMS USED IN THE TITLE OF THIS SCROLL, *HEIEKI YŌHŌ*

Commentator one

Points on the ideograms 兵役 used in the scroll title, *Heieki*:

兵

Hei

This means an entire army and all of the soldiers within it.

役

Eki

This means the services assigned to those soldiers.

Within this scroll is a summary of all military positions, their manners and customs, including those for the *taishō* and high-ranking retainers, all the way down to every soldier and servant. Therefore, it is named *Heieki Yōhō* – Important ways on military duties.

Commentator two

This writing describes the appointed tasks of each position found within an army, from generals all the way down to the humble, and contains: leadership over an army, military schemes and plans, the way of protesting, remonstration and arguments and also of rewards and punishments. High-ranking retainers should conduct their primary roles in accordance with this writing.

In addition, this scroll will give an outline of instructions on the use of soldiers and servants, including the likes of *sarugaku* performers and even outcasts. Understand that those who simply learn these teachings without obtaining a proper understanding of them will not reach the required level of sophistication.

Issui-sensei says

Sun Tzu says:

> *The art of war is of vital importance to the state. It is a matter of life and death, a road either to safety or to ruin. Hence it is a subject of inquiry that can on no account be neglected.*

Commentator one

Taking the above into consideration, you should understand in depth [the Five Constant Factors, which are:]

1. *dō* 道 – way
2. *ten* 天 – heaven
3. *chi* 地 – earth
4. *shō* 将 – leadership
5. *hō* 法 – regulations

Mastery will become evident after you fully understand the different military services. Take heed and know that this scroll should not be ignored.

CHAPTER TWO

手柄
Tegara

ACCOMPLISHMENTS

Commentator two
These are discussions on exploits by high-ranking retainers.

ARTICLE ONE
士卒ヲ能ナツクル事
Shisotsu wo yoku natsukuru koto
BUILDING AN ATTACHMENT BETWEEN [A LEADER] AND HIS SAMURAI AND SOLDIERS

There are two ways to make other *samurai* become attached to you. These are:
1. *ōdō* 王道 – the path of the true sovereign
2. *hadō* 伯道 – the path of the conqueror

Commentator one
Ōdō, the path of the true sovereign, is to flow with normal human ways based on the true nature of human beings (人心ノ性). It is to influence people to naturally follow a leader without trying to take overt control of their minds. In this way the followers have no feelings of excitement but instead are always left feeling safe and stable.

Alternatively, the people ruled by a *hasha* (伯者) – he who follows *hadō*, the way of the conqueror – cannot live with a safe and stable feeling but instead feel excitement within the moment.

Consider these words from Mencius for yourself:

> *Under the rulership of a hasha – the conqueror type – people appear excited [in the moment], while under the rulership of an ōja – a true sovereign type – they have an air of deep contentment.*

Generally, those who discuss warfare these days tend to mix the above concepts up and try to learn the way of *ōdō* superficially and without understanding the meaning behind the words and therefore cannot grasp the essence of military affairs. To truly know a subject deeply is beyond any comparison in this world. Without becoming embedded and 'lost' [inside of a subject], how can you gain a true understanding?

Commentator two

People of the present day [in this land of peace] do not feel attached to lords who take the way of *ōdō*. Therefore, *hadō* should be used where you need to influence your men and have them decide whether to fall or prosper with you.

Examples of *hadō* include:
- If there is a single bean, a general should share it with his men.
- If there is soup of an insignificant amount, share it equally.
- When the men do not cook, [the leader] should not eat either.
- In rainy weather the general should not have war curtains raised.
- The general *should not* experience pleasure before the lord above him, but *should* endure grief before others.

Hasha – those who use the way of the conqueror – should keep the above in mind to enchant other people.

ARTICLE TWO

事ヲ不破全納ル事

Koto wo yaburazu subete osamuru koto

SMOOTH THINGS OVER WITHOUT SEVERING TIES

Commentator one

It is easy to break a situation off, but it is difficult to come to a settlement.

Commentator two

Losing your mind because of sudden anger indicates a lack of determination. It is only brute courage and has no value. Han Xin crawled between the legs of a hooligan because it was only a small humiliation compared to his later, great achievements for the Han Dynasty. Remember, it is usually easier to sever a tie than to settle a dispute. You should attain achievement by taking the difficult way, rather than ruining yourself by taking the easy way out.

ARTICLE THREE

士卒之高名能吟味シテ兵ヲ取立ル事

Shisotsu no kōmyō yoku ginmi shite hei wo toritateru koto

HAVE PROPER JUDGEMENT ON THE ACHIEVEMENT OF SOLDIERS; WITH CAREFUL EXAMINATION PROMOTE THEM APPROPRIATELY

Commentator one

Consider deeply the achievements of *samurai* and help them to develop themselves. Military codes state that if a general thirsts for those who are capable, then strategies can be conducted.

The *Three Strategies* (三略) says:

> *When rewarding, do not delay.*

Commentator two

As stated in the scroll *Ippei Yōkō*, make sure to issue reward and punishment only after careful examination. Without proper examination, the achievements of soldiers will be wasted, and soldiers will develop grudges against the lord and leave him in the end.

The *Three Strategies* says:

If the good and the evil are treated alike, the praiseworthy will grow weary.

ARTICLE FOUR
臨事不動轉驚騒事
Koto ni nozomi dōten kyōsō sezaru koto
WHEN AN EMERGENCY ARISES, DO NOT PANIC OR BE STARTLED

Commentator one
If you remain undaunted, why would you panic or become startled?

Commentator two
Being panicked or startled results from a soft and weak mind. If the general is like this, a disastrous defeat will ensue. If you have a brave and strong mind, you will not be startled or make a fuss over anything.

ARTICLE FIVE
軍備能敵知テ権ヲ不失事
Ikusa zonae yoku teki shirite ken wo ushinawazaru koto
WHEN ARRANGING THE FORMATION OF YOUR ARMY, KNOW THE ENEMY AND MAINTAIN RESPONSIVE BALANCE (KEN)[1]

Commentator one
Sun Tzu says in the chapter 'Laying plans':

---

1   See glossary for more details about the concept of *ken*. The formations are listed here (page 13) to show that a *samurai* commander must understand each one to adapt to any situation on a battlefield.

If circumstances are favourable, one should modify one's plans.

[Chinese battle] formations are the eight formations of:

1. *ten* 天 – heaven
2. *chi* 地 – earth
3. *kaze* 風 – wind
4. *kumo* 雲 – cloud
5. *ryū* 龍 – dragon
6. *tora* 虎 – tiger
7. *tori* 鳥 – bird
8. *hebi* 蛇 – snake

The Japanese version consists of:

1. *minote* 箕ノ手 – the crescent blade
2. *hōshi* 鋒矢 – the arrowhead
3. *wangetsu* 彎月 – the crescent moon
4. *ichimonji* 一文字 – the single line
5. *gankō* 雁行 – the flying geese
6. *suginari* 杉形 – an arrowhead with horizontally expanded lines
7. *gyorin* 魚鱗 – the fish scale
8. *kakuyoku* 鶴翼 – the crane's wing

Commentator two

Fully study the formations and choose the appropriate one for the situation at hand. If your strategy addresses the strength and number of the enemy, you will gain victory.

The Japanese formations are:[2]

1. *gyorin* 魚鱗 – the fish scale
2. *kakuyoku* 鶴翼 – the crane's wing
3. *hōshi* 鋒矢 – the arrowhead

---

2   The two commentators' lists differ by one name: commentator one lists *gankō*, whereas commentator two mentions *ichigyō*.

4. *ichigyō* 一行 – the single column
5. *suginari* 杉形 – an arrowhead with horizontally expanded lines
6. *ichimonji* 一文字 – the single line
7. *minote* 蓑手 – the crescent blade
8. *wangetsu* 彎月 – the crescent moon

Issui-sensei says

It is considered an achievement to administrate an army and maintain order by following the above articles.

軍戦之時堅可慎事三カ条
Gunsen no toki kataku tsutsushimu beki koto sankajō

THREE THINGS [A LEADER] SHOULD BE FULLY AWARE OF IN BATTLE

ARTICLE ONE
自分ノ働キ不可為事
Jibun no hataraki nasubekarazaru koto
DO NOT TRY TO CONDUCT YOUR OWN COMBAT

Commentator one

Generals (*shō*) should not try to enter combat themselves. Even if they attain personal achievement, they risk being killed and such an outcome would cause the men to fall into disorder, which would be extremely disloyal. It is said that large fish do not swim in shallow water.[3]

---

3   People should keep to their own responsibilities.

ARTICLE TWO
采拝能可遣事
Saihai yoku tsukau beki koto
HAVE GOOD COMMAND OF THE WAR BATON

Commentator one
Zen words say:

> 春色無高下花枝自ラ短長
> *Everything is equal in spring at its peak, though some branches*
> *in blossom are long and others are short.*

There are other secrets in the scroll on the *saihai* war baton – refer to that writing.

A poem states:

> 春さめの分て夫とハ降ねとも生る草木ノ己か品々
> *Spring showers fall equally upon the land, which allows*
> *various trees and grasses to grow in their own ways.*

Another poem states:

> 白露を紅葉におけハそのままに　おのが形をくれないの玉
> *All dew drops when appearing on autumn leaves will turn red*
> *within their own shapes.*

Commentator two
Details on the war baton are written in the scroll concerned with the *saihai* war baton.

The basic principles are:
• Point to the enemy with the top of the baton.

- Point to allies with the end of the handle.
- To order an attack pass the baton from right to left.
- To withdraw pass the baton from left to right.

To call for *toki* war cries (鬨), turn the baton above your head three times, but to call for *tsukegoe* call-and-response war cries (付声), tap the tassets of your armour with the baton.

There is an oral tradition called *kokoro no saihai* (心ノ采拝), meaning 'the mind of command', but this is not explained here.

The basic idea is just as Zen teachings state:

春色無高下花枝自長短

Everything is equal in spring at its peak, though some branches
in blossom are long and others short.

This means that, just like in a spring landscape where everything under heaven benefits equally from rain and dew to bloom and grow, so everyone should work together equally under the *taishō*'s command.

Poems state:

春雨ノワキテソレトハ降ラストモヲヽル草木ノ己カサマザマ

Spring showers fall equally upon the land, which allows
various trees and grasses to grow in their own ways.

庭ニ生ルチリヂリ草の露マデモ一ツモ日の宿ラヌハナシ

Of every single dew drop upon the leaves of various plants in the garden,
there is none that does not have the sun reflected within it.

千万ノ兵大将ノ下知ヲ受テ強弱一ハイノ働ヲスル

Upon the lord's order, vast numbers of soldiers, both strong and weak,
fight to their fullest.

This is just like the following poem:

白露ヲ紅葉ニヲケハソノママニオノカ姿ヲ紅ノ玉

All dew drops when appearing on autumn leaves will turn
red within their own shapes.

In our school, this is called *yōensui no narai* (陽炎水ノ習) – the teaching of water evaporation[4] – and is transmitted in the scroll *Kōketsu*.

ARTICLE THREE

備之手組手分手配者可隋時事

Sonae no tegumi tewake tehai ha toki ni shitagau beki koto

BUILD GROUPS OF FIVE PEOPLE AND CONSTRUCT TROOPS
BASED ON THE NUMBER FIVE AND LAY OUT THOSE TROOPS IN
APPROPRIATE FORMATIONS BASED ON THIS PRINCIPLE OF FIVE
IN ACCORDANCE WITH EACH SITUATION[5]

Commentator one

Sun Tzu says in the chapter 'Laying plans':

> *The general who wins a battle makes many calculations* (廟算) *in his temple before the battle is fought. The general who loses battles makes few calculations beforehand. This means that making many calculations leads to victory, but making too few leads to defeat.*

Commentator two

Sun Tzu says:

> *If there is no calculation then defeat is assured.*

---

4   This most likely means that the leader (the sun) can encourage unified vibrations and energy from his troops (in this case the water). The leader brings energy to the troops but all have different talents below him.

5   The references to the number five do not appear in the original text but were added by commentator one.

You can foresee who is likely to win or lose by paying attention to this point.

Consider the above three articles well and evaluate high-table battle strategy and have a clear picture of the upcoming battle itself. This should be the same [for the general] as it is for the lord (*shushō*).

CHAPTER THREE

人數積之事
Ninju tsumori no koto

ESTIMATING THE NUMBER IN AN ARMY

一軍
Ichigun
A division

This means 12,500 soldiers (*zōhyō*).

三百人武者
Sanbyakunin musha
Three hundred warriors

This means a total of 300 mixed soldiers, including fifty mounted warriors.

A group of 300 men comprises the following among others:
- *yumi* 弓 – archers
- *teppō* 鉄砲 – musketeers
- *hata* 旗 – flag holders
- *itte no taishō* 一手ノ大将 – commanders of troops
- *teaki* 手明 – unassigned men
- *umatori* 馬取 – grooms

千騎

Senki

One thousand soldiers

This means various kinds of soldiers (*zōhyō*), of which 150 will be *samurai*.

Commentator one

The estimation of the number of men has been put here to establish how many men there are in an *ichigun* single division, and how many [different types of people] there are in a *sanbyakunin musha* – a battalion of 300 warriors.

Traditionally, a *sangun* is a full force of three divisions each comprising 12,500 men, making a total of 37,500. However, any force that is subdivided into three units is generally called a *sangun* regardless of the total number of men. Types of *sangun* include:

- those under the control of the *jō-shōgun* – supreme leader
- those under the *sa-shōgun* – general of the left
- those under the *u-shōgun* – general of the right

Commentator two

To judge whether a troop is a *sanbyakunin musha* (battalion of 300 people), know that if it is it will consist of fifty mounted warriors, each of whom is accompanied by five assistants. The principle for a thousand-strong troop[6] is the same. [Each mounted warrior will have five assistants with him.] The five assistants are:

1. *kuchitori* 口取 – first groom[7]
2. *kuchitori* 口取 – second groom
3. *wakatō* 若薰 – assistant
4. *yarimochi* 鑓持 – spear-bearer
5. *gusokumochi* 具足持 – armour bearer

---

6 The troop actually adds up to 900 people: 150 warriors with five attendants each.

7 The original just states that there are two grooms, but we have itemized them separately.

備際之歩數
Sonaegiwa no hosū

CONCERNING THE DISTANCE BETWEEN UNITS IN FORMATION

- For an army of 10,000, the vanguard is positioned 60 *ken* away from the second unit.
- For an army of 5,000, the vanguard is positioned 40 *ken* away from the second unit.
- For an army of 3,000, the vanguard is positioned 30 *ken* away from the second unit.
- For an army of 1,000, the vanguard is positioned 17 *ken* away from the second unit.

For other army sizes consider the numbers above.

According to tradition, the distance between the vanguard and the command group (*hatamoto*) should be 3 or 4 *chō* maximum, even in a huge army of tens of thousands of people. However, remember that the nature of the topography will also determine positioning.

Musha warriors should march in two columns. However, marching in a single column is sometimes necessary – for example, if the road is narrow.

Commentator one
The main text describes the ancient way of determining distance between units in a formation. However, be aware that much depends on how large or small, steep or flat the area is.

If the distance between the command group and the vanguard is too great, it will become difficult to issue signals or communicate verbally.

Commentator two

It is a principle to leave space between the first and the second units. If the vanguard collapses and slides back into those behind, then both units will collapse and will be unable to withdraw. Leaving a space will avoid such a situation.

If the command group is positioned too far away from the vanguard, passwords (*aikotoba*) or signals (*aizu*) become difficult to convey. Therefore, it is a principle not to put too much distance between the *hatamoto* and the vanguard.

押次第
Oshi shidai

THE ORDER OF MARCHING

Commentator one

Since ancient times the ways of marching have been named as:

- *jūni-oshi* 十二押 – the march of the twelve units
- *jūni-dan* 十二段 – the twelve phases of the march
- *jūni-zonae oshi* 十二備押 – marching and defending in groups of twelve

PHASE ONE
先物見段々出事
MAZU MONOMI DANDAN NI DASU KOTO

Repeatedly send out *monomi* scouts at the head of the army. Shields march at the front.

The first phase of the march should include:

- *ōmatoi* – the large standard
- *samurai-daishō* – *samurai* commanders

Commentator one
Details on scouting are described in the scroll *Monomi no maki.*

Commentator two
Whether the first phase includes the *ōmatoi* (larger standard) or the *komatoi* (smaller standard) depends on the lord's clan. In either case, the standard is used to bring the army together.

PHASE TWO
軍備ノ惣旗奉行并旗持
IKUSA ZONAE NO SŌHATA-BUGYŌ NARABINI HATAMOCHI
The second phase should include:
- *sōhata-bugyō* – the chief flag commander for the formation of the army
- *hatamochi* – flag bearers

These should form two columns and should be followed by spare horses for *samurai* to ride.

Commentator one
The above troops should choose the *tachi* (great sword). There should also be *teaki* (unassigned men). The right-hand column contains men who are on duty, while the left-hand column contains those who are off duty. Helmets should be carried on the inside, while spears should be carried on the outside [of the double column].

The horses are led in a single column in the centre of the roadway.

Commentator two
The flags are for individual units. The flag bearers should be chosen for their strength and have *teaki* (unassigned men) to assist them. In older times, flags were held on horseback.

The spare horses are for ordinary *samurai* to change their mounts.

PHASE THREE

足軽大将幷弓鉄炮　次二与力

ASHIGARU-DAISHŌ NARABINI YUMI TEPPŌ TSUGI NI YORIKI

The third phase should include:

- *ashigaru-daishō* – the leader of the foot soldiers
- *yumi teppō* – archers and musketeers
- *yoriki* – captains who are attached to the *ashigaru-daishō* and who support him

Commentator one

Those leaders who have *yoriki* (attached captains) are called *ashigaru-daishō*, while those without *yoriki* are called *mono-gashira*.

PHASE FOUR

長柄奉行幷長柄持

NAGAE-BUGYŌ NARABINI NAGAEMOCHI

The fourth phase should include:

- *nagae-bugyō* – the commander of the pikemen
- *nagaemochi* – pikemen

Commentator one

Nagae can also be called *kazuyari* – loaned pikes. Labourers use pikes.

Commentator two

Pikemen are of the *ashigaru* – foot soldier class.

PHASE FIVE

持足軽大将幷弓鉄炮

MOCHI ASHIGARU-DAISHŌ NARABINI YUMI TEPPŌ

The fifth phase should include:

- *mochi ashigaru-daishō* – the commander of those foot soldiers who own their weapons
- *yumi teppō* – archers and musketeers

Commentator one

Mochizutsu (持筒) are musketeers who own their guns and *mochiyumi* (持弓) are archers who own their bows.

Commentator two

These are also called *teyumi* (手弓) archers and *tezutsu* (手筒) musketeers.

PHASE SIX
使番
TSUKAIBAN
The sixth phase should include:

- *tsukaiban* – the lord's messengers

PHASE SEVEN
持鑓奉行幷鑓持
MOCHIYARI-BUGYŌ NARABINI YARIMOCHI
The seventh phase should include:

- *mochiyari-bugyō* – commander of the *samurai* with spears
- *yarimochi* – spear-bearers

PHASE EIGHT
押太鼓螺両脇ニ武者奉行
OSHIDAIKO HORA RYŌWAKI NI MUSHA-BUGYŌ
The eighth phase should include:

- *oshidaiko* – marching drums
- *hora* – conch shells
- *musha-bugyō* – *samurai* commanders, one at each side

PHASE NINE
旗奉行中通ニ纏
HATA-BUGYŌ NAKADŌRI NI MATOI
The ninth phase should include:

- *hata-bugyō* – flag commanders
- *matoi* – standards

The *matoi* move down the centre line.

Commentator two

The standards referred to here are the *komatoi* (小マトヒ) – small standards.[8]

PHASE TEN

馬験次二軍配者

UMAJIRUSHI TSUGI NI GUNBAISHA

The tenth phase should include:

- *umajirushi* – the general's battle standard
- *gunbaisha* – esoteric tacticians

The *gunbaisha* follow after the battle standard.

Commentator one

The *umajirushi* represents the position of the army commander-in-chief. However, the location of the commander-in-chief should not always be the same.

Commentator two

As a measure of caution [in certain situations], the location of the *taishō* should vary [and be disguised] so that the enemy cannot tell where the *hatamoto* command group is.

PHASE ELEVEN

歩侍一面二横二並

KACHIZAMURAI ICHIMEN NI YOKO NI NARABU

The eleventh phase should include:

- *kachizamurai* – soldiers on foot

They cover the whole roadway.

---

8   There is a single large standard (*ōmatoi*), but multiple lesser standards.

PHASE TWELVE[9]

侍大将　次使武者二人　其両脇ニ手明ノ中間小者

SAMURAI-DAISHŌ TSUGI TSUKAI-MUSHA FUTARI SONO RYOWAKI
NI TEAKI NO CHŪGEN KOMONO

The twelfth phase should include:

- *samurai-daishō* – *samurai* commanders
- *tsukai-musha* – warrior envoys, two in number, accompanied by *chūgen* (unassigned men) and *komono* (servants) on both sides

These are followed by:

- *shoshi*– various *samurai* in two columns
- *kiba* – mounted *samurai* in two columns

Who are followed by:

- *norikake* – mounted packhorses
- *konida* – packhorses (in two lines)

At the very rear are:

- *shiriharai*[10] – rear protection troops (in two lines)

Off-duty *kashira* captains should move back and serve at the rear.

If the force is of a smaller number its packhorse train may not require a commander (*konida-bugyō*). The *shiriharai* rear protection troops, mentioned above, may be able to carry out this function.

The above describes the marching order of a single force led by a general. The marching order of a full army led by the lord (*shukun*) is described in another writing.

---

9   None of the original transcriptions lists the position of the twelfth phase; this has been inserted.

10   尻拂.

押前傳法
Oshimae denpō

TRADITIONAL WAYS OF MARCHING

Commentator one

The following points are essential for high-ranking retainers to know.

Issui-sensei says

Never let your guard down and frequently send out *monomi* scouts, especially in enemy territory where you are not familiar with the landscape. Also use guides, but remember that those guides may be spies for the enemy and may intend to lead you into a disadvantageous position.

Sometimes it is best to divide your men into two and take two different routes when marching. In this case use flags as signals between the two forces. If darkness falls and it is difficult to see these signal flags, use fire to communicate. This is done in order to rejoin forces and make camp.

Commentator one

Use flags during the day, and fire and drums during the night.

Issui-sensei says

Be aware that there are invariably ambushes to be found in:

- mountains
- valleys
- thick woodlands
- grasses

Take extra care in these places. In such a case, as well as *monomi* scouts, choose twelve *samurai* who are good at riding horses in the mountains and the valleys and also twelve soldiers on foot who have an aptitude for running in mountains and steep areas. Match one mounted *samurai* with one soldier on foot and send them to observe an area.

When upon flat land move forward while sending normal *monomi* scouts out.

Commentator one

Sun Tzu says:

> *These are places where men in ambush will wait or insidious spies are likely to be lurking.*

Commentator two

For this task, choose one mounted *samurai* and one soldier on foot from each section. The total number does not always have to be twelve; it should depend on the size of the area.

Issui-sensei says

It is sometimes the case that an army unexpectedly encounters the enemy while marching to war. Thus, prior arrangements should be made for the formation to be taken should this situation arise.[11]

When the enemy comes upon you all of sudden, do not move in surprise but follow these rules:

- If the enemy is well prepared and moves to attack while they remain firm and controlled, then also you should not rush and you should remain controlled.
- If the enemy is surprised by your presence, attack immediately.
- If you are against [a strong] wind, do not move forward, but if you have the wind at your back, advance upon the enemy.

---

11 This section was originally positioned after the section concerning the estimation of enemy army size. However, it seems more appropriate to place it here. The relevant commentaries have also been moved.

Commentator one

When marching and you come across the enemy all of sudden, you need not be afraid if you have planned in advance the correct formation to take.

It is not always the case that you should not move forward if the wind is against you. There are other factors to take into account.

Commentator two

This is for when the wind is strong and sweeping against you. In such a case you should not be the first to launch a strike. If you are attacked, of course you have to fight. You should not launch an attack [if the wind is against you] unless the enemy attacks you first. If the wind is a tailwind, it is beneficial for you to advance to attack.

三段ノ不意
Sandan no fui
THE THREE FORMS OF SUDDEN ATTACK

It is said that a *samurai* named Tada Sanpachi once told Takeda Harunobu [Shingen] that there are three oral traditions for sudden encounters.

直指ノ不意
Tadazashi no fui
THE START OF A SUDDEN ENCOUNTER

Commentator one

Take advantage of speed in this situation.

Commentator two

The initial part: a sudden encounter happens when both sides are approaching each other and one side [immediately] attacks the other where it is not well defended.

直中ノ不意
Tadanaka no fui
THE MIDDLE OF A SUDDEN ENCOUNTER

Commentator one
This is done just like when cutting a string that is stretched out.

Commentator two
The middle of a sudden encounter: this is a sudden chance in the middle of an encounter, where one side attacks when the other has not managed to settle, just like cutting a string that is stretched out.

復乗ノ不意
Norikaeshi no fui
THE LAST PART OF A SUDDEN ENCOUNTER

Commentator one
This is used when both sides have settled [after contact] and the initial pressure of the encounter has passed.

Commentator two
For a surprise attack that has settled down: do not enter combat straight away when you come across the enemy, but deaden their energy and attack them when they are insubstantial. This is to dampen and undermine the enemy's courage.

These are called *sandan no fui* – the three forms of sudden attack.

Issui-sensei says
Be fully aware of the above and conduct a sudden attack. Also, it is a well-known and commonly used tactic to attack the enemy when they are exhausted, so it is not mentioned in detail here.

Commentator one

Sun Tzu says:

Attack where they are unprepared, appear where you are not expected.

This is an example of the concept of *sho chū go* – the first, middle and end phases.

Commentator two

The *samurai* Sanpachi, mentioned above, was a retainer of Takeda Shingen and also called Awaji no kami. As Sun Tzu says in the chapters 'Substantial and insubstantial' and 'Laying plans', if you attack where you are not expected you can gain victory over an army that is larger than yours, because you will be attacking where it does not have proper defensive measures.

A poem states:

ヲノツカラ理ハアリ明ノモノナカラ開ク扉ニ月ソ入ケル
*You may be certain of your victory with the coming of dawn,
but the moment you open the door, a ray of moonlight will enter.*[12]

Issui-sensei says

When coming across an enemy, do not try to construct formations without having planned them. First, form a circle and then start constructing your formation with the rear unit. Do this without making fuss.

Tradition says that in such a case you should not pay attention to lower-ranking warriors, but give consideration to the commander-in-chief (*taishō*), generals (*shinka*) and captains (*kashira*).

Commentator one

In a sudden encounter with the enemy while you are on the march, it is a general principle that formations should not be built in haste, but time and consideration should be taken.

---

12 This poem is also found in the *Shōninki* manual.

Commentator two

If you encounter the enemy while marching, build a circular formation. This will make it harder for the enemy to attack. If the front line is close to the enemy, confusion tends to set in; therefore, you should first establish a strong foundation [starting with the rear troops].

HEAVY SNOW FALL

Issui-sensei says

If heavy snow falls while you are marching, everyone should dismount and have the horses lead [each warrior] of the army.

Commentator one

There is a theory about the use of old horses concerning this point.

Commentator two

Have horses go ahead to tread down the snow. This is also connected to ancient episodes about old horses.

AMBUSHES

Issui-sensei says

If you think that the enemy is going to attack in a large number [based on the number of troops you have observed], but in actual fact they attack in a smaller number than anticipated, then you should expect an ambush or troop stationed to attack from your rear. Also, consider the number of troops in an ambush. If the number about to engage you is too small, know that more people will be stationed elsewhere. Attack only after careful consideration.

Commentator one

The art of *tachikurabe* – a rough comparison of numbers – is required in a case like this.

Commentator two

This estimation is called *tachikurabe no san* – estimation by comparison – and is a tradition found in the scroll *Dakkō Shinobi no Maki*. It involves estimating the enemy number based on their resources.

MOUNTAINS

Issui-sensei says

In high mountains, deep valleys and those places where people have difficulties moving, only the vanguard should go forward. Once they have passed such a place, they should move into [a defensive] formation. They should leave a space for horses to advance, and prepare themselves as if facing an enemy. After this, the rest of the troops should pass through in order. The rear units should hold in formation [in their original position] until the troop containing the *taishō* has passed through; again they should act as if facing an enemy. After the *gogun* (五軍) Five Divisions have passed the difficult place in question, move forward in the correct order, starting with the vanguard.

There are other points within the traditions, but as there are no special notes for those elements they have been omitted here.

Commentator one

The above method should also be applied when crossing a river.

Commentator two

The vanguard should move into formation when they have crossed a difficult area, while the rear group should maintain a tight formation until the *taishō* has crossed over. The *gogun* (五軍) Five Divisions consist of:

1. *zen* 前 – front
2. *go* 後 – rear
3. *sa* 左 – left
4. *yū* 右 – right
5. *hatamoto* 旗本 – command group

Tradition says that when you come upon a marsh, build lattices of bamboo by tying them together and putting straw mats over them to cross the marsh. If there is no bamboo, tie spears together instead.

It is said that when you are on an enemy mountain in an enemy province to which you have never ventured before, consider the element of the unfamiliar mountain to know if you can get your army through without getting stuck.

Generally, a mountain is least steep on one side and steepest on the opposite side.

[The elements connected to mountains:]

- A mountain facing[13] east is of the Wood element.
- A mountain facing south is of the Fire element.
- A mountain facing west is of the Metal element.
- A mountain facing the north is of the Water element.
- A mountain facing in the direction of the ox, ram, dragon or dog is considered to be of the Earth element.

If you climb a mountain of the Wood element from the east, then you will be climbing up the least steep side, which means that your army should not become stuck. If you climb it from the west, you will be approaching from the steepest and most difficult side. The other types of mountain should be considered in the same way.

Furthermore, there is another type of mountain, which has a central summit that is flat both to the front and to the rear.

WEST   EAST   CENTRE

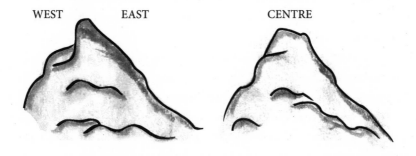

---

13 In this list, the shallowest side of the mountain is described as its front, so the direction in which it faces is the least steep side.

A mountain is characterized by the direction where it has a wider base. Details are written in the scroll *Jūzan no Maki*.

Commentator one
The above teachings are found in the *Kōyō Gunkan* war epic.

Issui-sensei says
Although there are many theories concerning marching, the above teachings should be used as principles. Adapt them according to the situation.

凡押前ニ臨テ諸士可申渡事

Oyoso oshimae ni nozomite shoshi ni mōshiwatasu beki koto

ANNOUNCEMENTS TO MAKE TO ALL *SAMURAI* BEFORE MARCHING

Commentator one
These announcements differ from one clan to another and they may vary depending on the mind of the general (*shō*). Older methods have been outlined here.

Issui-sensei says
During a campaign, make sure that all soldiers, high or low, march in a good order and in proper rows and never go against the orders of the general (*shō*). If someone becomes ill on the march while still in your own province, leave them in a residence along the road and have someone stay behind to take care of them. This will help them to rest and recuperate. Once recovered from the illness, they are required to rejoin the rest of the force. Anyone who does not do so should be convicted. If the person dies from the illness, the other person left

to care for them should see to the corpse. Know that even though they have not died in battle, they should be treated as if they had. The captain and his group should organize prayers for the dead as if he were a part of their own family. Not giving the dead a proper burial should be considered a sin as serious as abandoning a friend.

Commentator one

There is a tradition called *atarikuji*, meaning to draw lots, and this is the system you should use to select the person to be left behind to take care of the sick person.

Commentator two

If someone falls ill on the way, leave someone behind to care for them. However, warriors, who are motivated to fight, will not want to carry out this duty, even if they share the same surname and clan as the sick person. Therefore, a lottery system should be used. There is a tradition called *atarikuji* – to draw lots.

The 'group' mentioned above means the five-man squad that the dead person belonged to.

Commentator three

I think that any *samurai* would prefer to remain with the fighting force than stay behind to take care of an ill person, even if the ill person were a colleague from the same group. Do not decide who should stay behind without due care and attention. This is an example of one of the systems that should be put in place before departing for war. Each squad of five should draw lots between them. There is an important tradition for this.

Issui-sensei says

Unauthorized pillaging is forbidden. In the case of authorized pillaging, there should be arrangements concerning the order in which different units pillage.

Commentator one

A lot system can also be used for this situation.

Commentator two

Details are mentioned in the scroll *Ippei Yōkō*. There are rules for when each troop can pillage – the first unit followed by the second unit, etc. It should not be done without full control. The first thing to be collected is military gear, then food and finally gold and silver.

Issui-sensei says

While marching the following should be prohibited:

- *noriai* 乗合 – skirmishes between mounted warriors
- *kenka* 喧嘩 – brawling

Commentator one

Know that these fights stem from personal grudges.

Issui-sensei says

When putting straw shoes on a horse, lead the horse to either side of the road and fix the shoes in place. Whenever issues of this nature arise, move to the roadside and return to the correct position within the procession afterwards. When servants have to change straw sandals, it should be done in the same manner. It is a chargeable offence to create disarray.

Commentator one

The above should be repeatedly instructed.

Commentator two

Even if you have many servants, take only two or three with you when you have to leave the procession to attend to a matter, then return to your original position. Make sure not to become separated from your armour and spear-bearers at any point.

Issui-sensei says

Each soldier should carry rations on his waist. Anyone who does not should be charged.

Commentator two

Katō Kiyomasa once discovered that one of his page boys (小姓) was not carrying rations with him. Kiyomasa was enraged and scolded the boy, saying that a preference for graciousness or elegance was totally inappropriate in such a situation and that it was considered an act of misconduct not to carry rations during a campaign.

Issui-sensei says

[When marching] strictly follow the [instructions of the] signal flags and drums given from the vanguard and wait for any reports.

Commentator two

The *taishō* should give the order that signals from the vanguard are to be followed so that there is no confusion. If any instructions are given, do not make a fuss and do not lose your concentration.

Issui-sensei says

Until you receive a report from the vanguard [confirming the matter], do not assume that the enemy are upon you and do not fall into confusion by jostling each other, clashing with armour boxes, etc. Remember that signals will come from the vanguard and that you must deal with any situation appropriately. Armour box carriers and spear-bearers should not leave their master's side. This should be strictly enforced as a rule beforehand and charges should be brought [against those who fail in this duty].

Also, be wary of riding a vicious horse.

Commentator one

Vicious horses can injure not only the rider but also other people.

Commentator two

Vicious horses may cause trouble not only to the rider but also to other people. Judge them appropriately before marching. Details of this are written in the scroll *Ippei Yōkō*. Make sure that you are aware that vicious horses should be avoided.

Issui-sensei says

It is prohibited to fight over position, to argue, to speak loudly or to speak ill of others. It is also prohibited to be startled by the enemy.

Commentator two

Do not fight over position, but defend the position to which you have been assigned. It is prohibited not to take the precise position allocated to you.

Issui-sensei says

When marching, keep quiet so that the drums or conch shells can be heard easily, and be careful not to cause the procession to fall into disarray.

Commentator two

Do not cause the procession to fall into disarray as the enemy will take advantage of this.

Issui-sensei says

Furthermore, when marching depart at the hour of hare (5–7am) and stop to lodge at the hour of ram (1–3pm), but this can be altered according to the situation. The [daily] marching distance is 5–6 *ri*. If approximately 1,400–1,500 people – including mounted and other soldiers – march in one line, it will extend for 24–5 *chō*. This is calculated from the estimation of 1 *ken* per person with horse.

Commentator one

These are estimates and should not be treated as definitive.

Issui-sensei says

The above selection of points should be strictly adhered to. Have good judgement and make new rules if the situation demands it.

Tradition says that it is a principle that after travelling 5 *ri*, the first two units should secure their position. The general (*shō*) accompanied by approximately ten mounted warriors and thirty foot soldiers[14] should investigate a surrounding area of 2 *ri* square.

All soldiers are to be forbidden from constructing and entering camp huts before the general returns [from his investigation of the area]. When the general returns, he himself should go around the camp to check the huts [after they have been constructed] and give instructions for the defence of the guardhouses and gates. Without an order from the *taishō*, no one should be allowed to enter any huts or unsaddle their horses.

備形間積之事
Sonaegata kenzumori no koto

ESTIMATING THE SIZE OF AN ARMY BY THE AREA IT OCCUPIES WHEN IN POSITION

An army that occupies a space measuring 60 *ken* in width and 30 *ken* in depth is estimated to include 2,700 people. This is based on a square of 2 *ken* being able to accommodate one mounted warrior and his five attendants.

Commentator two

Divide the width of 60 *ken* into squares of 2 *ken* and you will end up with thirty squares along the front edge. Next, divide the depth of 30 *ken* into squares of 2 *ken* to get fifteen squares down the side and multiply by the thirty squares along the front. This gives a total of 450 individual squares of 2 *ken*. If a single 2 *ken* square can contain six people – one master and his five servants – then 450 squares will contain 2,700 people in total.

---

14 The Tōkyō transcription states that there should be thirty mounted warriors and ten foot soldiers.

Issui-sensei says

The same size square can contain 16 foot soldiers. Tradition says that the measurement of 1 *tsubo* can contain four warriors.

Commentator two

Alternatively: a 60 *ken* by 30 *ken* area is equivalent to 1,800 *tsubo* and since 1 *tsubo* can contain four people, the total number will be 7,200 people.

Issui-sensei says

A circular formation will tend to contain a larger number of people than estimated, because of the space inside the formation.[15] However, if you apply the above method you will not go too far wrong.

Each clan has its own way of estimating numbers of people; there is no universal method.

It is essential for generals (*shin*), captains (*kashira*) and commanders (*bugyō*) to have a good command over all the *samurai* and soldiers and a good understanding of responsive balance (*ken*). Not following orders given by a general should carry an instant charge without having to report the matter to the *taishō*. If any captain or commander gives priority to his own combat over [taking responsibility for] his men in battle, he should be punished immediately.

If a general entrusts more people to a *samurai* than he is able to manage, then it is the general who is at fault. For example, if a *samurai* wants to be entrusted with 100 men, consider the capability of the *samurai* and entrust him with about half that number. If he is entrusted with fewer men than would be expected, it will improve his ability to advance and retreat [and give him mobility in battle]. With a small number of men he will not be beaten, even if the enemy force is large. A saying goes: 'In the use of people, 1 *shaku* may be too short in some places while 1 *sun* may be too long in another.'[16] Tai Gong's method for selecting warriors teaches that you should assign roles to people according to what they excel at.

---

15 This text is not entirely clear, but the point may be that, because the number of soldiers in a circular formation is harder to calculate, you need to be careful not to underestimate the total.

16 Use things and people appropriately according to their abilities.

CHAPTER FOUR

選士法
Senshi no hō

THE WAY OF SELECTING *SAMURAI*

ARTICLE ONE

Assemble those who resent being poor and who are endeavouring to gain achievement, that is those whose first priority is to increase their wealth when opportunity presents itself even at the risk of their lives. Use them where an intense assault is needed to smash the enemy.

Commentator two

Examples include the warriors Oyamada Tarō and Sano Genzaemon [who are mentioned in the *Taiheiki* war chronicle].

ARTICLE TWO

Assemble those who are young, light-footed and good at running. Have them detect ambushes, scout at a distance and other such tasks.

Commentator two

There are lots of examples of *samurai* of this kind, such as the warrior Hiramatsu Kinjirō.

ARTICLE THREE

Assemble those who have superiority over other people in bravery and are strong. Use them to attack castle gates, break fences, backfill moats and other similar tasks.

Commentator two

During the battle of Miidera on the sixteenth day of the first month in Kenmu 2 (1335) when Hosokawa Zenjō led an army of 60,000 people, the warriors Kuryū Saemon, Shinozuka Iga no kami, Hata Rokurōzaemon and Watari Shinzaemon crossed over the moat and the bridge and succeeded in breaking through the gate.

ARTICLE FOUR

Assemble those whose talk is fluent and who are intellectual. Have them encourage other warriors or work as spies (*kanchō*).

Commentator two

One example is the warrior Ina Zusho. Also [remember the episode of the] seventy-two castles during the Qi Dynasty of China, which were brought to surrender through just speech [not force].

ARTICLE FIVE

Assemble those who have expertise in archery and gunnery and use them when you need to sweep away [the enemy].

Commentator two

Examples include the warriors Honma Magoshirō and Sōma Shirōzaemon. Also the thirty warriors who served Lord Kusunoki and the sixteen warriors who served [Nitta] Yoshisada. Furthermore, consider the Four Heavenly Kings who serve generals.[17]

ARTICLE SIX

Assemble those who are accomplished in *bugei* martial arts and who excel in bravery. Use them to fulfil any urgent commands that the *taishō* has and to carry out sudden, unexpected attacks.

---

17 Originally deities, but in this context key people who protect a lord or general.

Commentator two

This is a reserve troop for irregular purposes.

ARTICLE SEVEN

Assemble those who are courageous, tend to take matters seriously and do not fear death. Have them serve as *fuse* ambush [troops], *sakigake* leaders in attacking or *shingari* rear troops.

ARTICLE EIGHT

Assemble those who are cowards and who are timid and use them as gate keepers, watch-fire keepers and members of night patrols.

Commentator one

The ideogram for coward – 臆 – represents those things that should be avoided concerning matters of *bu* (military service). Sometimes it may be the case that people are just ill or exhausted. Furthermore, for night patrols use those who are hardworking.

Commentator two

These people have their own captain to direct them.

Commentator three

This also applies to those who are feeling hesitant because of illness or tiredness and cannot fight fiercely. For night patrols, hardworking *bushi* should be used.

ARTICLE NINE

Assemble those who are old or ill and have them administer the rations, gunpowder and so on.

ARTICLE TEN

Assemble those who have a good knowledge of other provinces. Send them to those places that they are familiar with and use them as *kanja* spies or guides.

Commentator two

These people include:

- *shinobi no mono* – infiltrators
- *Kōka no mono* – men of Kōka
- *bu* – lower soldiers[18]
- *chūgen* – lower people

They are not *bushi* warriors.[19]

ARTICLE ELEVEN

Assemble those who are experienced at swimming and those who perform sneaking and thievery (細入)[20] including those who are thieves themselves (盗). Have them hear what the enemy say and observe the situation of the enemy province. Also they should be used for crossing rivers.

Commentator one

These people include:

- *shinobi-mono* – infiltrators
- *Kōka no mono* – men of Kōka
- *kachi* – those on foot
- *chūgen* – lower troops

Are these not *bushi* warriors?[21]

Commentator two

Just like in the previous article, these are not *bushi* warriors.

---

18 The ideogram for this category of soldier is 夫. It is different from the other meaning of *bu*, pertaining to *samurai*.

19 The commentators are writing after the fall of the *shinobi*, when professional *shinobi* such as the men of Kōka and Iga had been relegated to a lower class, and the commentaries relate solely to this later period. It should be noted that the commentary directly contradicts the *Shōninki*, which states that the role of *shinobi* should be carried out by a *bushi* warrior. Commentator two is sure in his position that this is not a role for *bushi* – compare with Commentator one's more uncertain note on article eleven.

20 The text states the pronunciation of these ideograms as *sei*. However, they are commonly read as *hosoiri* and mean 'sneak-thief'.

21 It appears in this commentary it is asking, should they be *bushi* or not?

ARTICLE TWELVE

Assemble those who have been charged as criminals in an enemy province and who have fled to your own province. Interrogate them on the status or mindset of the enemy, the way of their ministers and other points and then have them join the vanguard.

Commentator one

In the Kōshū-Ryū school, it is said that it is most effective to put those who surrender in the vanguard.

Commentator two

In the Kōshū-Ryū school, those who surrender and *karimusha* temporarily hired warriors are positioned in the vanguard. Details are mentioned in the scroll *Ippei Yōkō*.

ARTICLE THIRTEEN

The following and other such [specialists] are to be positioned where they are needed:

- *isha* 醫者 – doctors
- *gakusha* 学者 – scholars
- *tenmonsha* 天文者 – astrologists and astronomers
- *gunbaisha* 軍配者 – esoteric tacticians

Furthermore, craftsmen (細工人) should also be positioned where they are needed.

Commentator one

These four types of people are attached to the *hatamoto* command group. This teaching is from the *Kōgun Suchi* (行軍須知) manual.

ARTICLE FOURTEEN

Assemble those who have a good command of dialects from different provinces and use them for strategy and where they need to be mixed in with the enemy.

ARTICLE FIFTEEN

Assemble left-handed archers. Use them to attack the enemy by shooting from both sides.

Commentator one

This is taken from the *Sashiteikō* (左師堤綱) text.

Commentator two

There are not many left-handed archers [in Japan], but there are a lot in China.

ARTICLE SIXTEEN

Assemble descendants of *daimyō* and prestigious families that have fallen on hard times. This [fall from grace] makes them ambitious and eager to follow their ancestors by accomplishing great exploits. They are called *shitō no shi* – *samurai* who fight to the death.

Commentator two

There are many examples of *samurai* of this kind, such as those at the siege of Ōsaka castle. The warrior Kiso Yoshinaka is another example.

ARTICLE SEVENTEEN

Assemble descendants of those who were killed in battle and who are anxious to avenge their ancestors. They are called *shifun no shi* – death-enraged *samurai*.

Commentator two

Examples include the warriors Minamoto no Yoritomo, Minamoto no Noriyori, Minamoto no Yoshitsune, Nitta Yoshimune, Nitta Yoshioki and Wakiya Yoshiharu.

ARTICLE EIGHTEEN

Assemble those whose ancestors brought dishonour upon themselves, as their descendants wish to clear such disgrace by dying with good grace themselves. They are called *kōyō no shi* – *samurai* who are eager to be used.

Commentator one

The above is taken from the manual *Goshi Heikan* (呉氏兵鑑) by Wu Zi.

Commentator two

Itō Kurō Sukekiyo is an example of this. The above is mentioned in the document *Heikyō* (兵鏡) by Wu Zi.

Issui-sensei says

I think that the last three types of people will all readily risk their lives. Use them when the situation is difficult and the enemy is strong.

CHAPTER FIVE

Li Gang[22] says that when a society enters into turbulent times, it is always the case that rogues and commoners who have left their homeland band together and become thieves. Do not try to put each of them to death, as it is impossible to kill and destroy them all. Instead, invite such thieves into service and use them for your own interests.

THE FIVE ADVANTAGES OF USING THIEVES

ADVANTAGE ONE

No one will suffer from thievery in your own province.

ADVANTAGE TWO

You can use thieves to defend against the enemy.

Commentator one

Thieves are determined and energetic and will risk their lives to take treasures, but employing too many of them may be a mistake. Use them to set fires on the enemy camp and other such acts [of subterfuge].

ADVANTAGE THREE

If people of good nature have been threatened [and forced] to work for the thieves, allot paddy fields to them. This will result in there being no wasteland.

---

22 Of the Southern Song Dynasty (1127–1279).

ADVANTAGE FOUR
Thieves who demonstrate bravery while in service can be promoted to *samurai*.

Commentator two
This is what happened to the warrior Ise no Saburō Yoshimori.

ADVANTAGE FIVE
As thieves are basically expendable, if they succeed it is a positive outcome and if they die they will not be missed. It is essential that the *taishō* should control such rascals to fulfil his wishes. He should command them with spirit so that they will become appreciative and be indebted to the lord, and feel an attachment to him.

Commentator two
Break rascals in as you would a horse, so that they feel truly indebted and well disposed to you.

THE FIVE DISADVANTAGES OF USING THIEVES

DISADVANTAGE ONE
Thieves have an egotistical and violent mind and little by little it has to be straightened.

DISADVANTAGE TWO
They are accustomed to taking other people's property, which they will eventually do one way or another. It is difficult to restrain such a greedy mind.

DISADVANTAGE THREE
If the *taishō* is replaced, thieves may form doubts and turn traitor.

DISADVANTAGE FOUR

If you do not apply military codes correctly to them, they will easily turn to betrayal.

DISADVANTAGE FIVE

If you show thieves too much favour, they will become arrogant and if they have an overbearing nature, they will turn to anger and be difficult to manage.

Following the above teachings, the *taishō* should treat thieves with both favour and dignity so that their minds will naturally reform and become as normal people's are.

GATHERING TROOPS

When things are turbulent in all the provinces, it is desirable to gather as many people together as possible.

Commentator one

The *Three Strategies* says:

> *If the state is governed well and families are kept in safety, the trust of the people will be gained. If the state is lost and families ruined, the trust of the people will be lost.*

Issui-sensei says

He who invites and gathers ten *rōnin* should be assigned as the *kashira* captain of ten people, and he who invites and gathers 100 people should be the *shō* commander of 100 people. This will mean that people invite and gather more troops and soon [another] general will be needed. When gathering *rōnin* do not spare gold and silver, rice or money; this is called *seiroku* (征録) – campaign stipend.

Commentator two

This is found in the *Hokuseiroku* (北征録) manual.

Issui-sensei says

Generally, one who is superior over ten people should be assigned as *kashira* captain of ten people; one is superior over 100 people should act as the captain of 100 people; and one who is superior over 1,000 people should serve as the captain of 1,000 people. It is vital for the *taishō* to select the correct people. Sometimes, nine out of ten elements should be thrown away because of a single element, while in other cases a single element should be thrown away over the nine.[23] For that which is good or bad, remember the ratio of six to four, use it according to the situation.[24] Use people according to their abilities: for example, deaf people burn and keep watch fires, while blind people operate signal clappers. The *taishō* should be discerning in his use of people so that none of their abilities is wasted.

Commentator two

It is the *taishō*'s prerogative to ignore nine benefits [in a person] to avoid one flaw, or to ignore nine flaws to gain one benefit, or they may instead choose the concept of a four to six ratio. Remember, hawks are useless in water, while cormorants are not built to ascend a mountain.

---

23 In an otherwise praiseworthy person, there may be a single negative element that stops a commander using them; or, conversely, a commander may overlook a person's many bad points because that person has one important positive quality. This 90/10 principle may be weighted towards either the positive or the negative, meaning that even the worst person can be used for something or that the best applicant for a position may be refused because of a single failing.

24 This 60/40 principle is a less extreme version of the 90/10 principle.

CHAPTER SIX

BATTLE FORMATIONS

Details of essential military skills (*gunjutsu*) are given in the chapter 'Shō no maki' ('The ways of the general'), which is also known as the scroll *Kundō Yōhō*. As these details are in depth, they will not be mentioned here.

Formations and the designation of warriors are to be transmitted later.

It is a general principle to apply *ken* (権) responsive balance in warfare. Also, the setting out of warriors and military formations are dependent on the mindset [of the lord].

If the politics [of the lord] are on the right path, soldiers will automatically be obedient and keep to the rules and be well mannered. A lord who follows the correct path will achieve victory without fail, while one who is not on the correct path and who leads a band of rascals will lose without fail. According to the writing *Gunpō Denju* (軍法傳授), the formal way for the allotment of warriors is to use *seiden no hō*, the ancient Chinese way of allotting land by dividing a large square into nine sections.

[The ideogram *sei* represents the division of fields.]

Use this [the ideogram above] as a basis and then construct a formation upon it. Alternatively, apply Zhuge Liang's (孔明) eight Chinese formations as a starting point. It is said today that formations should be adapted according to the situation and that there is no established method. However, know that there are sixty-four formations. These are described in another writing.

Formations can be based on units of five, starting with a group of five people.

This principle is used in the eight Chinese formations. An *itte* single troop is constructed of combinations of groups of five – there is a tradition for this.

If you assemble troops [from groups of five], you can create a *shibukōjin* (四武衡陣) formation. This positions the *taishō* in the centre and then the troops on the four sides [surrounding the *taishō*] are allowed to move [in accordance with the situation].

This is also called *shihō* (四方), the four ways, and consists of the following:
1. *senjin* (先陣) – front position
2. *kōjin* (後陣) – rear position
3. *ujin* (右陣) – right position
4. *sajin* (左陣) – left position

These can interact [with the enemy] in all eight directions (八方) [giving all-round protection].

These are just the basic principles and can be adapted according to the situation and the needs of the battle.

Commentator two

Use the concept of *ken* (権) in warfare: *ken* refers to the weights used on a scale, thus the concept involves positioning [your forces] with 'good balance' according to how strong and substantial the enemy is. On a balancing scale, one *sen* coin perfectly balances with one *sen* coin, and 100 *sen* coins balance with 100 *sen* coins. The arrangements for positioning warriors or for a battle formation should wholly depend on the mind of the *taishō* and can be adapted according to the situation. Therefore, do not transmit rigid, unchangeable formations.

As described earlier [in the main text], a wise lord-general can command an army of soldiers with excellence and bring them together under his command. When serving under such a leader, troops can advance or retreat in accordance with any changes, and they can defeat an enemy of a large number, even if they are few. This is a sure way to achieve victory.

If the *shō* general is wicked and not correct, he cannot properly administer to his forces and the *shisotsu* soldiers will not be united under him and they will not be under correct command. As they are not under correct command, they cannot advance or retreat in order and they will be defeated by a small number even if they are in fact large in number.

The arrangements for positioning warriors should be based on the concept of *seiden no wari* (井田ノ割). This is transmitted in the scroll *Hachijin no Maki*.

The diagram below represents the concept and formation of *seiden no wari*.

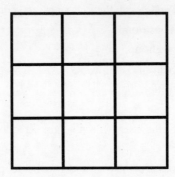

The way of formations should be based on Zhuge Liang's (孔明) eight Chinese formations. These are:

1. *ten* 天 – heaven
2. *chi* 地 – earth
3. *fū* 風 – wind
4. *un* 雲 – cloud
5. *ryū* 龍 – dragon
6. *ko* 虎 – tiger
7. *chō* 長 – long [bird]
8. *da* 蛇 – snake[25]

In this way an army is arranged in the eight directions and these eight battle formations are based on the *hakke* – the eight trigrams [found in the *I Ching*] and they are as follows:[26]

---

25 This list differs from other versions and some are matching pairs, i.e. heaven and earth, wind and clouds.

26 These are the eight basic Chinese trigrams, which are presented here with the Chinese transliteration first, then the Japanese equivalent in brackets. See also *The Book of Samurai: Fundamental Samurai Teachings*, pages 251–7.

1. *qian (ken)* 乾 – heaven
2. *dui (da)* 兌 – marsh
3. *li (ri)* 離 – fire
4. *zhen (shin)* 震 – thunder
5. *xun (son)* 巽 – wind
6. *kan (kan)* 坎 – water
7. *gen (gon)* 艮 – mountain
8. *kun (kon)* 坤 – earth

[The basic building blocks of the universe are] the *gogyō*, the Five Elements:
1. *sui* 水 – Water
2. *ka* 火 – Fire
3. *moku* 木 – Wood
4. *kin* 金 – Metal
5. *do* 土 – Earth

Create bodies of men based on the number five, but know that this also represents a human being as each human has five fingers on each hand.

Furthermore, consider the four factors of:
1. *dai* 大 – large
2. *shō* 小 – small
3. *chō* 長 – long
4. *tan* 短 – short

By taking the above into account, [an army] will work correctly.

Therefore, a single troop is called *itte*, which means 'a single hand' – this refers to the way of assembling troops in units of five and follows the Five Elements principle, which highlights the exquisiteness of nature.

To assemble a formation in the way of *shibukōjin*, as mentioned previously, means to position the *taishō* in the centre and put regular and irregular elements in all four directions [around the *taishō*]. This is so the front can protect the rear, and the right can protect the left, and any direction can function as the front line. This is an exquisite and unequalled formation that can cope with any situation when applied in conjunction with the principle, discussed by Sun Tzu, of the head and tail working together. In addition to this is the principle of *sotsuzen no sei* (卒然ノ勢) – sudden strike forces – but all will be transmitted in the scroll *Hachijin no Maki*.

The idea of facing all directions is known as *happōshōmen* (八方正面) – to have a front in all eight directions. Know that this means that [when in a square formation] it should be solid on all four sides and have structure at all four corners. Know also that castle turrets apply the concept of *happōshōmen*, meaning that they are well defended and secure all the way around, and the same concept is applied in castle grounds. In all cases it means to be solid on all four sides and at all four corners [and to observe all eight directions].

The diagram below represents the concept and formation of *shibukōjin*.

If the enemy attacks from the top, the right will work as irregular and win a victory. Thus every direction can be the front line troops.[27]

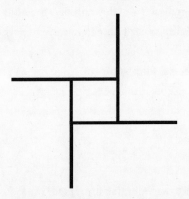

Tradition says that when considering the options listed below, know that they are decided by nothing but the time of heaven, the advantage of earth and harmony among the people.

---

27 The idea here is that no matter which direction the enemy attacks from, the allied formation is flexible enough to counter the attack from another side rather than just meeting it head on.

- attacking (懸) or standing by (待)
- regular (表) or irregular (裏)
- correct order (順) or reverse order (逆)
- straight (直) or twisted (曲)
- detached (離) or joined (逢)
- to employ (用) or to discard (捨)
- moving (動) or still (静)
- good (善) or evil (悪)
- easy (易) or difficult (難)

Remember that all these are subjective matters and based on the concept of *setsu* (節) timed judgement.[28] They should all be understood in relation to the enemy. No one perfectly understands the correct time for change, because all things that occur under heaven and on earth are dictated by laws that are beyond human nature.

Commentator two

'Time of heaven' includes, among other factors:
- *nichiji* 日時 – date
- *shi* 支 – the twelve-sign zodiac system
- *kan* 干 – the ten celestial signs
- *ko-kyo* 孤虚 – auspicious and inauspicious directions
- *ōsō* 王相 – the energy of each season

'Advantages of earth' include:
- distant (遠) or close (近)
- steep (険) or flat (易)
- large (廣) or small (狭)
- life (生) or death (死)

28　This term is extremely difficult to convey in English and deeper or alternative meanings can be attached to it.

'Harmony of people' means that all people, both upper and lower, are united as one body.

All will depend on the general's decision. It is appropriate to fully understand these principles and always to be flexible. Understand the concept of *setsu* (節) balanced judgement; this is to be completely flexible in accordance with the situation, being and doing neither too much nor too little. Details are mentioned in the chapter 'Heisei' (兵勢), 'The energy of the army', in Sun Tzu's *Art of War*.

Issui-sensei says

There are generals (*shin*) who are excellent at devising tactics and plots. While it is said from ancient times that they are rare, it is also said that they can be acquired if the *taishō* wishes to have them and seeks them out.

I think those who create excellent tactics and plots also need to maintain an exquisite understanding of the righteous principles and *budō* – the path of *samurai*. They need to be very thoughtful, wise, resourceful, fluent of speech and have the ability to construct plans. This is why they are so rare.

Commentator two

Kanchō spies are people who look for disorder and change, perceive and reveal people's emotions and seek to uncover the enemy's intention.

Good generals get the most out of their men without exploiting them. The warrior Matsudaira Izu no kami was such a good general that he became a regional lord.

An old saying goes that there are no strong or weak soldiers, but there are good or bad generals. Therefore, generals should be carefully selected. Good tactics are essential (*hon*), while bravery should be less important (*matsu*).

Issui-sensei says

Battles on flatland are the same as normally discussed.

CHAPTER SEVEN

The following topics are discussed in other writings:

- *suisen no koto* 水戦之事 – aquatic warfare
- *morijiro no koto* 守城之事 – defending castles
- *funaikusa no koto* 舩戦之事 – ship battles
- *yamaikusa no koto* 山戦之事 – mountain battles
- *youchi no koto* 夜討之事 – night attacks

城責之事
Shirozeme no koto

ATTACKS ON CASTLES

There are no additional details on this subject given here. Strong castles should not be attacked with intensity, whereas weak castles should be subject to surprise raids. Furthermore, you should consider the possibility of [enemy] reinforcements.

Commentator one

The issue of enemy reinforcement troops matters when you are attacking a weak castle, because if there are no reinforcements on their way you do not have to rush the attack. If attempting to attack by direct force, mistakes will occur.

Commentator two

It is said that strong [castles] will not fall [so easily]; therefore, attack them very 'softly' to make the soldiers in the castle negligent. Weak castles should be attacked at once before reinforcements arrive.

When attacking be aware of how to defend, and when defending be aware of how to attack.

Issui-sensei says
When besieging a castle it is a principle not to surround a castle in all directions but to leave one direction open.

Commentator one
It is a principle to not besiege a castle in all directions but to actually leave one direction open.

Commentator two
If you surround a castle completely, the enemy will become desperate. Therefore, clear one direction to create an opening for them. However, you should completely surround the castle at first and then later on create an opening. Do not leave an opening at the beginning.

Issui-sensei says
If reinforcements are expected to arrive to defend the castle, it is an established tactic to occupy the area 300 *bu*[29] around the fortification itself.

It is important to note that when capturing soldiers who are trying to flee from the castle, treat them kindly and ask them for information on the status inside the castle and the best way to create divisions among the *bushi* inside the fortress.

Use flood tactics and conduct attacks by setting fires just as you would on a battlefield.

---

29 This is different from the common *bu* measurement, which is equivalent to 3 millimetres. The *bu* unit can also be (1) a unit of length equivalent to 6 *shaku*, which is 1.8 metres; or (2) a unit of area equivalent to 6 *shaku* square, which is 3.3 square metres. Here, it appears to be referring to a unit of area, the instruction being to occupy an area 300 *bu* (i.e. 990 square metres) around the castle.

Commentator one

Tradition says to look for an appropriate place and build a *mukai-jiro*, a strategic castle,[30] close to the enemy fort.

In addition, first, surround the enemy castle in all directions, and then after a few days clear one direction and position good men as guards at a remote distance to block the soldiers [from actually escaping].

If the castle has plentiful supplies, attack it as soon as possible even if you are a small number. If it is not well provisioned, attack slowly.

Commentator two

To divide those in the castle means to divide the lord and his high-ranking retainers and also to divide colleagues. Details are mentioned in the scroll *Dakkō [Shinobi] no Maki.*

During the Tenshō era (1573–1593), Lord Hideyoshi flooded castles such as Takamatsu castle in Bitchū and Ōta castle in Kishū. Takamatsu castle belonged to the Mōri clan, and was defended by the warriors Shimizu Muneharu, Kiyo Nyūdō, Shimizu Tarō, Naniwa Denbei and so on. The attack on Ōta castle occurred during the rebellion of the Ōta clan.

Issui-sensei says

You can tell if a castle is abandoned by using *hichō no narai* – the teaching of flying birds – as well as war cries, messengers and so on.

Commentator two

Sun Tzu says that if birds gather around a position, this means that it is unoccupied. In the 'tiger strategy' of his *Six Secret Teachings*, Liu Tao says the following on the subject of unoccupied fortresses:

> *If many birds can be seen flying above a fortress without becoming startled and there seems to be no chi in the sky, it means the enemy has set up as if there were people actually inside but it is a ruse.*

---

30 This is equivalent to a *tsuke-jiro* (付城), as found in *The Book of Samurai: Fundamental Samurai Teachings*, page 216.

[To check for this kind of enemy trick,] shoot muskets all of a sudden and make war cries and look for any movement, then send scouts to investigate.

Issui-sensei says

Be aware that the key to attacking a castle is knowing how to defend a castle.

Commentator two

If an attack is not proceeding quickly, study the topography around the castle and build a *mukai-jiro* strategic castle to hold the enemy in check. Alternatively, surround the castle in all directions and hold position for a few days, then create an opening in one direction with guards watching along that route. If the enemy maintains plentiful rations, you should attack quickly, even if you are a lesser number. If they do not have stocks, remain quiet and observe the castle, speculate on how they are defending the internals and come up with a way to defeat them.

Issui-sensei says

If [those defending a castle] burn the inner side of the outer enclosure and retreat into the main and the second enclosure, you should *not* automatically assume that they have become determined [to make a last stand]. Before you move forward, after the fires have died down, have warriors on foot check if there are pitfall traps.

Commentator two

When a castle falls, if you are not vigilant other allies may take advantage of your intended route of attack, and if you are not careful you will make mistakes. To achieve your aim you must time your actions carefully. There are teachings on proper timing in this context.

To dampen the spirits of the enemy inside the castle when their morale is high, offer a reconciliation and retreat from any points of possible attack and other such measures – this movement may reduce their confidence.[31] Even if

---

31 When the enemy is in a state of rising power, step back and retreat. Let that power wane before moving to attack.

they do not accept the offer of reconciliation, let [the enemy troops] observe your messengers going back and forth a few times. This will cause the enemy troops to become doubtful and will lower their morale.

Yakiharai, burning the inside of a castle, is associated with the skill of *jiyaki* (自焼) – setting fire to your own [castle].

To explain the context of the previous text concerning the enemy retreating inwards after setting fire, know that when many of the enemy have been killed, the remaining forces may burn areas of their own castle. This is because it is difficult for them to defend the entire castle with the small number they have left.

城代役之事
Jōdaiyaku no koto

CONCERNING THE CASTLE STEWARD

There should be only a single person in this position.

The castle steward is of primary importance in military tactics. The person chosen for this role should be skilled in the way of defending castles when besieged.

When the *taishō* is advancing to another province, [the steward should] send supplies and rations out to him; there are important ways of estimation for this. If generals (*shō*) [who are on campaign] are lacking troops, those left in command [of the castle] decide on the allocation of soldiers who have been recruited from the province.[32] They then send such troops [to aid the general]. In doing this there is a tradition that needs to be considered and this is called *morijiro no mushawari* – the deployment of warriors when defending a castle.

---

32 That is to say, how many soldiers they can spare while still keeping the castle well defended.

Commentator one

Concerning the castle steward: the first true castle keep was built in the time of Nobunaga. So were the [first true] stone walls. Before that, they were constructed of earthworks and embankments.

Concerning the deployment of warriors: it is transmitted that generals (*shō*) and brave warriors should be positioned in the area around the *ōte* – the main castle gate. Wise and loyal men should be positioned to both sides, while newcomers and close retainers should be at the gate(s). It is also a principle that the brave and the wise should be the main forces, while the aged and weak should be used as irregulars and secure the rear areas (*ura*) of the castle. This principle is called *shidō no wakachi* – the four ways of distribution.

Commentator two

There is also a teaching called *kuruma okuri*, sending carts [of rations], but this is to be orally transmitted.

The art of *morijiro no mushawari* mentioned above is to position warriors to defend each gate as well as the *koguchi* area just inside the gate. This is the same principle as that followed when building a battle formation.

Also, assemble a reserve troop with warriors allocated from other groups.

Details for the above are in the scroll *Hachijin no Maki*.

The castle steward is of primary importance in warfare and the role should be carried out by a single person who represents the will of the lord. Having more than one castle steward leads to prolonged councils, whereas with only a single leader tactics are quickly decided in an emergency.

Issui-sensei says

There is a traditional way on secret communication using a *taishō*'s identification mark (印符) and letters (書簡); this is called *hakushi no hō* – the way of blank paper – and is kept as a secret for military families.

Commentator three

This secret is mentioned in the scroll *Kōketsu*.

Issui-sensei says

When the *taishō* departs for war, everything from the beginning to end should be agreed upon and arranged before he leaves. Also, when the *taishō* is away at war, people should gather together inside the castle, and labourers should be summoned from every village to come to the castle.

Commentator two

Labourers should be summoned based on a ratio system per 100 *koku* in area. Typically this works out as one labourer per 100 *koku* – but this proportion may vary.

Issui-sensei says

It is also a principle that everyone, including *samurai*, foot soldiers, commoners and so on, should recall their fathers, mothers, wives, children, brothers and sisters [back home from other areas]. This way has been transmitted from ancient times. They are to be used as hostages.[33]

人衆ヲ積テ扶持方ヲコムル事

Ninshū wo tsumorite fuchikata wo komuru koto

BUILD UP PROVISIONS THROUGH ESTIMATING THE NUMBER OF PEOPLE

At the same time [as preparing provisions for the correct number of people], be prepared with bows, muskets, bullets and gunpowder. Such weapons should always be amassed in a castle in advance; there should be no lack of them. Check these items again and again and accumulate as much weaponry as possible.

城代可心得事

Jōdai kokoroeru beki koto

THINGS THE CASTLE STEWARD SHOULD KEEP IN MIND

- Never let anyone from another province into the castle.
- Do not allow drinking parties or pleasure with women – this goes not only for *samurai*, but even lower people.

---

33 This is to ensure that the *samurai* under the lord maintain loyalty.

- Do not receive presents sent from other provinces.
- If an express messenger or the like brings a message from another province, let the group captains (*kashira*) know what it was about as soon as possible.
- Strictly prohibit access by ship and keep watch over the boundaries of the province including the mouths of rivers.
- Solidify defences by thoroughly inspecting them, by building up *yagura* turrets, and by paying special attention to moats and walls.
- When the *taishō* is leaving for war, use the teaching of *mushawari* – the deployment of warriors within a castle. Each samurai should be allocated a specific position; this way there will be no gap [in the defence].

Commentator two

Detecting someone from another province: this is to prevent them getting inside the castle. [Discover whether a person is from another domain] by questioning him about the group he belongs to and who he is retained by.

When defending a castle compound, assign each group a specifically defined place, showing them the boundaries from point to point. This is done so that it will be hard for *kanja* spies to gain access. If the enemy approaches and attacks the castle, even if a certain group falls [under pressure from the enemy] and all is in danger, other groups [along the wall] should *not* move to help them, as this will make it difficult for the reserve troop to give assistance.[34]

Issui-sensei says

Tradition says that the enemy will come at you with various plots from neighbouring provinces, each aimed at deceiving you. Therefore, never let your guard down. They sometimes try to divide good *samurai* within the castle. There will also sometimes be unexpected riots that occur in various villages. In such cases, the castle steward should not leave the castle himself without giving careful consideration, but instead should send appropriate *samurai*. It is essential to settle such matters before they become critical.

---

34 When a troop guarding a section of the castle is falling, other groups should not disengage to help them. Only the reserve troop should move up to give aid.

Sometimes a castle may be flooded with river water or raided at night in conjunction with an arson attack. It is a principle to plan for these situations before they happen.

Commentator two
Groups will establish in advance how and when they will come to each other's aid, but this will depend on the situation. In order to pre-empt riots, send scouts out to all areas. If there are signs that a riot is being initiated, attack and kill the ringleaders; the others will scatter to the four directions.

Issui-sensei says
It is sometimes the case that wells are poisoned and *naikan* internal spies are used to confuse people's minds. There is a way to use poisoned water and also a tradition to know who is an internal spy.

Commentator one
Naikan, the internal spy, will:
- conspire with the enemy
- use the way of lust
- use speech to avoid detection

Commentator two
It is a task of internal spies to poison castle wells. Thus, identifying internal spies is mentioned in the scroll *Dakkō [Shinobi] no Maki*.

It is said that poisoned water can be detoxified by filtering it through adzuki beans or by adding red clay.[35] Each group should conduct strict examinations [to detect any internal spies in their midst].

Position guards at each castle well and secure the wells with a lockable lid. This will make it difficult to poison them.

---

35 赤土.

籠城可入置物

Rōjō ireokubeki mono

THINGS TO BE KEPT IN A CASTLE WHEN IT IS UNDER SIEGE

[Weapons and other equipment:]

- *yumi* 弓 – bows
- *ya* 矢 – arrows
- *tsuru* 弦 – bow strings
- *teppō* 鉄炮 – muskets
- *tama* 玉 – bullets
- *kusuri* 薬 – gunpowder
- *yari* 鑓 – spears
- *kai* 貝 – conch shells
- *kane* 鐘 – bells
- *taiko* 太鼓 – drums
- *kin* 金 – gold
- *gin* 銀 – silver
- *kome* 米 – rice[36]
- *zeni* 銭 – money
- *daizu* 大豆 – soy beans
- *bagu* 馬具 – horse gear

Food items:

- *arame* アラメ – seaweed
- *yakijio* 焼塩 – roasted salt
- *warabi* 蕨 – bracken[37]
- *umeboshi* 梅干 – salted plums
- *katsuobushi* 鰹節 – dried bonito
- *goma* 胡麻 – sesame
- *tōfukasu* 豆腐糟 – tofu lees
- *adzuki* 小豆 – adzuki beans

---

36 One might expect rice and soy beans to be in the food list. However, most likely they are in the first list due to their absolute necessity.

37 *Pteridium aquilinum.*

- *hoshizakana* 干魚 – dried fish
- *momigome* 籾米 – rice in its husk

The items in the above list and other similar items should be stored up [before a siege]. Things that do not have a long shelf life should not be stored. Things that can be used as a food substitute are recorded elsewhere.

城郭ノ法
Jōkaku no hō

THE PRINCIPLES OF CASTLE CONSTRUCTION

Tradition says that each area [of the castle] *must* be built with consideration for the concept of *jōkaku no hō* – the principles of castle construction.

Commentator one
Tradition says that it is advantageous for a castle to leave one-third of its total area as open space. There are four main uses for open space within a castle:
- for the positioning of archers and musketeers when attacked by the enemy
- for keeping hostages in
- to limit the spread of fires
- to resist storms and earthquakes and for making sandbags

Issui-sensei says
Do not allow the residences outside of your castle to have *neribei* walls[38] surrounding them.

Do not make castles bigger than they need to be. Also, the fortifications

---

38 *Neribei* (ネリ塀) are walls constructed out of layers of tiles, stone and clay. They provide advantageous places for the enemy to defend themselves when besieging a castle.

should be appropriate for the number of people [the castle has to shelter], and make sure that the exterior walls are not low in height.

The roads within the castle compound should be smooth so that people can move around without difficulty.

Commentator two

Neribei walls withstand fire and thus the enemy can use them for cover during their siege. There are also points to be considered when planting trees. A castle should not be made larger than required or beyond the resources and status [of the commander]. If the number of people [based at the castle] significantly increases, additional enclosures or fortresses should be built to accommodate the additional people. Generally it is a principle to allocate one-third of the castle grounds to open space when designing a castle.

Some advantages for this are:

- easy arrangement of archers and musketeers including arrow and gun ports
- fewer casualties during typhoons, earthquakes and fires
- space for accommodating hostages
- makes it easy to construct sandbags
- facilitates manoeuvring of troops when advancing and retreating

This is transmitted in the scroll *Jōsei no Maki*.

The outer wall should be 6 *shaku* 5 *sun* in height for a flatland fortification, or 5 *shaku* 5 *sun* for a mountain fortification. If it is too low, it will be easy to cross over it; but if it is too high, it will be inconvenient to defend for those inside. If you do not know such things, you may face difficulties.

Backfill most of the wells outside of the castle and poison the few that you leave open.

Commentator three

Leave bamboo groves and woods in place around your castle if you judge that they will be useful for firewood or as shelter for your forces. However, if you think they will be more useful to the enemy – for example, as cover for enemy *shinobi* – then you should cut them down.

Issui-sensei says

Make an observation of the area from your castle and consider where the enemy will lay their siege, where they will approach from, where they will position musketeers and where they will place catapults. Sometimes the enemy will use miners, so as a precautionary measure bury jars in the ground to know if they are digging [as the containers will echo with the miners' sounds]. Know that in such cases the enemy will always fiercely attack [with a diversionary troop] to drown out the sound of any resonance [which echoes in the buried jars]. Therefore, position guards by these jars.

Commentator two

During the siege of Shiraga castle in the province of Ūnshū, there was an incident called *shiraga-jō anashiyori jūbanyari* – the tale of the ten spear fights in tunnels. The besieging army employed tunnelling tactics and ten spear fights took place [in the tunnels themselves].

If the besieged castle has strong *yagura* turrets that cannot be captured, it is sometimes the case that the besieging army estimates the distance to the turret and then builds a tunnel to it so that they can lay gunpowder in barrels or jars beneath the turret. Then they ignite the gunpowder with fuses so that the turret will collapse.

Issui-sensei says

At the front and the rear of the main keep, the *taishō*'s larger flags, bows, spears and other items should be displayed. Curtains should be erected along with the items displayed. It is a principle that the curtains should be constructed on all sides of the castle keep and in five or seven layers.

Commentator two

Those items mentioned above should be displayed as spectacularly as possible. War curtains should be constructed in the same location. Know that the first ever keep was built at Azuchi castle in Gōshū. Also, in older days high stone walls did not exist as they do today; earthworks were used instead.

Five layers of curtains should be constructed one by one around the castle keep, the same should be done with seven layers.

Issui-sensei says

It is a set custom to stand *umajirushi* standards in the direction of the enemy. [However,] there is an old custom – shown below – and this is used in conjunction with other forms of ritual.[39]

- In spring [the direction is] *tatsumi* 巽 – south-east.
- In summer [the direction is] *hitsujisaru* 坤 – south-west.
- In autumn [the direction is] *inui* 乾 – north-west.
- In winter [the direction is] *ushitora* 艮 – north-east.

Commentator two

Until around the period of Eiroku (1558–1570), *umajirushi*-style standards did not exist. They first appeared early in the Genki period (1570–1573) and they became the primary banner, which is how they continue to be used even now.

Tradition says that such standards should be raised in the direction facing the enemy.

Issui-sensei says

The *matoi* army standard should be stood by the *chakutō yagura* – the turret of arrival.

Commentator two

The turret of arrival mentioned above is built in a large space between the main enclosure and the second enclosure. It is here that records of *samurai* service are written down in ledgers and troops receive their orders for deployment. Also, this is where the *taishō* inspects the heads taken by soldiers.

---

39 The direction in which you set flags can be either auspicious or inauspicious. For example, according to the list, the auspicious direction in spring is the south-east, and so on.

Issui-sensei says

High-ranking *shin* retainers and *kashira* captains should have their *umajirushi* standards displayed at their respective positions, including the main enclosure, the second and third enclosures, etc.

    Large planks should be erected in the following positions:

- *jōnai yamamichi* 城内山道 – mountain pathways within the castle areas
- *jōgai* 城外 – the outside areas of the castle
- *tekiai* 敵合 – the external areas between the allies and the enemy

Commentator one

Concerning the boards to be erected: thick planks should be used to enclose areas.

Commentator two

If an area is open to enemy view, raise boards at disadvantageous positions [to obscure the view].

Issui-sensei says

When creating *yazama* arrow ports in walls, build viewing windows in the upper part of the wall.

Commentator one

Arrow ports should be 1 *shaku* 2 *sun* in height and 4 *sun* wide. They should be inset at knee height for an average man. They can be placed a little lower but not any higher.

Commentator two

There is a custom called *ōtakezama* – larger bamboo arrow loopholes. These are usually covered with bamboo cylinder shutters.

Issui-sensei says

There is a type of arrow port called a *fukurozama* – dropping port. These should be employed at every fifth port. They are 4 or 5 *shaku* wide and 5 *shaku* in height.

[Dropping ports] should be built [with the opening pointing] downwards and should be located at each corner.

Commentator two

Fukurozama (袋サマ) dropping ports should be created at places which are advantageous for lateral attack [on invading enemies].[40]

Issui-sensei says

The advantage of narrow arrow ports is the protection they give against return fire from the enemy. However, they are hard to see out of. There is a specific method of building ports into a thick wall; this is orally transmitted.

Commentator two

Arrow ports should be narrower on the inside and widen out towards the opening on the outside. This method is called *hachimonji no narai* – the teaching of the ideogram of the number eight (八).

Issui-sensei says

Arrow ports should be constructed at intervals of 1 *ken*. *Yagura* turrets should be constructed at intervals of 70 *ken*. There are important points to be considered for using arrow ports to drive the enemy back.

Commentator one

Tradition says that the outer boundary of a castle should be surrounded by two layers of walls, one of which should be a suspended fake wall.

Arrow ports should be set at breast height when standing; this is so that they give a full view when you are in a kneeling position (すわりテ). In Kōshū-Ryū it is said that the interval between arrow ports should be 5 *shaku* 5 *sun*.

Gun ports should be set 8 *sun* above breast height when crouched down.

---

40 *Fukurozama* are small dropping ports built into walls, particularly at the corners of fortifications. They allow things to be fired or dropped down by troops on the inside. However, here it is saying that when they are positioned correctly on an outer wall the dropping ports can be used to shoot arrows laterally, creating a cross fire to put the enemy in difficulty.

These ports are used when in a half-kneeling firing position (地ニ居テ). They are positioned around 1 *shaku* 8 *sun* above the ground. The shape should be triangular and each side should be 8 *sun* 3 *bu*.

Commentator two

Arrow ports should *not* be furnished with sliding covers (引戸), because covers do not allow for a free range when shooting arrows. Instead they should have *tsukiage mado* – vertical covers.

Tradition says that there should be two layers of walls around the castle and one of them should be a *tsuribei* suspended fake wall.

Arrow ports should be positioned at a height that will allow an average person to have a view when kneeling on one knee with the other knee raised (立ヒサタケ居).

Gun ports should be set 8 *sun* up from the breast for an average person in a kneeling position. They should be triangular in shape, with each side measuring 8 *sun*.

Issui-sensei says

Yagura turrets [and walls] should be constructed in one of the following styles:

- *chigiri no kane* (チキリノカネ)
- *gangi* (雁木)
- *oribei* (折塀)

For each of these there are traditions.

Commentator two

チキリ

Chigiri

雁木
Gangi

折塀
Oribei

Issui-sensei says

- It is best for stone walls to be relatively narrow at the base.[41]
- If there are heights outside of the castle area, they should be flattened.
- It is said that all bamboo or woods within 1 *ri* of a castle should be cut down.
- The outermost parts of the castle should be fortified by building enclosures (総構).
- Prepare by making the roads wide and build *kakemawari* (駈廻) free passage areas. This is done so that people and horses can move around freely.

Commentator one

Tradition says that paths (切通) cut through constructions within a castle are called *nukemichi* (抜道) rat runs, or *kageana* (陰穴) hidden passages.

The *horiguchi* – the inlet for the water within a moat – should be:

- 10 *ken* wide – first grade (*jō*)
- 15 *ken* wide – second grade (*chū*)
- 20 *ken* wide – third grade (*ge*)

---

41 If the base of a stone wall is too wide, it makes it easier to climb. This is why narrow-based, steep walls are preferable.

Also, consider the following aspects:

- *koguchi* 虎口 – castle entrance
- *in-yō no nawa* 陰陽ノ縄 – elements of *in* and *yō* in castle layout[42]
- *horikiri* 堀切 – moat

One text[43] says that the moat should be 10, 13 or 15 *ken* wide. However, it can be wider if the general desires.

Castle moats should be constructed with a base that is either *hakobori* (箱堀), meaning square, or *yagen* (薬研), meaning v-shaped. If a v-shaped moat is built below high stone walls then the stone walls will collapse. If a moat is 10 *ken* wide and 25 *ken*[44] deep, you should know that the soil extracted from the moat will make embankments 3 *ken* high and more than 8 *ken* [wide].

Commentator two

Details on castle construction are transmitted in the scroll *Jōsei no Maki*.

Burn down the immediate area outside the castle when defending, so as to destroy any areas the enemy may use to shield themselves.

合戦之習傳法
Kassen no narai denpō

TRADITIONAL TEACHINGS ABOUT SIEGE WARFARE

The above are all methods on how to tightly secure existing castles. The traditions for establishing new castles are mentioned in a different writing.

---

42 There are two types of castle design: *in no nawa* and *yō no nawa*. An *in no nawa* castle is easier to defend, while a *yō no nawa* design facilitates outward attacking.

43 The name of the manual is not given.

44 Such a depth seems excessive. This may be an ideal depth hard to achieve in practice, a transcription error or a harking back to ancient China.

What is discussed here is how to prepare a castle to defend it against siege.

When you receive information that the enemy is advancing [to attack your castle], undertake the following actions within a radius of 5 *ri* around your castle:

- Cut down all of the woods, forests and bushes.
- Destroy bridges.
- Destroy houses.
- Burn surplus firewood.
- Fill wells and springs with poison, faeces, soil and the like.
- Bring into the castle rice, salt, miso, cattle and horses, martial equipment and anything else that might be useful.
- Instruct local farmers, commoners, etc. to hide in the mountains and other such places.
- Burn down all remaining houses.
- After you have done all this, wait for the enemy.

Pay extreme attention to all entrances and make sure that they are well defended. Position men inside and along the walls with the idea of having one person for every *ken* of wall length.

If numbers are no object then assign:

- fifteen people for every 10 *ken* of wall
- a *kogashira* sub-captain for every 5 *ken* of wall
- an *itte no shō* unit commander for every 100 *ken* of wall

This is what has been set down in old methods. Be aware that in case of a battle each area [inside and along the wall] will be defended by the troop assigned to it. Therefore, once the troops are assembled, they should go immediately to their positions and defend.

Commentator two
The above is one outline [of the number of people required to defend a wall]. This can be varied according to the number of soldiers you have at your disposal.

Issui-sensei says

Those who guard gates should take turns performing watches during night and day.

Commentator one

The duration of day and night watches will depend on the situation and is discussed below. People should switch regularly, because performing full day or night shifts is considered to be wrong.

Commentator two

Know that if guards change watches frequently, it is difficult for them to conspire with the enemy.

Issui-sensei says

In addition to those soldiers who defend the inside of the walls, one or two reserve troops should be kept back to be deployed wherever the enemy is attacking most fiercely. It is common when besieging castles to attack fiercely from one direction while others move to the rear to strike with a sudden attack from behind. Be on your guard against this type of strategy.

There are special teachings on how to assign roles to warriors – specifically, those soldiers under the *taishō*'s direct supervision.

Commentator two

The *taishō*'s direct troops usually comprise very loyal retainers, relatives with different surnames and brothers.

Issui-sensei says

If the enemy is fiercely attacking, some of the soldiers defending within the castle may develop a double mind [meaning that they wish to aid the enemy]. Be aware of this and frequently redeploy them. This is a traditional way. For example, switch them every one or two days, every three or four days, or even once or twice a day, according to the situation. If this is done, it will be difficult for any individual to exchange promises with the enemy outside.

If the enemy shoots fire arrows into the castle, the soldiers defending behind the walls should *not* draw back from their positions but should extinguish the flames. In addition, any reserve soldiers assigned there should also help to extinguish the fire. Prohibit soldiers defending behind the walls from leaving their assigned positions or moving around without good reason.

Do not erect anything that is as tall as a pole and can be seen from outside the castle. Such constructions are not a problem when they are close to the wall, but you should not allow anything tall and distinctive to stand out from within the castle. Also, avoid piping or sounding any instrument apart from [official] conch shells, bells and drums, which are used to announce the *taishō*'s wishes. Making noise with any other instrument is prohibited. Generally, avoid any speaking in loud voices or making any other noise so as not to give away information on the status inside the castle.

Commentator one
Tradition says that sometimes at night *monomi tōrō* viewing lanterns were lit, but know that they were beneficial not only for the allied side but also for the enemy. This is to be orally transmitted.

Commentator two
The above should be prohibited because they allow traitors a way of discreetly giving signals to an enemy from inside the castle.

Issui-sensei says
Sometimes one or two people may secretly come to a gate, saying that they wish to see acquaintances or relatives within the castle. Even if their identity is without question, never let anyone attend to a personal errand. As a rule, make sure to report this to the *kashira* section captain, who in turn will report to the *taishō*.

If a letter fixed to an arrow or the like has been shot inside of the boundary [of the castle], immediately report this to the unit leader in charge of that area and do this without moving it from where it landed. Next, the leader of the troop should seal it[45] in full view of everyone and pass it to the general. No one who is not in a position of command should open such a letter without good reason.

Commentator two

Yabumi letters attached to arrows should be presented unopened to the lord, but know that situations may change. For example, remember that at the Siege of Odawara the [opposing] warriors Ukita Hideie and Hōjō Jūrō Ujifusa exchanged letters that were attached to arrows [and resolved the whole conflict in this way].

To create a *yabumi* – letter attached to an arrow: write [the message] on paper, roll it around the shaft of the arrow below the fletching, and secure it with glue at the end. Alternatively, write the message in a circular format directly onto the shaft. The name of the receiver should be written within the fletching. The arrowhead should be removed. The message is written in a circular way so that the words do not wear away [when being shot from the bow].

Issui-sensei says

Generally, rules should not be changed once they have been established. The *taishō* should have sensible judgement and establish proper rules from the start. This is mentioned in the book *Wujing Zongyao* (武経惣要).

If your castle is besieged and fiercely attacked by the enemy, and you are expecting reinforcement from a neighbouring province, try to defend the castle firmly without engaging the enemy. When the reinforcements have arrived, start raiding both from inside the castle and also from behind the enemy. This should be done upon a prearranged signal. If you are not expecting any forces from a neighbouring province to come to your aid, know that your own troops will tend to be too hasty and rush to action. It is fundamental [in siege-craft] to wait for the enemy to exhaust themselves while you maintain a firm defence of the castle. Be aware that if you defend well and [the siege] is prolonged, the enemy will without doubt fall into exhaustion.

If the enemy is surrounding the castle but clearing a single area [so that it

---

45 Possibly 'wrap up', 'secure' or 'mark' in such a way that it cannot be tampered with.

appears unoccupied], know that there will be a strategic intention behind this. Also, if the enemy is striking ferociously from the east but the attack is weak from the west, do not let your guard down. Furthermore, if the enemy attacks strongly then suddenly draws back 2 or 3 *ri* and takes up position there, know that they actually intend to wait for the right moment [within their strategy] to return and capture the castle. In this case make sure to have an excellent strategy in mind. If you see them retreating for real, then you should pursue them in order to attack them while they are withdrawing.

If you cannot establish for certain their real intention (*kyojitsu*) – whether they are withdrawing to attack later, or retreating for real – then do not venture out to attack them. Prioritize defending your castle over striking the enemy.

Commentator two

In a real retreat the enemy will use the formation called *seiden no sonae* (正殿ノ備), whereas in a fake retreat the enemy will often look backwards [towards your forces]. Observe them carefully for these and other signs of their true intentions and act accordingly.

If they dissolve their entire formation but the vanguard (先勢) is positioned to defend the retreat, they will retreat for sure. Also, if the unit of packhorses (小荷駄) retreats first, followed by the troops that were in the centre (中備), then the left and right flanks (左右), and finally the rear unit (後陣) withdraws quietly, then know that they are truly retreating. Conversely, if the five units retreat quickly and people within the units often glance backwards, or to the left or the right, know that this is a fake retreat.

Issui-sensei says

Make sure not to waste bullets, gunpowder and arrows while the enemy is at a distance. People of old said that defending at a distance of 1 *jō* is better than defending from a distance of 1 *ri*, and defending at 1 *shaku* is better than defending at 1 *jō*. Indeed it is a known fact that defending from a long distance is exhausting, while striking an enemy that is close enhances your strength.[46]

---

46 Meaning not to overstretch your forces. It is better to stay compact instead of spreading out over a distance.

Commentator two

The five principles of night raids are listed in the scroll *Gunshū [Yōhō]*.

Issui-sensei says

Allied troops defending a castle will become weary if there is no combat for a long period. To keep them vigilant, send out *ashigaru* foot soldiers to perform forays on the enemy flank, unexpected attacks and night raids – these are all done to create skirmishes. There is another method, which can be used during the day or the night, that involves making loud noises with bells and drums, having men, women and even children raise war cries, and shooting muskets in a barrage. This is done to make the enemy think that you are about to attack, and that they must respond by accepting such a 'battle'. The purpose is to exhaust the enemy. In this scenario, the muskets should not be loaded with bullets.

There are many more ways of battles and these will be mentioned in other writings. Therefore, they are not written here.

城中禁罰之次第
Jōchū kinbatsu no shidai

PROHIBITIONS AND PUNISHMENTS IN A CASTLE

When troops return after combat or a night attack, the first thing to remember is to keep the gate closed, keep the guard tight behind the walls, and make sure to maintain full caution. Have those entering state the required password before opening the gate. If anyone allows the troops access without care, both the one who let them enter and those who came in should be punished. This should be strictly enforced.

Commentator two

Although there is a method called *tachisuguri isuguri* – body movements that accompany passwords – the enemy may still become mixed with the people within your castle. There is the method in our school of *warifu* – split tallies.

Issui-sensei says

Those who move treasures to other places upon the news of the enemy approaching should be considered as having dual loyalty and should be punished by death and executed without delay. Generally, it is prohibited to move treasure in such situations.

Those soldiers who defend behind the walls should not leave their positions to return to their homes. If they must return, then they should report to their commander and state that they are going but that they will return to their position behind the wall as soon as possible. If someone has not returned by the time the enemy advances and attacks, then that person should be accused [of cowardice].

Moving out of the castle to pillage is prohibited, unless there has been an order to break into enemy territory to replenish the castle stockpiles.

Commentator two

Pillaging should be regulated through signal bells and drums and take place in an arranged order. For example, first group, then the second group, then the third and so on. This should be done with control.

Issui-sensei says

All men, high or low, are away defending the walls, the *yagura* turrets and other positions. Only women are left at home. Know that there will always be scoundrels who break into people's houses to steal things or rape other people's wives. Such people should be killed as soon as they are seen or you are informed of them. However, those thieves who steal to eat the food from people's houses should be questioned first. If it becomes clear that they have not been given enough provisions, they should be pardoned.

Commentator two

When the warrior Oyamada Tarō Takaie had his men reap immature wheat [even though this was prohibited, the lord Nitta] Yoshisada not only forgave him but also sent rations and a *kimono* in response. Oyamada Tarō Takaie was immensely grateful and later he died saving Yoshisada's life.

Issui-sensei says

Anyone who has heard or seen anything of the status of the enemy and has information that might benefit the allied side should immediately report to their superiors, no matter how low or base a person they are. If a person conceals that which he knows and it is revealed later, he should be charged.

Drums should be used to signal the hours within a castle. Someone should be assigned to listen to any drum beats for signalling (*tsugedaiko*) within the castle. This is because if there is someone who is cooperating with the enemy it is likely that they will sound a certain number of drum beats as a prearranged signal that the enemy should attack. Therefore, if the listener hears an incorrect number of beats, this should be reported to the *taishō* for investigation.

Commentator two

Tsugedaiko drums are used to signal the time and such things as an enemy approach.

降参人質之作法之事
Kōsan hitojichi no sahō no koto

CONCERNING CUSTOMS REGARDING HOSTAGES AT THE TIME OF SURRENDER

[Upon the surrender of the enemy,] both sides should withdraw until there is a 6 *chō* gap and then take up positions. Any hostages will be led towards you in a column and a senior counsellor from your side should meet them at the halfway point, bow to them, and then guide them to meet the *taishō*. The *taishō* should sit on a *shōgi* stool, attended by a war-baton bearer to the right side, a *tachi* bearer to the left, and rear and side guards, as is the case on the field of battle. Two ministers (*shin*) should be positioned one on each side in front of the *taishō* and the senior counsellor escorting the hostages should act as the intermediary. Curtains should be erected 15 or even 20 *ken* in front of the *taishō*. Any servants accompanying the hostages or enemy senior counsellors should not be allowed to pass through the curtains.

HOSTAGE
SERVANTS

CURTAIN

HOSTAGES

ESCORT
SENIOR COUNSELLOR

GENERAL
(SHIN)   GENERAL
(SHIN)

SIDE   SIDE
DEFENCE   DEFENCE

LORD

COMMANDER

SWORD   WAR BATON
BEARER   BEARER

REAR
DEFENCE

The *taishō* then takes off his helmet, picks up a pottery cup and pledges his oath while sitting on the stool. After the promises are given, the ministers – who are in position on the left and the right – should bow when the hostages withdraw and then take their seats. The senior counsellor who acts as the intermediary should be entrusted with the hostages.

HOSTAGES IN A SIEGE

When defending a castle against a siege, significant hostages should be selected and taken from the allied and branch castles that have pledged to be under the *taishō*'s command.[47] Two-storied quarters in rows should be built at an appropriate place in the second or third enclosure and the hostages should be kept there. They should not be completely free to roam within the castle.

Needless to say, anyone who goes against the general's orders and rules should be punished, but those who act in loyalty should be rewarded.

The above are the major points concerning defending a castle. There are plenty of other elements to consider but they are mentioned in other writings. It is a principle from ancient times that *samurai* and soldiers (*shisotsu*) should be used according to their capabilities. The old, the very young, the unwell and healthy women should all be used for the tasks related to rice rations and other food stuffs.

The following people should be made to leave:

- those who have come from other places but stay when the castle appears to need defending against a siege and nobody knows where they or their relatives have come from
- those who have no brothers or any other relatives within the castle
- monks, nuns, commoners and others who are not useful in combat and consume food

This applies only when defending a castle against siege.

城ヲ請取事
Shiro wo uketoru koto

TRANSFERRING OWNERSHIP OF A CASTLE

Be it a residence or a castle [that is being transferred to you by the enemy], you need to go there to receive it. Those leaving the castle should do so in a line and

---

47 These are hostages from the allied forces who are held to ensure loyalty.

those coming in from the outside should also be in line. Those giving the castle and those receiving it should exchange bows between the lines [as seen in the image below].

INSIDE THE CASTLE

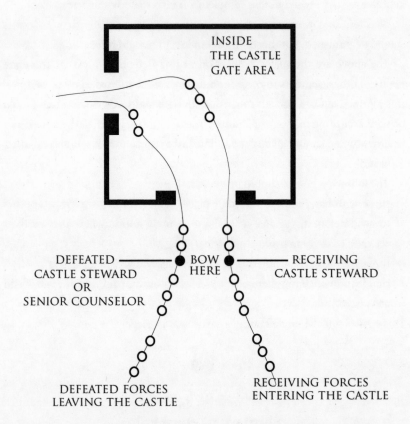

INSIDE
THE CASTLE
GATE AREA

DEFEATED
CASTLE STEWARD
OR
SENIOR COUNSELOR

BOW
HERE

RECEIVING
CASTLE STEWARD

DEFEATED FORCES
LEAVING THE CASTLE

RECEIVING FORCES
ENTERING THE CASTLE

OUTSIDE CASTLE GATE

CHAPTER EIGHT

士大将
Samurai-daishō

SAMURAI COMMANDERS

For a troop of fifty to one hundred soldiers, only one of this position is required. However, in some clans there are two of them.

Some say that this position is the same as *ikusa-bugyō* – minister of war. In ancient times, Kurō Yoshitsune went to Kyōto and a warrior named Doi Jirō Sanehira accompanied him as *ikusa-daishō*,[48] a position that is said to be equivalent to the present-day rank of *ikusa-bugyō*. As *ikusa-bugyō* ministers of war still exist today, the position of the warrior Sanehira in the above example should be considered as equivalent to *ikusa-daishō*. Simply be aware that the position mentioned here is equivalent to *samurai-daishō*, but is *not* one of the six *bugyō*.[49]

Commentator one
The military writings of Kōshū-Ryū state that a person commanding more than fifty *samurai* is called a *samurai-daishō*. A *musha-daishō* warrior commander must be of the social position of *shin*. Remember, *musha-bugyō* is the same as *ikusa-bugyō*.

---

48 This is an example of how titles can become confused with each other, meaning that they are at times used interchangeably. This manual has two different opinions on the position of *taishō*: one has it as commander of 50 or more men; the other as commander of a whole army.

49 The point here hinges on the word *bugyō*, which denotes a very high rank. However, the term should not be confused with the six *bugyō* leaders in the army (see pages 114–30).

Issui-sensei says

When marching, *samurai-daishō* should be mounted and take up position behind the *ōmatoi* – greater banner. Also, they will give orders concerning the *tekiai* – the land between the two armies. In other provinces and at the time of a battle, the *samurai-daishō* is in charge of *shōko* flags. It is a rule that this position should be performed by a *samurai-daishō*.

Shōko flags give information to the troops at the rear concerning the topography of the land. This is done with the five colours. In addition, sometimes two flags, one to the left and one to the right of the marching columns, are used to tell the rear section that the enemy is attacking and to relay the method of the assault.

When in battle formation, the person in this position takes command of reserve troops.

Commentator two

The *ōmatoi* larger standard should be positioned at the front when marching, but moved to the side during combat. This standard is used to rally forces in disarray.

Issui-sensei says

When on campaign the [*samurai-daishō*] should examine and take command of mixed *samurai* and soldiers (*shisotsu*), and the *rōninzamurai*.[50] If there is only a small number of soldiers, the *ikusa-bugyō* war commander can do this instead.

[*Samurai-daishō*] should fully understand *shihō no gi* (士法ノ儀), the codes and manners of the *samurai*, and when needs arise they should give orders relating to all matters – this is done in cooperation with the six *bugyō*. Therefore, codes for reward and punishment are to be transmitted [and are given below].

I think that an entire army (*sangun*) can be invincible when the soldiers are brave and keen. The soldiers are the essence of an army; it is the general's responsibility to get the most out of them. Whether they will be able to truly fulfil the commander-in-chief's intention will depend on the minds of the generals (*shō*), commanders (*bugyō*) and captains (*kashira*).

---

50 These are professional warriors not conscripted commoners.

If one of the above breaks the rules or lets an advantage slip, it may have been done out of loyalty. Furthermore, it is wrong to report every tiny violation to the overall commander; such small issues need not be settled by the commander himself. Therefore, close examination will be required to discover what has actually happened and to what level [up the chain of command] it should be reported.

賞法
Shōhō

CODES FOR REWARD

LEVELS OF CAMPAIGN

上陣

Jōjin

Upper-level campaign

This is when you fight with a small number against an army of a larger number and gain a victory without incurring [many] casualties.

中陣

Chūjin

Middle-level campaign

This is when both sides are almost equal in number and your side prevails.

下陣

Gejin

Lower-level campaign

This is when you fight with a large number against an army of a smaller number and gain a victory.

MANAGEMENT OF EXPENDITURE

上獲

Jōkaku

Upper-level management of expenditure

This ranking is assigned if the enemy numbers roughly 100,000 and more than 40,000 of them are killed. Also, if only about 10,000 *koku* of finance is actually required to gain victory over the enemy while the estimated expenditure was forecast to be 100,000 *koku*.

中獲

Chūkaku

Middle-level management of expenditure

If the amount of loss for the enemy is estimated to be more than that for your side.

下獲

Gekaku

Lower-level management of expenditure

If the amount of loss for the enemy is estimated to be equivalent to that for your side.

The above rankings relate to the achievements of generals. Achievements are assessed in terms of numbers and classified into upper, middle and lower levels and should be rewarded accordingly. Although success in battle can be measured in terms of the number of enemy heads taken and the amount of gain the allied forces receive, remember that the killing of enemies should not be that which is the most appreciated; instead, defeating and ruining the enemy should be most valued. This is how a battle should be assessed. Captains (*kashira*) of each unit should be rewarded with a bonus in the form of gold, silver, rice, money or other valuables. Be aware that an increase of fief should entail a change of position.

Although lower generals and rank-and-file *samurai* should also be rewarded, each should be discussed according to their position. *Heishi*-class *samurai* who have achieved extraordinary feats in combat should be judged as having reached a high level of attainment.

上功

Jōkō

HIGHEST LEVELS OF ACHIEVEMENT

The achievements of *ippei* independent soldiers are evaluated as follows.

ARTICLE ONE

To evaluate: the eight levels of achievements for a *bushi* warrior.

Commentator two

[The eight achievements are] as follows:

1. *ichiban-yari* – the first spear fight
2. *niban-yari* – the second spear fight
3. *yarishita no kōmyō* – being assistant to the victor of the spear
4. *kumiuchi* – grappling and striking
5. *ichiban-nori* – being the first to arrive
6. *shingari no hataraki* – protecting a retreat
7. *hitori no hataraki* – helping the injured and taking heads
8. *shukun no yaomote* – standing in front of the lord to take arrow fire

Details are in the scroll *Ippei Yōkō*.

ARTICLE TWO

To evaluate: the taking of heads and impressive fighting.

Commentator two

- *mogitsuke* – to take the head of a warrior with a helmet
- *kumiuchi* – grappling and striking
- *shōuchi* – to take a general's head
- *kubikazu* – the number of heads taken

ARTICLE THREE

To evaluate: each of the *kokorobase* – achievements through intention.

Commentator two

The concepts of *kokorobase* are:

- positioning dead bodies
- helping someone else to take a head
- bringing back a banner someone else has left behind
- achievements in scouting
- burying allied warriors

ARTICLE FOUR

To evaluate: the capturing of enemies alive.

Commentator one

[When assessing rewards,] consider whether a single man has captured one man or if he has taken two men, and also consider who the captives are.

Commentator two

[Things to be discussed are:]

- capturing an enemy with two or three people
- capturing an enemy singlehandedly
- the types of those captured

ARTICLE FIVE

To evaluate: the venturing into places where it is difficult to travel such as steep mountains, through woods and so on.

ARTICLE SIX

To evaluate: achievements where allies could not follow.[51]

---

51 The original text has five points but says six, but the final is divided into two sections. Therefore, the commentary may relate to both points.

Commentator two

Examples include:

- [performing in the] vanguard
- crossing rivers
- [performing as] *shinobi*

The above six points are classified as *jōkō* – upper-level achievements.

中功

Chūkō
MIDDLE-LEVEL ACHIEVEMENTS

ARTICLE ONE

To evaluate: whether you followed the *taishō's* orders completely, or whether you [disobeyed them by attacking] when you thought you should attack or by retreating when you thought you should retreat.

Commentator two

It is hard to have correct judgement on this matter. For example, if you are ordered not to attack when the vanguard is riding in an aura of victory and pursuing an enemy, it is difficult to bring [your men] to a halt as the order requests you to do. Also, when your allies are collapsing and close to defeat, [it is difficult to] endure and stand fast, maintaining order.

ARTICLE TWO

To evaluate: infiltrating [the enemy] during a battle during daytime so as to perform night attacks by breaking fences and to return after threatening the enemy deep in their area.

Commentator two

- *Yoikusa* night war is conducted with entire armies of thousands or even tens of thousands of people at night.
- *Youchi* night attacks are skirmishes with one or two troops (隊).

- *Yogomi* night raiding involves discreetly infiltrating an enemy camp or fortress for pillage.

[Times of attack and infiltration:]
- when the enemy have returned from a day of fighting
- when they are in a deep sleep late at night
- when they are preparing at dawn
- when they are constructing camp huts
- in rain and wind
- at the occurrence of a fire
- on a night when reinforcements have arrived

According to Sun Tzu:

> *A wind that rises in the daytime lasts long, but a night breeze soon falls.*

ARTICLE THREE

To evaluate: keeping soldiers in formation and defeating the enemy. This should be considered as an achievement even if heads are not taken.

ARTICLE FOUR

To evaluate: a charge into a number of enemies where heavy damage is inflicted. This should be considered as an achievement even if heads are not taken.

ARTICLE FIVE

To evaluate: eliciting secret enemy information by acting extremely covertly. This should be considered as an achievement.

ARTICLE SIX

To evaluate: killing or capturing enemies with two or three allies. This should be considered as an achievement.

The above six points are classified as *chūkō* – middle-level achievements.

下功

Gekō

LOWER-LEVEL ACHIEVEMENTS

ARTICLE ONE

To evaluate: the elements of the light and brisk way of the mind. Those *samurai* who say something to benefit the allies, even if it is not impressive, should be discussed.

ARTICLE TWO

To evaluate: taking equipment from the enemy. This should also be considered as an achievement. This should be classified into upper, middle and lower levels according to what items are brought back.

Commentator two

- *jō* – upper level: curtains and flags
- *chū* – middle level: helmets and armour
- *ge* – lower level: weapons

For example, three flags from a warrior named Nagoya[52] at the battle for Chihaya castle were taken with tactics. Also, Suda Ōi's men took valuable curtains with the *Saddharma Pundarika Sutra* [upon them] and also curtains from the Date clan that had the *kuyō* crest upon them.

ARTICLE THREE

To evaluate: those who, even only in an emergency, deliver a message on a battlefield. They should be considered for an achievement according to the manner by which it is done.

ARTICLE FOUR

To evaluate: those killed in battle. This should be considered as an achievement even though the person is dead. The classification of *jō*, *chū* and *ge* also applies to this.

---

52 Possibly Nagoshi.

Commentator two

For example, after the warrior Ishikawa Heisuke was killed in battle his nephew Oimatsu was given a reward by Hideyoshi. Another example is the warrior Hosokawa Yoshichirō Tadaoki, who was killed at the battle of Komaki (1584).

If five people fight together and one of them dies, the remaining four should not be rewarded. Remember, a general must be kind enough to mourn and have compassion for even a servant who has died in order for soldiers and servants to become attached to him.

ARTICLE FIVE

To evaluate: those injured in an unsuccessful attempt to kill an enemy. They should also be discussed for a *jō*, *chū* or *ge* classification, according to the number of strikes [they have received].

Consideration should also be given to the number of heads that have been taken and which enemy has been killed. Some cases can be classified as a *jō* achievement.

ARTICLE SIX

To evaluate: if a father, child or brothers fought and attained an achievement but were killed, even if the rest of the family have made no achievements, the achievement of death should be inherited [by a surviving family member].

Commentator two

An example of this is when the achievements of the warrior [Satō] Tsugunobu were transferred to his brother Tadanobu at the battle of Yashima (1185).

The above six points are classified as *gekō* – lower-level achievements.

Rewards should be given based on a discussion of the above points and should be announced to the troop generals and to high- and low-ranking soldiers only after the six *bugyō* have thoroughly examined all cases presented to them. Furthermore, the *taishō* may give an additional consideration in some cases.

CHAPTER NINE

罰法
Batsuhō

CODES FOR PUNISHMENT

重罪
Jūzai
SERIOUS CHARGES

DECREE ONE

Those who leave their own troop to achieve distinction by being first, when it is expressly against the *taishō*'s orders, should be killed.

Commentator two

Du-zi, who was one of Wu-zi's generals, succeeded in taking the heads of three generals, but in doing so he moved against the orders given. As a punishment for overstepping military commands, Wu-zi beheaded Du-zi while shedding tears for him. Military orders should be strictly maintained, as is shown by this example.

DECREE TWO

Those who waste bullets and gunpowder or arrows by shooting at the enemy from a distance [should be killed]. Those who do not seem eager to fight or shoot their muskets or bows while the enemy is closely approaching should also be killed.

DECREE THREE

Those who feign illness just before the battle should be killed.

DECREE FOUR

When staying in a battle camp, those who go out or come in from other places besides the main gate should be killed.

DECREE FIVE

Those scouts (*monomi*) who have not thoroughly observed or even seen important points, or those who divulge to other people elements of their report intended only for the *taishō*, should be killed. Also, those who reveal any of the *taishō*'s writings should be killed.

DECREE SIX

Those who talk about allied tactics should be killed.

DECREE SEVEN

Those who flee when facing the enemy should be killed.

DECREE EIGHT

Those who alert the enemy by talking loudly while hiding [in position] should be killed.

DECREE NINE

Those who steal even a small amount [from the allies] during a battle should be killed.

DECREE TEN

Those who set even a small fire [without authorization] in battle should be killed.

DECREE ELEVEN

Those who abandon any allies who are fighting the enemy and flee to let them be killed should themselves be killed.

DECREE TWELVE

Those who rape women or who kidnap them from the local area and bring them into the battle camp should be killed.

DECREE THIRTEEN

Those who take signals from allies wrongly and those who deceive allies should be killed.

The decrees listed above are serious charges. Perpetrators should be killed without discussion.

中罪

Chūzai

MIDDLE-LEVEL CHARGES

DECREE ONE

Even in an enemy province, those who set fires or kill men and women without orders should be charged.

DECREE TWO

Those who are slow to report anything should be charged.

DECREE THREE

Those who return after the general of a division has been killed should be charged.

DECREE FOUR

Those who kill servants without good reason should be charged.

DECREE FIVE

Those who have caused accidental fire within a battle camp should be charged.

DECREE SIX

Even in the event of arson, those who leave their positions and go to other places should be charged.

DECREE SEVEN

Those who open a letter attached to an arrow before presenting it to the lord should be charged.

DECREE EIGHT

Those who testify to something they did not actually see should be charged.

DECREE NINE

If people of achievement neglect to mention that they have witnessed other soldiers fighting a hard fight but left them without help, they should be charged.

DECREE TEN

Those who gamble during the campaign should be charged.

DECREE ELEVEN

Those who discuss the strength of the [opposing] forces with their colleagues should be charged.

DECREE TWELVE

Those who neglect their night patrols or guardhouse duty should be charged.

The above are middle-level charges. These should be dealt with case by case.

下罪
Gezai
LOWER-LEVEL CHARGES

DECREE ONE

Those who become drunk and violent.

DECREE TWO

Those who visit other sections of a battle camp for entertainment when encamped in position.

DECREE THREE

Those grooms who let horses loose or those who cannot manage to control their horses.

DECREE FOUR

Those who talk idly or speculatively.

DECREE FIVE

Those who lend gold and silver for personal profit.

DECREE SIX

Those who run around a battle camp and make a fuss without good reason.

DECREE SEVEN

Those who speak loudly or make other noise for no reason.

DECREE EIGHT

Those who neglect *bugei* martial skills and show disrespect towards *budō* – the way of the *samurai*.

DECREE NINE

Those *ashigaru* foot soldiers who sleep while working in the guardhouse.

DECREE TEN

Those who have gorgeous weapons or armour that exceed their status.

DECREE ELEVEN

Those who criticize or ridicule the *taishō*'s orders.

DECREE TWELVE

Those who have been assigned important tasks but leave them for others to do and please themselves.

The above are lower-level charges. They should be investigated and light fines given.

My opinion is this: if the codes for rewards and punishments are not clear, military order will be difficult to maintain and ineffective. There should be fewer rules for an army than for civil society, but they should be enforced more strictly. Therefore, be warned [and be careful about how you treat your troops as] it is necessary to retain as many soldiers as possible and reduce the number of troops you lose – avoid this option as much as possible.

POINTS ON REWARDS AND PUNISHMENTS FROM THE *XING LI QUAN SHU* (性理大全)

Guishan (亀山), also known as Yang Shi (楊氏), says that laws should be established and orders given so that people can avoid violating them without difficulty. Someone who violates them should not be excused no matter what their rank. Follow this way and ensure that laws and orders are maintained without exception.

Wufeng (五峰), also known as Huhong (胡氏), quotes the philosopher Xunzi (荀子) in stating that it is man who rules, not laws. The man who tries to settle turbulent times of war and bring about order must act as if crossing a sea or river. The law is the 'ship' and the man is trying to make his way across the water on that ship. If the ship is wrecked and the oars are broken asunder, it would be impossible to successfully cross [the sea] even if the man were of unequalled competence in the world. Therefore, during turbulent times of great chaos, laws should be changed in accordance with the situation. Nobody can bring about great peace without changing laws.

Commentator two

'It is man who rules, not laws.' There are people who can settle great turbulence and bring peace by governing people, but there are no eternal laws by which you can govern. As the above text says, it is just like crossing a sea. If you run into a storm upon the waves, then even if there is a man of incomparable skill on board, the outcome will be the same. No normal ways will keep the ship on its course. To survive the storm you will have to cast away cargo to lighten the load, replace rudders and check the rigging. Similarly, in a time of [political] turbulence, you cannot govern with the laws for peace.

Issui-sensei says

Yuan-cheng (元城), also known as Liu Anshi (劉氏), says that a lord should establish orders to ensure correct conduct by those people who follow such rules. If the orders meet righteous principles, they should be kept in effect and should not be changed. If they do not meet such principles or they go against the wishes of the people, they should be revised. It is not the way of the sage to leave in place something he once ordered if he knows it is not beneficial; this is not a positive move. It is the way of the sage to employ that which is positive and move forward with it. Know that the rise or fall of a state or the status of the court is dependent on this matter. Do not conduct anything that goes against the mind of the people, to any degree.

Zhu Xi (朱氏) says that the lord has a responsibility to give orders, but that he should always take counsel from his ministers and discuss with advisers to examine such laws thoroughly so that they are established based on public welfare. After this the laws should be presented to the imperial court, and then to the public. The lord should do all this dispassionately.

Cheng Hao (程子) says that the *Book of Documents*[53] praises emperors Yao and Shun because they stated that those found guilty should not always be punished [severely], whereas those who have attained achievements should always be rewarded. They believed that if there was a doubt concerning the charge, a lesser punishment should be handed out, but that people should always be rewarded generously, even if there was a doubt over the achievement.

---

53   One of the Five Classics (五經) of ancient Chinese literature.

Even though sometimes this relaxation of the laws will result in too much mercy being given, it will also prevent killing the innocent.

Wei Yang Fan (華陽范) says that if all the people flatter the lord when he gives out rewards and they fear him when he gives out punishments, this does not mean that he has won over millions of people; it is simply that his actions were reasonable. Be warned, all the people in the state will turn to disobedience if the unworthy are promoted and may form grudges if the innocent are killed. Although, this will not destroy [the stability of] the entire population, there will be a degree of inequality caused by such a situation.

Wu Yi (武夷) says that a lord should praise or reward according to the correct path of the lord (王道), not because he conceives a liking for a certain person's way of service. Conversely, he should dislike people only according to the correct path of the lord and not punish them just because he has a grudge against them.

A lord should be aware of the above quotes on principles. Matters concerning *samurai* and *shisotsu* soldiers should be investigated thoroughly through the correct command structure of lower to higher.[54] Rewards should be given even for minor achievements, but minor charges should be dropped.

During a campaign, issues should be presented to the six *bugyō* for consideration before they are reported to the *taishō*. If an issue is brought [to the *taishō*] without careful consideration, it can be regrettable. However, dependent on the situation, all information concerning the enemy status should immediately be reported to the *taishō* without discussion. Be aware of the above regarding issues within your own clan.

---

54 Do not take matters directly to the top, follow the proper process.

CHAPTER TEN

番頭
Bangashira

CAPTAINS OF THE TROOPS[55]

The number of these varies and this position is also called *samurai-gashira*. The army should also have *itte no shō* troop commanders. The *taishō* assigns the positions [of *bangashira* – captain of the troops] according to each situation. Be aware that the areas they are to take control of should not be fixed beforehand.

Those who lead *samurai* should not give thought to fighting for themselves but instead should be aware that their achievements derive from:

- having a good command of the *samurai* and soldiers below them
- having a rational and correct grasp of the way of combat
- dying a proper death
- not disrupting order

Commentator two

In Japan there is a principle called *san no saihai*, the three ways of military command (三ノ再拝). The following are the three ways of military command for the *taishō*:

- To have good judgement on people's abilities and to give orders according to such judgements.

---

55 A *samurai* who becomes a captain of a group. However, the *samurai* under them are not his retainers but are just given to him to command. Later, *bangashira* became the term for a captain of a group of castle guards.

- To always discuss the achievements of brave warriors, in their own province or other provinces, and carefully decide, with proper judgement, the amount of reward for such attainments.
- To plan formations and strategies of attack, to manoeuvre troops by simulating with *go* pieces or figures, and to know the types of combat and the formations and situation of warriors.

Senior counsellors keep a careful eye on all *kashira* captains and *bugyō* commanders and also have good judgement on all details concerning right or wrong.

Points that a *bangashira* captain of the troop should keep in mind:

[A captain should] encourage the *samurai* of his unit by regularly talking to them.

Commentator two

The *bangashira* should often give words of encouragement to the men in his group and always try to endear himself to them so that they are inspired to give their all for him. [Someone in this position] should always make sure that there is no discord between himself and his men.

Issui-sensei says

Deal with the soldiers of the unit and consider their respective competences.

Commentator two

Samurai achievements should be assessed based on a judgement of the strengths of each man. This is to ensure that rewards and punishments are attributed with a proper sense of proportion.

Issui-sensei says

Teachings for the time of spear fighting: for close combat performed by *ashigaru* foot soldiers, understand enemy procedures well and train your own soldiers beforehand.

Commentator two

Details on spear fighting are written in another scroll.

Issui-sensei says

There are positions for the *kashira* captains when the army takes formation. *Samurai* and soldiers should form up quickly. These things are transmitted in the scroll *Kōketsu*.

Make sure to give thorough consideration to the above points and be fully aware of them. Also make sure not to slight your soldiers.

CHAPTER ELEVEN

The following five articles contain points that should be determined internally among *samurai* for use in their respective units.

ARTICLE ONE
How to signal with a war baton

Commentator two

Signalling with a war baton was discussed previously. Therefore, here this point is mainly concerned with [its use in relation to] an agreement with a group.[56] For example, arrangements may be made for your group not to attack upon a signal that looks [to everyone else] like a command to attack. If the war baton appears to signal a retreat, it may actually mean [that your group should] advance, or if it appears to signal an advance, it may actually be a signal to retreat [for your group]. In such a case, if the *taishō* questions why you did not attack when he ordered an attack, you should say that despite the order to attack it was not possible because of poor footing, or some other such pretext [to keep the arrangement secret].

In Korea, there were approximately 300 enemy war ships, so Ban Dan'emon, a retainer to Katō Yoshiaki, divided [from the main force] and took a waterborne force out to attack. Katō Yoshiaki said to the commander-in-chief, a warrior named Ukita Hideie, 'It is unpardonable that my retainer sneaked out to achieve distinction. I will signal him to return.'

Katō Yoshiaki then signalled with his war baton [with the gesture to have them return]. However, [unbeknown to others,] he and Ban Dan'emon had previously arranged for Dan'emon to continue to attack even more fiercely upon this signal. Yoshiaki pretended to be angry and said, 'This is outrageous. I

---

56   That is, a special, secret arrangement made between the leader and one particular group.

will move out to kill him myself.' He moved out by ship and went on the attack while pretending to call him back. This is an exact example of this particular way of using a war baton, where [what appears to be] an order from the *taishō* should not be accepted.

ARTICLE TWO
Attacking an enemy

Commentator one
[The skill of] attacking three enemies with five.

Commentator two
[This is also the skill of attacking one enemy with three men.] Some instructions should be given to the group beforehand. These include making a subgroup when fighting with an enemy so that two or three members of the group attack a single enemy together. One member fights with a spear, one member takes the opponent's head, the other fights against other enemies who are attacking them. In this way three people will be able to take one head, and if they repeat this three times each of them will gain an enemy head. This way will allow everyone to take a head without fail. Otherwise, strong *samurai* will always attain achievement, while weak soldiers attain nothing. The brave and the coward should be teamed up in this way.

ARTICLE THREE
When an army loses a battle

Commentator one
[Within a group] pre-arrange a meeting point so that all can reunite there.

Commentator two
Instruct where all personnel should regroup if the battle is lost, especially if there is no *matoi* standard. If there is a *matoi* standard [in view], know that it will help people rally easily.

ARTICLE FOUR
Internal arrangements and passwords within the unit

Commentator two
If passwords are not arranged for each group that are separate from the [password] for the entire army, it will be difficult for the group to come together. Other groups of allies will mix in during a *youchi* night attack or *yoikusa* night battle [which may lead to confusion].

ARTICLE FIVE
Mutual communication within a castle

Commentator two
If a group of fifty people is assigned to defend a certain area from (insert place name) to (insert place name), it is desirable to divide the group into two sections of twenty-five people, who take turns to defend the area. Also, everyone in the group should share details beforehand on what to do if they suffer a night attack, if the enemy approaches, and so on.

Issui-sensei says
The above are teachings concerning the use of soldiers and these should be transmitted. Those holding this position [of *bangashira* – captain of a troop] could be assigned various services and they should investigate numerous matters by asking for details concerning many areas.

軍奉行
Ikusa-bugyō

MINISTERS OF WAR

There are two of these and together they make up one pair of the six *bugyō* commanders. They can also be called *musha-bugyō*.

The *ikusa-bugyō* control everything within an army. They consider everything in discussion with the *hata-bugyō* flag commanders and the *yari-bugyō* spear commanders. Their task is to give orders concerning combat.

During battle, they move around to see each unit, so they are also described as *uki-musha* – floating warriors. They ensure that the formations are correctly constructed, check the *samurai* troops and give them direct orders, discussing any concerns with each unit. Particularly in an army of a small number, they sometimes take command of a unit wherever it is deemed to be necessary, although this varies from clan to clan.

When attacking deep into an enemy province and when withdrawing, *ikusa-bugyō* ministers of war ride around and control the movement of their forces to avoid being attacked or followed by the enemy. This is a difficult task commensurate with the seniority of this position.

When retreating, use the teaching called *kuribiki* – phased withdrawal. However, if it is not possible [to withdraw] due to topography, then use the concept of *kurikomi* – tucking your troops into areas that the geography allows – and move the troops into certain areas, as seen in the drawing below.[57]

Kurikomi

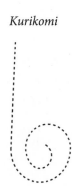

---

57 The term *kuri* (繰) means: to fit into an area, to tuck in, to fold within, to move section by section. The idea is to move and mould troops into the natural features of the land. Therefore, a general either uses phased withdrawal or he tries to 'tuck' the men into the landscape because the area is tight.

Commentator two

Kurikomi (alternative version one)

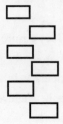

Kurikomi (alternative version two)

Kuribiki

Issui-sensei says

This is not to be used in a position that has shady places.[58] In such situations you should instead use *gankō* – the wild goose formation – or a blocking unit to allow the *taishō* to retreat first.

---

58 The ideograms here imply limited visibility due to foliage.

Below is an illustration of the left and right formations of *gankō* – the wild goose formation.

Commentator one
'Shady places' means woods, bushes, footpaths between rice paddies, etc.

Commentator two
The above tactics [*kurikomi* and *kuribiki*] should not be used in bushy areas between rice paddies or watersides with reed grasses. In these cases, have blocking forces in place or use *gankō* – the wild goose formation – to enable the *taishō* to retreat.

Issui-sensei says
The six *bugyō* should discuss the details of each formation. Also, they should estimate [enemy] numbers through calculation.

Our school contains the subject of *zabi* (座備) formations. One formation is known as *shichidan no hō* – the way of the seven-layered formation [as described in the next article]. Although this kind of principle falls under a *taishō's* remit, it has been placed here so that the deployment of warriors can be discussed.

Commentator two
The concept of *zabi* is also discussed in another writing.

七段之法

Shichidan no hō

THE SEVEN-LAYERED FORMATION

1. *ichi no saki* 一ノ先 – the first troop [vanguard]
2. *ni no saki* 二ノ先 – the second troop
3. *wakizonae* 脇備 – flanking troops
4. *hatamoto* 旗本 – command group
5. *ushirozonae* 後備 – rear troop
6. *konida* 小荷駄 – logistics and baggage train
7. *yūgun* 遊軍 – reserve troop

The above are the seven layers of troops. In an eight-layered formation (*hachidan no wari*), the *shingari* – the troop that defends the retreat – is added.

Commentator two

In an eight-layered formation, a *shingari* – retreat-protecting troop – is added.

人數割之法

Ninjuwari no hō

THE DEPLOYMENT OF TROOPS

A division of 10,000 people should be divided up as follows:

- 3,000 should stay within the castle
- 7,000 should venture out to fight

The 7,000 people who venture out to fight should be divided up as follows:

- vanguard – ten units each of 300, which adds up to 3,000
- command group – six units each of 500 [which adds up to 3,000]
- logistics – two units each of 300, which adds up to 600
- scouts – the remaining 400 should make up one unit

Take two of the ten vanguard units, one unit from the command group, and one unit from logistics: this equates to 1,400 people. These should be used as reserve forces, which are called *kenbutsu no sonae* (見物ノ備) – observing troops. In a winning battle they are called *shimari zonae* (シマリ), finishing troops, and they also serve as *shingari* – troops who defend the retreat.

The above way of assignment is for a force of a small number. For a large number, calculate from the numbers above. If the overall number of troops is smaller than the above example, divide accordingly. However, in the case of a large number, troops themselves sometimes are divided, but this all depends on the situation.

Eight points on the assignment of 20,000 people:

1. Five thousand stay to defend the castle.
2. Three thousand form the *hatamoto* command group.
3. Seven units each of 500 should be the first troop; this adds up to 3,500.
4. Seven units each of 300 should be the second troop; this adds up to 2,100.
5. Six units each of 500 should be the flank troops stationed on each side of the *hatamoto* command group; this adds up to 3,000.
6. Three units each of 300 should be the rear troop; this adds up to 900.
7. Five units each of 300 should be the reserve troop; this add up to 1,500.
8. Two units each of 500 should be logistics; this adds up to 1,000.

The above method should be used to examine the assignment of the troops of an army. The details of the army should be devised by the commander.

六奉行相談合詞可定事

Roku bugyō sōdan aikotoba sadameru beki koto

THE SIX *BUGYŌ* SHOULD DISCUSS AND CREATE PASSWORDS

Do not use passwords that have existed since ancient times. Change them daily, or even two or three times a day, according to the situation. Create such passwords that people cannot directly understand why they are associated with each other but that are still easy for even lower people to remember. Avoid the kind of password used by the Takeda clan in older times – examples include 'mountains' to 'woods', or 'mountain peaks' to 'pine trees'. However, ones that are too complicated are difficult for lower people to remember. Also be aware that people will always make a mistake with passwords that are similar to common words, especially at hectic times. Make a list of them beforehand and present the list to the *taishō* for his reference. Sometimes passwords are used in combination with gestures. In this case, create combinations that are easy to remember but are difficult for others to associate with each other.

The position [of *ikusa-bugyō*] can even be taken by young warriors if they possess benevolence, courage and talent. Also, lesser-ranking people can take this position if they are sons of well-known people. If this is the case, accompanying warriors (添武者) should be appointed to guide them.

On the subject of *hiroi-fu* (拾符) stamped paper markers, tradition says that if 100 people venture out for a night attack, the *ikusa-bugyō* minister of war should prepare 101 pieces of paper each measuring 4 *sun* square and carrying his stamp. The general (*shō*) of the troop should give each of his men one of these pieces of paper. Checking the papers at the *masugata*, the square inner compound,[59] when the soldiers return will prevent the enemy from following them back and infiltrating.

Commentator one

It must be said that here the ideogram *hiroi* 拾 from *hiroi-fu*, which means 'to pick up' does not make sense to me. [In my opinion] this is what is called *ai-fu* (合符) identification marks or *in-fu* (印符) identification tallies. Therefore, I think that [the ideogram used previously] should be *sute-fu* (捨符), which means 'throw away markers', but I think this was mistakenly written by the author or transcriber.

Small bamboo strips can also be used for this purpose. Such tags are sometimes lost; therefore, ensure that the troops do not lose them.

Commentator two

One hundred pieces of paper are to be delivered to one hundred people and one piece is kept as the master slip for checking. When the people return, their stamps are compared against the master slip to make sure they are genuine.

---

59   A 'killing zone' inside a gateway.

旗奉行
Hata-bugyō

FLAG COMMANDERS

There are two of these and together they make up one pair of the six *bugyō* commanders.

This position is essential in an army and they are without question indispensable when a battle is about to start. For example, even if your allies fall into confusion, if the banners and flags are held firmly in their positions and do not move, people who once collapsed will be able to regroup by finding the flags again. This is called *ryū* – the dragon. Dragons have the energy of *yō* (positivity) and accomplish the greatest of achievements. Also, the flags are where the gods of war reside and such gods like to be at a height. However, I would like to suggest that the flags are positioned high up so that they can be seen easily by everyone, rather than because this is where the gods reside.

When attacking a castle, a large number of flags should be set up like a forest so that they stand out, and as the saying goes they should be without gaps from east to west.

旗ヲ東西ニナビカス

Flags should stretch from east to west.

When warriors move forward to attack, for every ten flags accompanying them three should go forward in front of the horses and the rest should go at the rear. Flags should be positioned at regular and wide enough intervals when attacking so that it looks like there are more people than there actually are. Do not have too few flags, as this will cause the forces to fall into disarray.

Be aware, when breaking through enemy forces with horses, that you need to rearrange the flag layout quickly so that about three out of ten flags accompany the horses on both sides while rushing into the enemy ranks.

Commentator two

Breaking in with horses is an extreme action to be taken when the enemy is in a tight formation, making it difficult to attack them with spears. This action will drive [the enemy] into disarray so that your spear units can tear into them. Choose fast horses and good riders and have 300–500 horsemen.[60]

There are [a few] ways to break in with horses:

- Break through the enemy and ride on.
- Break through the enemy and return through them.
- Break through the enemy and peel off to the left and right.

Use flags to signal to the *hatamoto* command group, so that the command group knows how far the horses have advanced.

Issui-sensei says

When defending a castle against a siege, position as many flags as possible around the castle so that an immense number of them can be seen. Position one flag for each *ken* in distance along the castle wall. Also, raise up as many flags as possible at each *yagura* turret. This is called *sōbata* (惣旗) mass flag raising, or also it can be known as *kazubata* (数旗) universal flags.

As for raising flags in a battle camp, create a sacred area by building and tying a frame of wooden posts together into a grid consisting of five verticals and four horizontals, to be positioned one on each side of the outer area of the fortification gate. The number of flags to be tied to the lattice is not definitive and depends on the clan; most likely it will be seven, ten, fifteen, twenty and so on. It should be decided according to the resources of the clan, but this kind of number would be appropriate for most provincial lords.

---

60 The text is ambiguous at this point. We have assumed that the figure refers to the number of riders. However, it could be a reference to some other element.

Commentator two

A five-by-four grid represents the *kuji* grid of protection. This is a practice to dispel evil spirits and drive away the enemy.

Issui-sensei says

On a battlefield, flags are also placed in front of the *taishō*, which is why the area where the *taishō* is positioned is called the *hatamoto*.[61] Add [flags] to the front, rear, left and right. However, there is no set rule for this – use them according to the situation. The flags for the vanguard should be placed behind the *samurai* and when a battle has finished, and [the warriors] return, [flag bearers] should be repositioned, moving around the returning men to the area at their rear.

Commentator two

At the battle of Nagakute during the Tenshō period (1573–1593), there was a *rōnin* from the area of Kōshū called Ogiwara Kenmotsu – he was at that time the captain of the *chūgen*. He stepped forward [before the lord] and said: 'The *ashigaru* foot soldiers are the "fence" for the pikemen (足軽ハ鑓ノ垣), while the pikemen are the "fence" for the *samurai* (鑓ハ士ノ垣) and the *samurai* are the "fence" for the flags (士ハ旗ノ垣), so [in essence] there should actually be no battle around the lord's flag.[62] This flag should be positioned behind the lord's horse, while only a standard (小円居) in the shape of a fan should be placed in front of the lord's horse.'

When these words were heard, the flag was moved backwards to the rear of the lord.

---

61 Literally, *hata* 'flag' and *moto* 'central area', meaning 'place of the flag'. However, in this series we have translated *hatamoto* as 'command group'.

62 This gives three layers of protection for the main command group. The problem here is the term 'pikemen': the original text uses the word *yari*, which means 'spear'. However, in other sections the word *yari* has been used to mean 'pike'. Therefore, by context we have adopted the word 'pikemen' here.

TRADITIONAL WAYS FOR THE STATUS OF FLAGS

Cover the area with flags and make sure that they are arranged relatively densely without [too much] space between them, so as to make them look numerous. This gives the vanguard an infusion of energy with which to attack the enemy.

When passing out through a gate you should lead with the top of the flag, but when returning lead with the bottom of the flag.

When you come across a river during a march, [flags] should not go to the rear but should advance without changing position.[63]

For the flag pole, fresh bamboo should be straightened by burning [the surface] so that it will not break, even if blown by wind.

Flags are sometimes blown up in the air by wind so they should be fastened down with an *odome no kuda* (緒トメノ管)[64] [as shown in the illustrations below]. If the horizontal bar [at the top of the flag is in the style of] *origane* angled iron, use unforged iron. Another desirable style of flag crossbar is the *hishaku yokote*, which has a ladle-shaped upper bar. Further details are in the scroll *Hata no Maki*, so are not mentioned here.

Commentator two

[The two styles of flag crossbars mentioned in the text above:]

柄折ヨコテ

Hishaku yokote

Ladle-shaped upper bar

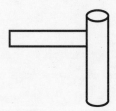

---

63 The key is for the flags not to retreat from the river.

64 The Koga transcription reads *saodome no kuda* (竿留ノ管). In either case, the device in question is a small set of cords and cylinders to keep the flag in place.

折金
Origane
Angled iron

竿留管
Saodome no kuda[65]
Flag-securing cylinder

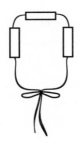

Issui-sensei says

Flag bearers are lower ranking than the *dōshin* class, which means they may have difficulty understanding orders. They readily fall into disarray, but you can actually assemble them relatively easily. However, without proper supervision they will allow the flags to become furled so that they are easier to carry when advancing. Therefore, the *yoriki* attached captain of each group should pay careful attention so as to maintain order [and to ensure the flags remain flying fully].

Commentator two

Generally, flags should be inserted into holders that are fixed to the rear. If it is windy, carry the flag to the front and insert it into a leather holder. A large flag

---

65 *Odome no kuda* (緒トメノ管) in the Tōkyō transcription.

should be fixed in a holder, carried over the shoulder and supported by two to four people.

Issui-sensei says

When advancing quickly, some people [holding flags] stumble and fall to the ground. Therefore, make sure to have spare flag bearers or *teaki* unassigned men to support them around the waist to keep them from falling. Also, sometimes poles break. If this happens, have the men splice the broken pole without it being noticed, then they should continue forward. In an urgent situation, they should carry the broken poles as they are and keep marching forward. Avoid making an issue out of this, or else there will be an argument among flag bearers.

Commentator one

In an urgent situation, broken flag poles should not be left behind but should be carried on without having been repaired.

GIVING AND RECEIVING A FLAG

When giving or receiving a flag, do not hold the pole at the bamboo joints. When the flag is brought inside [the camp, etc.], have the top pointed [in the auspicious direction of] south-east.

Commentator two

It is considered ill to hold a flag at the joints [of the bamboo pole], as *fushi*, the word for 'joint', reminds us of the phrase *fushi wo fusagu* – meaning 'blocking a good opportunity'. A flag should be placed with the top pointed south-east. Flags are essential tools so it is lucky if they advance and if they continue to advance it is classed as extremely lucky. Advancing is an element of *yō* and moving toward *yō* is auspicious.

鑓奉行
Yari-bugyō

SPEAR COMMANDERS

There are two of these and together they make up one pair of the six *bugyō* commanders.

This position commands the *mochiyari* self-owning spearmen, who should be combined in one unit. The number of troops is not definite.

Commentator two

These [men] are also considered as *dōnagae* uniformed pikemen. The term *mochiyari* does not refer to spearmen who are under the direct command of the lord [as they are different]. Therefore, different names are used for those [spearmen] in the vanguard and those [spearmen] in the *hatamoto* command group. *Dōnagae* uniformed pikemen and *tadanagae* simple spearmen are troops that are positioned in the vanguard.

Issui-sensei says

During a campaign, the six *bugyō* should meet to discuss matters each day. The *hata-bugyō* flag commanders and *yari-bugyō* spear commanders should be experienced older people and appointed only after careful consideration of their wartime career.

The position they should take in a formation depends upon the situation. Be aware that the enemy will surely have horses to break through your units, thus [people in this position] should know how to deal with this eventuality. The [*yari-bugyō* and his men] should take up position in front of the *hatamoto* command group.

Commentator two

Be aware that if the enemy is intending to break through [your formation] with horses they will have many horses in their vanguard. Usually both allied and enemy vanguards consist of archers and musketeers, so if you observe horses [stationed within the enemy vanguard], know that are planning to break through with them.

Issui-sensei says

Pikemen do not have to thrust but instead take up a position and strike down on the enemy only when [the enemy] breaks through with their horses. They are of the status of *chūgen* lower-ranking people and the like, so be aware that they may easily collapse. Form groups of three to five men and have them support each other, and also have replacements [standing by]. Make sure that their strikes are unified.

If your formation is weakened and the enemy is causing confusion and is breaking through, sometimes the *hatamoto* command group will make a sudden thrust forward. In such a case, the *yari-bugyō* spear commander should have the men under his command make unified downward strikes with their spears. This is just the kind of situation where the *yari-bugyō* should make use of his experience, as is shown below.

Tradition says:

- If the enemy horses break through [your side], have the men go down on one knee in line and attack the horses by sweeping them with [their weapons].
- If an enemy comes on suddenly, rushing in a charge, strike the horses.
- When striking give a loud cry and horses will give way.
- Pikemen should be used to eliminate the enemy when the enemy is crossing a river.
- They should also be used when your side is crossing a river. Be aware that when crossing a river, pole-arm troops should always be the first [of the main troops] to cross.

Commentator two

It is reasonable to use archers and musketeers to defend against a small enemy group crossing a river. However, if the number crossing is 1,000 or 2,000, you will need to resort to the more drastic measure of a unit of pikes. If you defend with pikes, the enemy will also use pikes, which will make it even more difficult for your force to defend with shorter weapons. Thus, pikes are the weapons to be used for [defending against a large enemy group] crossing a river.

Issui-sensei says

When securing a castle, position pikemen to defend the sides of gates, and also the corners.

When making spear rafts or stretching a rope to cross a river, the construction shown in the drawing below should be used.

Commentator two

As in the drawing, attach the handles to each other and use a barrel as a float.

Issui-sensei says

There is another commander called the *nagae-bugyō* – commander of the pikes. This position is not included in the six *bugyō*, but they command the *kazuyari* – men with loaned pikes.

Commentator one

Pikemen are mostly labourers but are important on a battlefield. How to control them is the same as described previously.

Commentator two

Pikemen are positioned to the front of *samurai* not only for defending against horses breaking through, but also so they can endure and hold firm with each other in critical situations. Know that [pikemen] should act just as *ippei* independent soldiers should act – this can be found in the scroll *Ippei Yōkō*. Take note, if it is difficult for them to attack independently, have the pikemen move forward hitting down with their pikes in unison.

Issui-sensei says

Be aware that [pikemen] should be positioned in the vanguard but the exact place they are positioned depends on the situation. Just like the captains of archers or musketeers [prepare their own men], have them prepared [and in position] before spear fighting starts.

THE SIX COMMANDERS

As seen above, the six *bugyō* are the primary commanders and control all aspects of the battle. They meet to discuss everything be it day or night in the *chakutō yagura* – the turret of arrival.[66] They discuss such aspects as war strategies, arrangements, the deployment of soldiers and instructions concerning signals by conch shell, etc.

---

66 A turret where the *taishō* watches and inspects the status of his army or the exercise of horse-riding.

KON

THE SCROLL OF EARTH

CHAPTER TWELVE

小荷駄奉行
Konida-bugyō

COMMANDERS OF LOGISTICS AND THE BAGGAGE TRAIN

Two of these are required.

This position is important, because the packhorses are one of the most profitable units for the enemy to capture.

If the general (*shō*) in charge is not good enough to undertake this position, the entire army can be affected and even defeated. Therefore, it is important for the *taishō* to choose people for this task carefully.

Tradition says that the word *konida-oshi* means 'packhorses that march and carry equipment for all soldiers'. The baggage train contains the youngest sons of those *samurai* in service to the clan, as well as *rōnin* and those who own no horse themselves, allowing them to travel mounted on a *norikake* horse.[67]

When the baggage train needs to take position in a formation [because the enemy is on the attack], have the baggage train commander act as a military leader so that he can command and prepare the people of that unit.

Commentator one

When Takeda Shingen drew back after attacking the warrior Hōjō Ujiyasu's castle in Odawara, the warrior Hōjō Mutsu no kami [Ujiteru] attempted to cut off his retreat. Takeda ordered his own warrior Naitō Shuri to take command

---

67 A packhorse that carries a person as well as a load.

of the baggage train, but Naitō declined the assignment. At this, the warlord Takeda said to him: 'I wish I had a replica of myself for I would like to take that position. As I regard you as the mirror image of myself, I order you to become the baggage train commander.'

Through this episode know the importance of the *konida-bugyō* – baggage train commander.

Commentator two

The *konida-bugyō* baggage train commander is a position for the high ranking to fulfil since it is of extreme importance. Takeda Shingen said that he himself would like to take this position during the battle of Mimase in Sōshū. Also, remember that [Tokugawa Ieyasu's] forces began to collapse from the baggage train as packhorses were attacked at the battle of Mikatagahara. The baggage train also came under attack at the battle of Kawanakajima. [Even the famous general] Naoe Yamashiro no kami Kanetsugu of Echigo province took command of the baggage train [because of its great importance].

The following are the various types of baggage trains:

別手ノ小荷駄押

Bette no konida oshi

This is a baggage train that marches in a single unit, marching at the rear of the entire army procession.[68]

一手押

Itte oshi

This is a baggage train whose units are separately connected to different sections of the army and therefore does not need a *konida-bugyō* – commander of the baggage train.

68　別手ノ小荷駄ヲシ.

Commentator two

In Kōshū-Ryū, there are methods called *itte no bette* and *bette no itte*.

一手ノ別手
Itte no bette
This is to have packhorses follow each separate group while in the army.

別手ノ一手
Bette no itte
This is to have all packhorses march together at the rear.

Issui-sensei says

Goods should have the marks of their owners on *shirushi* markings or on *aifu* – split identifying markers with stamped impressions. Remember, if anyone has something they must do outside of the procession, it is a rule not to disturb the order without good reason.

Commentator one

A *shirushi* is a form of drawn tag.

If someone [from outside the baggage train] has something to do [inside of the procession], he should get permission from the [baggage train] commander to do so.

Use the *i-ro-ha* phonetic alphabet[69] to mark the baggage.

小荷駄法度
Konida hatto
RULES FOR THE LOGISTICS DIVISION AND BAGGAGE TRAIN
Make sure that horses do not become uncontrollable, [which is a danger] because the section includes many lower-grade horses. Also, make sure that the intervals between horses are not too great, as the enemy will always attack those that become separated.

Much pilfering happens within a troop of packhorses. This *must* be prohibited.

---

69 Phonetic markers for easier reading.

If something has fallen off at the front of the baggage train, someone towards the rear should pick it up and pass it back up the train [to its original position].

It should be strictly prohibited to speak loudly, abuse others or even speak at all without good reason.

If you see the enemy, do not make a fuss; instead assemble and secure yourselves upon the general's order. While this rule also applies to the rest of the procession, it should be strictly observed by the baggage train above all others.

There are things to be kept in mind when marching in difficult places in enemy lands:

- Make sure the baggage train is kept in order.
- Have an assembly of *ashigaru* foot soldiers in front of it.
- Have any soldiers on *norikake* mounted packhorses [dismount and] march on foot, keeping themselves marching in unit order.

If the enemy is seen, make sure the procession is assembled properly and secure it. If the enemy attacks the centre [of the procession], one *taishō* at the front and one *taishō* at the rear should divide the procession into two sections at the place where the enemy has struck and those two parties should fight as two separate units with a *taishō* for each.

Commentator one

Each general should secure his front and rear. This is called *mukade-zonae* (百足備), the centipede's formation,[70] or alternatively it is called *ichiku-kuichi* (一九九一), the 19 and 91 formation.[71]

Commentator two

This method is used when [your force has] been split in the middle: in this case construct a front [troop], a rear [troop], a left [troop] and a right [troop]. In Kōshū-Ryū this is called *mukade-zonae*, the centipede's formation, or alternatively it is called *ichiku-kuichi zonae*, the 19 and 91 formation.

---

70 Meaning that it can divide into sections like the body of a centipede is articulated in sections.

71 Probably a reference to symmetry, 19 and 91 being near-mirror images of each other.

Issui-sensei says

If the enemy comes from behind, the commander at the rear should form the vanguard and the formation should be reversed without creating disorder. This is a secret tradition.

In a spacious field or other appropriate place, use the formation of *kurikomi no sonae.*[72] This formation may also be used by the baggage train. The principle is the same for the front and the rear [of the force].

While your army is fighting with the enemy, move the soldiers into position and place the lower people between the combatants; the luggage should go to the rear. Also, prearrange so that a certain number of people stay with the goods and staunchly guard them.

Commentator one

If there are 100 packhorses, the commander should assign 1,000 people [to defend] the baggage train. Thus, if the commander has a total of 2,000 people under him, he should have the remaining 1,000 to defend against the enemy. Also, soldiers who are on *norikake* mounted packhorses should be added to the troops defending [the baggage train].

Issui-sensei says

For the enemy, winning victory in the battle itself is important but so is winning the baggage train. Sometimes they attack just to capture your goods.

Groups of people from local villages may also rise up and attack to steal your goods. If you assume they are the enemy army, you may be puzzled by the way they fight. You should know who they are by the way they attack, so make sure to have a different way of defending against them. There are important points that the *konida-bugyō* baggage train commander should keep in mind regarding such matters. These are orally transmitted.

---

72 *Kurikomi* is normally to tuck into difficult areas, but here this means reducing the line length of the troops, making the formation more compact so that the enemy cannot easily break through.

Commentator one

Villagers do not attack in formation and their flags and banners are disorganized. As their primary objective is to steal goods, they first approach the packhorses and try to take [supplies] as quickly as possible. In this case, you should shatter them with arrows and muskets. If they are true enemies, they will attack by taking up a formation. During the Heiji rebellion (in 1160), Minamoto no Yoshitomo fled from Kyōto. At one point his force was surrounded by a group of rioters, to which Nagai Sanemori [one of Yoshitomo's generals] responded by throwing his helmet into the fray so that the rioters would fight over it. This enabled him to attack them and drive them away.

Commentator two

Village uprisings have no formations but simply come to steal the baggage. In this case, defend immediately and strongly. An enemy army will attack in a proper formation, so you should defend in a proper manner.

CHAPTER THIRTEEN

物頭之事
Monogashira no koto

VARIOUS CAPTAINS

Numerous captains are required. Units that have *yoriki* attached captains [are ruled over by a commander] who is given the title *ashigaru-daishō* – commander of the foot soldiers; whereas those units without attached captains have overall commanders called *dōshin-gashira* – captains of the *dōshin* class.[73] Also, there are differences [that captains should keep in mind] between archers and musketeers.

Commentator two
Yoriki (与力) are so named because they give aid to captains.[74]

弓足軽之事
Yumi ashigaru no koto

ARCHER FOOT SOLDIERS

These [troops] shoot at the start of a battle before the spear fighting begins.

---

73 This differs from the previous teaching (on page 24) where it stated they were called *mono-gashira*. There appear to be two names for the same position.
74 The ideograms mean 'giving' and 'aid'.

When the distance between the two sides closes up, there is an exchange of arrow fire and then at a prearranged point the archers peel off to each side. There are important points for the *taishō* to consider, but these are orally transmitted.

Commentator one

Archers and musketeers should fire about three shots before they give way [to the troops behind]. Whether they go to the left or the right will vary according to the situation. If the timing is not correct, momentum will be lost.

Commentator two

Tactics will vary according to the situation. This point is important for *ashigaru* foot soldiers [who move to combat] before spear fighting [begins]. If inappropriately timed, the motivation of the spearmen will diminish. There are important points to be considered.

Issui-sensei says

When positioned at the flank of the spearmen, [*ashigaru* archers] should attack [the enemy] and give support to the *yari* spearmen and *nagae* pikemen, as well as defending the flanks. If enemy horses break into your army, [archers] should gauge the spear combat and [at the correct time] engage them with arrow fire. Even the strongest enemy will collapse at this.

How the *ashigaru* foot soldiers at the front fight is of vital importance. The psychological advantage of your spearmen can be lost, depending on how the [*ashigaru* archers] are controlled. After drawing aside, [archers] should observe the spear fighting and know what to do if the enemy collapses or if the allies collapse. More to be orally transmitted.

Commentator one

If the enemy is on the retreat, [the *ashigaru* archers] should pursue them and fire [into their flank]. If your allies are collapsing, the archers should remain at the allied flank and fire at the enemy.

Commentator two

When your allies are collapsing, deliver side attacks [to the enemy] with archers; when the enemy is collapsing, follow and attack them [from the sides]. When doing this, it is important not to shoot your own allies.

Issui-sensei says

Use *nurigome* bows – that is, bows wrapped in rattan and lacquered. In ancient times, King Xunyin, also known as Minghe, said that you should carry entirely lacquered bows so that their wrapping will not come loose in the rain, the glue will not slacken in the heat, and they will maintain their aim, even if dropped in water.

It is also said that in battle archers should use bows that are strung a little less tautly than they can actually draw so that they can shoot as many arrows as possible [without getting tired]. This is found in the *Wubei Zhi* text.

For bow strings, use *sekizuru* – wrapped and lacquered strings. In ancient times and in our country, I think that everyone used *sekizuru*-style bow strings. This type of string is always lacquered as a precaution against rain. According to the *Huqianjing* manual, you should carry three strings for one bow.

Commentator one

Sekizuru strings should be wrapped with two or three layers of silk finishing line.

The *Huqianjing* manual is found within the document *Wubei Zhi*.

Commentator two

Sekizuru strings are so called because they were invented in Seki in west Seishū. One record talks about Kitabatake Noritomo [from Seishū], who, it is said, offered a bag of twelve strings of *jōjin* quality, claiming that they were produced in his own province – the province of Seki. This record also mentions how to use hemp strings.

Issui-sensei says

Arrows should be fletched and lacquered and the arrowhead should be of the *kanadōtōshi* (armour-piercing) type. Mao Yuanyi, author of the document *Wubei Zhi*, says that arrows should be fletched and lacquered for protection against rain.

鉄炮足軽之事
Teppō ashigaru no koto

MUSKETEER FOOT SOLDIERS

The use of musketeers should vary depending on the nature of the battle. However, like archers, musketeers are well used for defence by positioning them at the flanks of spearmen. There is a certain way to shoot before spear fighting begins.

Commentator one

According to the *Taiheiki* war chronicle, the emperor of the Yuan Dynasty sent 60,000 soldiers in ships of war to invade Japan during the eighth month of Bun'ei 2 (1265). Gunpowder was transmitted in Japan [at this point].[75]

A *yamabushi* named Ōryūbō from Odawara bought a musket from Sakai in the year Eisho 7 (1510) and presented it to Hōjō Ujitsuna.[76]

Commentator two

Make sure that the fire given by the foot soldier musketeers does not slacken. If it becomes slack, then the enemy will break through with horses and your forces will collapse; this is an important point. Muskets were first introduced in our country in Tenmon 12 (1543), when a western merchant ship brought them to Tanegashima Island in Gūshū province in the Kantō area. It is said that a *yamabushi* called Ōryūbō from Odawara also bought one in Sakai of Senshū and presented it to Hōjō Ujitsuna; this was the first musket in Kantō.

75 The term used here is *teppō*, which normally means muskets. However, we have translated it as gunpowder, as only crude firearms would have been available at this time and not the more advanced muskets brought to Japan in the sixteenth century.

76 This story is from the *Hōjō Godaiki* document.

Issui-sensei says

Regardless of how many muskets there are, the same principles should be used.[77]

Use *ashigaru-zutsu* muskets for foot soldiers and make sure they can be shot regardless of what kind of ammunition you have in store.

Commentator one

Before spear combat, musketeers should be controlled and not be allowed to shoot too early or too late. This is mentioned in the *Taishō Hyakusen* volume.

Commentator two

Bullets used in foot soldier muskets should be 6 *momme* in weight.

Issui-sensei says

If *ashigaru* foot soldiers are used properly as described above, even the most formidable enemy – one as strong as stone – will be defeated without doubt. Even if the allies are overwhelmed, proper use of foot soldiers can help the army to get back on its feet and regain strength.

One unit of *ashigaru* foot soldiers should include ten, fifteen, twenty, twenty-five, thirty or fifty people with *yoriki* – attached captains of an appropriate number. Orders to be given beforehand are to be transmitted.

Commentator one

Roughly speaking, there should be one *yoriki* attached captain per five people.

Commentator two

There should be one *yoriki* attached captain for five people. The *yoriki* is different from the *kogashira* sub-captain. *Yoriki* are external aids for the normal *kashira* captains. When *yoriki* are used for this purpose, they function as support troops.

---

77 The sentence is vague. It could mean to use the same principle no matter how many musket-carrying troops there are, but it is not clear on the specifics.

Issui-sensei says

Do not rush or get flustered before a battle. Make sure that there are no blank shots by musketeers or premature shots from archers. Try to sweep the enemy away before you have expended seventy or eighty per cent[78] of your ammunition.

Commentator two

Make sure that only seven or eight out of ten arrows and bullets have been used up; keep back three [out of ten] for emergency. This is an old teaching. There is also an old tradition of leaving some arrows with a person who has been killed. This is called *meido no yōjinya* – reserve arrows for your journey to the afterlife.[79]

Issui-sensei says

Arrows should be shot with the tips pointing upwards and muskets should be shot from the hip.

Commentator two

The Taikō [that is Lord Hideyoshi] ordered [musketeers to] shoot from waist height, while Shinkun [that is Lord Ieyasu] ordered them to shoot one grip [higher].

Issui-sensei says

[*Ashigaru* foot soldiers] should ensure that they take note of their captain's identifying marks and his war baton. They should loosen arrow heads and load bullets so that there is no gap between the bullet [and the cartridge].

Commentator one

If there is a gap between the powder and the bullet, the shot will be weaker and you will not be able to shoot downwards [as the bullet will roll out of the barrel if it is not rammed correctly]. For *otoridama* – smaller bullets [than the muzzle size] – force gunpowder [into the gap from the muzzle end].

---

78 The Koga transcription says 'eight parts in ten'.
79 冥土之用心矢.

Commentator two

Foot soldier bows are not so strong and may not have very much penetrating power, but if you loosen arrow heads [from the shaft] the arrow head will remain lodged in the enemy's body. If there is a gap between the bullet [and the powder], the force of the shot will be weaker. Therefore, put in a little extra gunpowder after the bullets themselves. Also, biting bullets to put teeth marks in them will help.

Issui-sensei says

Make sure that the match for the musket does not burn out.

Commentator two

Place the left foot one step forward when shooting.

SHOOTING ON A NARROW PATH

Commentator one

As shown in the drawing below, [shoot] in sequence.[80]

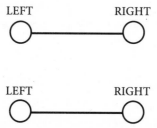

Commentator two

On a narrow path, those [who move up to the] front should crouch and shoot; this is repeated successively. Remember, the enemy will also do this. Loading gunpowder should be done with a signal word. This is called *tatamiuchi* –

---

80 This image and the next one appear to relate to the same teaching, but they differ and are not fully explained. It is unclear whether they show the way one soldier should position his feet or the positions of multiple soldiers.

shooting in sequence. Also, it is a fundamental principle in gunnery to keep fuses lit and make sure to perform this in *suisen* aquatic warfare, especially to secure *kirihinawa* cut fuse sections to a spare ramrod, carrying it on your back.

Furthermore, on a narrow path, there is a method for aligning the muskets [so that more men can shoot in a narrow space]. This is called *gankei* (雁形) – the flying geese formation.[81] Without understanding the proper methods it is difficult to arrange the unit correctly. Remember, the enemy will shoot your allies with *tatamiuchi* – shooting in sequence when on a narrow path.[82]

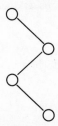

DEFENDING AGAINST AN ENEMY WHEN IT IS CROSSING A RIVER

Commentator one
[The enemy should be shot at when it is in the following positions:]
- preparing to cross the river
- in the [middle of the] river
- having crossed the river

WHEN ALLIES CROSS A RIVER

Commentator one
Have one group cross the river and have another group remain on the original side [to defend], then let the main troop make the crossing.

To let your allies cross a river, have *ashigaru* foot soldiers shoot to discourage the enemy. For example, [during the Winter Siege of Ōsaka castle] Satake's

---

81 This is considered the same as *gankō*, which also means the flying geese formation.
82 This commentary is partly theorized, as the original is ambiguous.

[besieging] army collapsed and was followed to Imafuku by an army led by the warriors Kimura Nagato and Gotō Matabei [who had come out of the castle to give chase]. The warrior Sugihara Hitachi, who was one of Uesugi Kagekatsu's commanders [and who was on the besieging side], had his foot soldiers shoot across the river to dampen the momentum of Kimura and Gotō's army.[83]

Commentator two
When your allies cross a river, first have one unit cross over and defend a position on the opposite bank. Leave one unit on the near bank and have the rest [of the troops] cross the river. Details are written in the scroll *Suisen Yōhō*.

SHOOTING WHEN THE ENEMY IS AT THE FOOT OF A TURRET[84]

Commentator one
Place one foot forward and the other one back [to shoot downwards – do not stand with your feet together].

Commentator two
When [the enemy is] below a turret, shoot with your feet turned inwards.[85] By doing this, it will be easier to shoot enemies who are below a *yagura* – turret.

SHOOTING AT AN ENEMY SHIP

Commentator one
Give instructions to shoot the sides of the ship and make sure to continue to steer [your own ship] correctly. [Shoot at the enemy waterline so as] to fill the ship with water.

---

83 Those inside the castle drove back the attacking side and followed them. The fleeing side crossed the river but used foot soldier gunmen to shoot back across the river to slow down the pursuers.

84 When defending a turret and the enemy is below.

85 From this position the shooter is shooting downwards. The knees should be slightly bent and the feet turned inwards for a more stable shot. This also naturally angles the gun downwards through turret shooting ports.

Commentator two

Make sure to shoot the side of the [enemy] ship while maintaining correct steering [of your own ship]. To penetrate the inside of the enemy ship, it is best to aim at the waterline.

SHOOTING FROM A SHIP

Commentator one

Have two people stand back to back and shoot out to both sides. Shoot at the waterline [of enemy ships].

Commentator two

When shooting from a ship, two people stand back to back and shoot out on both sides, aiming at the waterline of the enemy vessel.

FIGHTING ON FOOT

The method of passing muskets forward to shooters is called *okurizutsu no narai* (送筒習) – the teaching of rotating musketeers.

Commentator one

Send muskets from the rear to good musketeers [who are positioned at the front].

Commentator two

Position two or three excellent musketeers at the front, load multiple muskets with bullets and pass them forward for the musketeers to shoot.

This method should be employed when:

- attacking a castle
- aiming at something important
- operating in restricted space

CONCERNING MUSKET RAMRODS[86]

Commentator one

Have [musketeers] carry a spare ramrod at the waist with a string to attach it with. Make sure they use the main ramrods after they have discarded the spare ones.

TSURANE-UCHI SUCCESSIVE SHOOTING

Commentator one

This is also called *tatami-uchi* [and is to have lines of musketeers take turns in shooting].

SHINGARI – DEFENDING THE RETREAT

Commentator two

When the allies have collapsed and they are retreating out of formation, guard the retreat by moving [musketeers] onto both sides so they can shoot into the flank of the enemy. When withdrawing in formation, shoot to keep the enemy at bay while the allies retreat.

Issui-sensei says

The above are those points that should be transmitted.

HOW TO ASSEMBLE *ASHIGARU* – FOOT SOLDIERS IN LINES FOR SUCCESSIVE SHOOTING

Move them as shown below and form new rows. Also, there is a tradition for the position of *kashira* captain; this is to be discussed further.

Commentator one

The *kumigashira* group captains [should be related] – sons-in-law, younger brothers, nephews and the like.

---

86 This point and the following are missing from both the Koga and Odawara transcriptions.

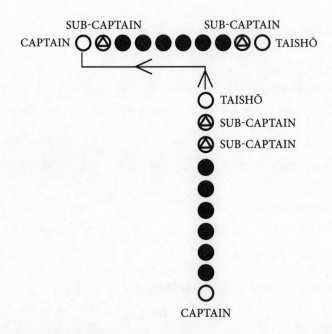

Commentator two

The tradition [for *kashira* captains] is to check the line from both sides and take up position on the right end and command from there.

Regardless of the number of people, three receiving soldiers secure the approaching *ashigaru* when they move and form up. One of these three [leaders] moves to the rear and straightens the line as he joins the other [leader] at the end. From these positions at each end of the line, they command the *ashigaru* on the shooting of muskets.

Issui-sensei says

Points on how to quickly build a formation are to be orally transmitted.

鉄炮打様之事
Teppō uchiyō no koto

HOW TO SHOOT MUSKETS

大連
Dairen
Full volley

小連
Shōren
Independent volley

Commentator two

In the above drawings, *dairen* full volley is for shooting in unison, whereas *shōren* independent volley is for shooting in sequence.[87] Which to use will all depend on the situation. Use a full volley to perform a full assault, and an independent volley for repeat shooting.

---

87 The literal translations of *dairen* and *shōren* are 'large sequence' and 'small sequence' respectively.

替打

Kawarichi

Rotating volleys

Rotating volleys require twenty-five people as shown below.

OOOOO OOOOO OOOOO

OOOOO

OOOOO

The distance between each row is 6 *ken*.

The above setup is for flat terrain, and should be changed according to the geography.

Commentator two

The first fifteen people at the front shoot and then peel off on both sides, moving to the rear so that those who were at the rear can move to the front, form a row and then shoot. At which point they also peel off in both directions and move to the rear. By doing this in turns the original people will return to the front. This does not have to be done only with twenty-five people.

DUTIES TO BE CARRIED OUT BY *ASHIGARU* FOOT SOLDIERS

In addition, *ashigaru* foot soldiers are responsible for construction work during a campaign. Although *fushin-bugyō* construction commanders work in cooperation [with the captains of the *ashigaru*], if the [captains of the *ashigaru*] are unfamiliar with this kind of work, confusion will arise. Therefore, refer to the later section concerning *fushin-bugyō* construction commanders. Remember, quick construction is essential in military service.

[*Ashigaru* foot soldier duties include the following:]
- construction while on campaign
- reaping rice fields
- pillage
- arson
- *jiyaki* – burning certain areas
- *okuri ashigaru* – outward protection
- *mukae ashigaru* – inward protection
- *keigo* – guarding
- *meakashi* – informing
- *sairyō* – supervision [of lower people]
- *bansho* – guardhouse duties
- *yomawari* – night patrols
- *kenshi* – inspection
- *osae ashigaru* – securing areas
- help in all cases
- service with the vanguard

Apart from the above, their duties include many other elements, each according to the situation. These should be considered when their achievements are discussed.

Commentator one

Okuri ashigaru is when a leader sends out a group of *ashigaru* foot soldiers to escort a messenger or scout when an area is thick with arrows and bullets.

Osae ashigaru involves protecting rice paddies to prevent [the enemy] reaping them and pillaging them (乱妨).

Commentator two

Okuri ashigaru is when scouts are sent out and find their way blocked by the enemy, and *ashigaru* are sent to defeat those enemies [to allow the scouts to leave].

Mukae ashigaru is for when scouts are returning and the enemy follow them and attack; here the *ashigaru* foot soldiers should be sent out to fight against the enemy to allow the scouts to return.

One of Lord Minamoto no Yoshitsune's poem says:

足軽モ段々ニ居テカワルベシタダ肝要ハ備タリケリ

Foot soldiers should be in layered ranks and ready to take turns;
what is essential is maintaining formation.

MARKING WEAPONS

Tradition says that to mark a bow you should cut paper into a strip of 1 *sun* [in width], tie it onto the upper curve of the bow (*toriuchi*), then untie it when an achievement has been attained. This is called *shirushi wo ageru* (印ヲ挙ル), the mark of success. Do the same for muskets and spears.

To mark an arrow, write your name one hand's grip down from the base of the fletching and in line with the *hashiriba* vertical fletching.

FORMING SPACES BETWEEN MUSKETEERS

To assemble fifty or one hundred *ashigaru* foot soldiers and bring them into formation, there are points concerning the opening up of spaces between them. By following these points, you can control risk when musket shooting.

Commentator one

[The drawing below] shows how to form spaces between musketeers.

♂ ♂ ♂

♂ ♂ ♂

♂ ♂ ♂

♂ ♂ ♂

Commentator two

When in a large area, you can form spaces among the troop in straight lines [without any problem. However,] the above points are for when you are in an area that is small and restricted. Make sure to maintain gaps between each line and use *gankō*, the flying geese formation. [This allows for more muskets to be fired at once like in the above image.] Also, have the men turn their feet inwards [to maintain a strong shooting stance].

DIVIDING A UNIT OF *ASHIGARU* FOOT SOLDIERS

To divide a foot soldier unit, separate them with mounted warriors by riding in the style of *ryūgo nori* (リウゴ乗) – the way of riding in the shape of a drum.

Commentator one

The shape of *ryūgo nori* is as shown below.

Commentator two

Ride from one corner to the opposite corner and then ride from the other corner to its opposite corner [which creates four equal sections], then form them into two groups, as shown below. If there are one hundred soldiers in total, this allows for the correct division into two groups of approximately fifty people.

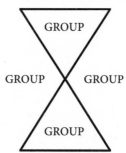

INTERNAL ARRANGEMENTS

内印

Uchijirushi

INTERNAL MARKINGS

The *taishō* should arrange internal markings beforehand. In addition to these, each unit should have their own markers prepared in advance.

Commentator one

[Examples of internal markings include] *sodejirushi* sleeve marks or a crest on the *haori* jacket.

内相詞

Uchiaikotoba

INTERNAL PASSWORDS

Apart from the passwords that the general gives through the six *bugyō*, other passwords for each group should be created internally by each captain.

内法度

Uchihatto

INTERNAL RULES

Commentator one

Each unit should have rules tailored to its particular setup, for only the captain truly knows [his men]. Examples of this would be rules covering gambling, drinking parties, pleasure, etc.

Commentator two

As in the above points, the leader should make rules for his own group, taking into consideration the type of men he has under his command.

内賞刑
Uchishōkei
INTERNAL REWARD AND PUNISHMENT

Commentator one

At the battle of Nagakute, the warrior Hori Kyūtarō announced to the *ashigaru* foot soldiers that if they killed one mounted warrior they would be given 100 *koku* in reward for this one killing. This is an example of an improvised reward.

Commentator two

The captain should make internal rules for rewards and punishments within his group to encourage and develop the men.

内組合
Uchikumiai
INTERNAL GROUPS

Commentator one

Make groups of five people, considering the elements of large and small, strong and weak.

Commentator two

As mentioned earlier, to attack enemies, make subgroups of a few people to work together.

Issui-sensei says

Captains should implement the above arrangements.

CHAPTER FOURTEEN

使番
Tsukaiban

MESSENGERS

Numerous messengers are required.

Messengers receive the *taishō*'s orders and distribute them throughout the army. They also receive information on any changes to the formation of units or tactics and then report this back to the *taishō*. They serve as messengers for various issues, so you need to recruit people who can understand the *taishō*'s wisdom and intention and who speak fluently. When the time comes, if they distort tactics or orders to their own ends, then know that such an action should be met with a serious charge. Be aware of this.

Commentator one

As an example of distorting tactics or orders, consider the following episode. At the siege of Ōsaka, the warrior Tōdō Izumi no kami Takatora, who served Shinkun [Tokugawa Ieyasu], was in command of the vanguard who were [attacking] the Dōmyōji gateway [of Ōsaka castle]. Watanabe Kanbei, who was in the vanguard, entered into combat with the warrior Chōsokabe Kunaishōshō Motochika, who was from the Ōsaka side. At this the warrior Takatora [moved back to the command group] to report to Shinkun. He said loudly that the vanguard had entered into combat with the Ōsaka forces. To which another warrior in the command group called Yokota Jin'emon responded, 'What a sluggish thing to say! My young warriors, drive him away.' Takatora heard this and immediately returned to his troop. After the incident a close retainer of

Shinkun named Hatakeyama Nyūan observed that young men [of his day] were inexperienced in battle. The former name [of Hatakeyama Nyūan] was Shimotsuke no kami.[88]

Issui-sensei says
Tradition says there are points to keep in mind concerning what messengers should wear.

Commentator two
[Messengers should wear] practical attire so that they will not stick out among other *samurai*.

Issui-sensei says
There are principles concerning banners for each clan.

Commentator two
There are no standard principles, as banners vary from clan to clan. For example, banners such as the *gonoji* (伍ノ字), the ideogram of five, or the *kaburo* (禿), the bobbed hair of a youth, would be used by [messengers who were from] the *hatamoto* class under the *shōgun*.

使行時可心得三箇条

Tsukai ni ikutoki kokoroeru beki sankajō

THREE POINTS TO KEEP IN MIND WHEN ACTING AS A MESSENGER

Observe and remember the topography around the castle compound of the enemy

---

88 While difficult to follow, this situation is an example of a messenger attached to the lord overstepping his authority. It was not the messenger's place to show disrespect to the warrior Tōdō Takatora and such words created undeserved shame for him. The retainer Hatakeyama Nyūan who spoke at the end of this episode was a well-respected warrior. By chastising the outspoken man in the command group, he was informing everyone that such behaviour was not acceptable.

Commentator two

The *taishō* may sometimes ask for such information. Make sure to give extra attention to the topography and the castle layout from a strategic viewpoint. Consider whether the castle is pregnable and observe how the castle is designed.

Issui-sensei says

Pay attention to what enemy soldiers discuss

Commentator two

By utilizing the teachings of the *Shōninki* scroll, speculate if the generals and soldiers are brave or cowardly, wise or ignorant.

Issui-sensei says

Do not accept gifts from the enemy

This does not apply to gifts given by the enemy *taishō* to your *taishō*. These should be received. Also be careful about how to talk when going to the enemy province.

Commentator two

If a messenger accepts a gift from the enemy, he will be suspected by his allies.

[When in the enemy camp] do not talk too much about great military achievements. Also, you should suggest to the [enemy] lord that he should feel free to discuss anything with you, opening up a frank dialogue. Also, there may be a chance for you to overhear rumours from among [the enemy] but [such rumours] may be misleading, so make sure that you understand the backgrounds of the generals and soldiers. Also, consider the positions of the mountains, seas and land.

[This is the end of the three points to keep in mind when acting as a messenger.]

Issui-sensei says

When going to the enemy province, conduct *togiki* external listening. Try to approach townspeople, farmers or *shukke* monks who reside in local villages and towns to obtain as much information about the terrain as possible. Also obtain information on everything about the clan, such as their laws.

When the army is in position, if a messenger moves to the vanguard to inform them to commence battle, it is a principle that the messenger should not return, even if the commander says he should. However, sometimes there will be a need to return, but this will vary according to the situation.

Commentator two

This is an ancient custom. Messengers can in fact return, but this depends on the situation and the timing. He should return if there are any issues [that need reporting from the vanguard.]

REPORTING THE NUMBER OF THE ENEMY AND THE ALLIES TO THE *TAISHŌ*

Such arrangements are sometimes made beforehand with the *taishō*, but if not there are set ways to be used in reporting.

Commentator one

Arrange in advance whether to report the number of allied troops as larger than it actually is and the number of enemy troops as smaller. This means a report on the number of enemy should meet with the lord's intention.

Commentator two

During the Ōsaka siege, when a messenger reported that the enemy was massive in number, Shinkun [the lord Tokugawa Ieyasu] became angry [because such talk risked discouraging the men]. In our school there is a teaching of subtracting three or five out of ten and adding three or five out of ten. For example, if the number of the enemy is 10,000 people, report it as 7,000 [or 5,000] by taking 3,000 or 5,000 away.

For the number of assembled allies, 7,000 should be stated as 10,000 by adding three out of ten. Five out of ten can also be added, so 5,000 can be stated as 10,000. There are things to be considered on this matter according to the lord's way of thinking, so it should not be done the same way each time.

RIDING AS A MESSENGER

Be aware that messengers, when they [leave the *hatamoto* group and] move into other formations of the army can take any position they wish.

When proceeding along a road, ride the horse at extreme speed. When moving into the formation, do so unobtrusively. There are traditions to be transmitted.

Commentator two

Messengers have an important duty, so they should carry it out with care. If they perform their duty calmly they will not make mistakes, but if they hurriedly and hideously ride into a troop, of either the enemy or the allies, they will be out of breath and have trouble speaking. Therefore, when they ride into a troop in position, they should do this unobtrusively.

The route a messenger takes when reporting and withdrawing

The drawing below shows how a messenger should move from the *hatamoto* group to the vanguard.

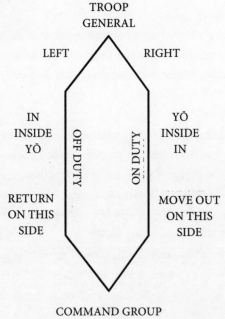

The right side is always full of the element of *in*. However, going on duty makes it become a case where the element of *yō* is inside the element of *in*. Alternatively, the left side is of *yō*, but because the left is off duty it becomes a case of the element of *in* within the element of *yō*.[89]

When a messenger returns [to the *taishō*] after following the method in the drawing above, if the *taishō* is on horseback the messenger should also report from horseback, whereas if the *taishō* is sitting on a stool the messenger should dismount to report. [When reporting to the *taishō*,] approach from the right and leave on the left. When receiving a message [from the *taishō*], take up position on the left side.

秘傳
Hiden
SECRET TRADITIONS

PASSING THROUGH CHECKPOINTS

Commentator one

Before you set off on your mission as a messenger ask the following question: 'It is likely that there will be new checkpoints as we are in a period of war, but what should I do to pass through them?' Ask for detailed information about the circumstances in which a checkpoint guard might not allow you to pass and also find out whether you should present them with documentation or not. When you actually reach the checkpoint, politely explain your purpose, and if they allow you to pass through, you should of course fulfil your mission as messenger. If they will not allow it – as is likely in a period of war – ask the checkpoint guard to pass on [your message].

---

89 In Japanese culture, left is *yō*, positive, while right is *in*, negative. But being on duty is active, making it *yō*, so performing duty on the right side leads to *yō* within *in* – a balance of positive and negative. The same principle applies to going off duty on the left side, in that it holds inactivity inside the element of activity. This is understood through the *taijitu* symbol (colloquially known as the *yin–yang* symbol).

Commentator two

In enemy territory, checkpoints may be erected where you do not expect them. When moving out on a mission as a messenger, think of how to get through a new checkpoint if you come across it. There are teachings on how to get through discreetly. The chapter 'Korō[90] no narai' – 'The teachings of foxes and wolves' – is to be found in the *Shōninki* manual.

PASSING THROUGH A PLACE THAT IS LIKELY TO HAVE *FUSEKAMARI* – HIDDEN AMBUSHES

Commentator one

To pass through a place that is likely to have ambushes hidden within it, you should make arrangements for signals with fans, horses or the like so that you can communicate with each other without alerting the enemy to your intent. Make sure to do this beforehand. If it is done poorly, the enemy will notice and attack.

Commentator two

If you have to go through a place likely to have ambushes, first you should consider the topography and work out a route that minimizes the risk. It is necessary to make a plan in advance, considering the pros and cons [of each route]. You should have prearranged plans for what to do if you do get ambushed, such as what route you will take to find your way out and which rivers you will cross on your return. Be aware that anything, including a particular way to ride a horse or use a war fan, can serve as a signal.

TAKING A MESSAGE TO THE ENEMY SIDE ON A BATTLEFIELD

Commentator one

Take off your helmet, raise up your fan when at a far enough distance and beckon the enemy with the fan, then, as you are approaching each other, ask them not to shoot. Take note, performing the action of *yari wo fusu* – making

---

90 The Koga transcription uses *kori*. This is possibly a transcription error as the *Shōninki* manual uses *korō*. We have changed it here to match the *Shōninki*.

the spear redundant – is a way for displaying actual surrender and therefore in this situation you should not use it. Instead simply take off your helmet.

Commentator two

Take off your helmet and ask for a ceasefire. Dismount when you are just outside of the formation. Remember, people use *tsuru wo hazusu* (弦ヲハツス), to unstring the bow, or they use *yari wo fusu* (鑓ヲ伏), making the spear redundant, to signal actual surrender [and so these actions should *not* be performed in this situation].

Issui-sensei says

[Messengers] sometimes need to perform as scouts, so those in this position should have a good knowledge on the subject of scouting.

検使
Kenshi

INSPECTORS

There are things to announce and keep in mind when operating as a *kenshi* – inspector [for ritual suicides].

Commentator one

Kenshi inspectors should wear both swords when announcing the charges of the condemned man. If the victim shows any resistance, [the inspector should] immediately kill the person. An example in old times is when the warrior Ina Zusho went mad [at the time of his ritual suicide] and the warrior Andō Tatewaki had to kill him.

Commentator two

In ancient times, [inspectors] spoke with their long and short swords on.

Today, swords should be placed to the side of you. If you meet any resistance, you need to kill the person [immediately].

目付之事
Metsuke no koto

OVERSEERS

Numerous overseers are required.

Metsuke overseers should not try to fight to gain achievement for themselves. If the general in the troop is killed, [the *metsuke*] should move among *samurai* [as a temporary leader] together with *tsukaiban* messengers. When in formation, they should stay beside the commander of the troop.

Tradition says to be aware that *metsuke* overseers are important and are of deep value for *samurai*. They can advance or ruin a soldier with just one word, no matter whether what they say is right or wrong. Primarily, they should investigate all elements concerning soldiers, including their achievements and loyalty, by taking their social status into consideration.

Commentator two

Metsuke overseers observe soldiers and establish if they are right or wrong, brave or cowardly, and so on. This is so that rewards and punishments can be properly handed out. Therefore, a single word [from a *metsuke* overseer] carries real weight. Also, they should judge each warrior according to his abilities and status, especially in cases such as two people killing one or one person killing two. Such matters should be given careful consideration.

QUESTION EVIDENCE FROM OTHER PEOPLE

There are important things to keep in mind when hearing from others if a warrior is right or wrong. Sometimes unregulated situations emerge and overseers need to consider the information in context.

Commentator one
An 'unregulated situation' here means an emergency. In such a case, respond to the emergency in the correct way.

Commentator two
If someone comes to talk about the rights or wrongs of other people, do not listen absent-mindedly [or jump to the wrong conclusion] as in most cases people will slander others because of a personal grudge or praise others because of favouritism. Some people just accept rumours without checking if they are true or false as they have a poor way of thinking. Be judicious in this matter. Generally speaking, those who talk about matters outside of their duties are evil and frivolous; do not listen to them on any subject. Even if someone has broken a law, reserve your judgement on what is actually right or wrong in that particular situation so that you do not make a mistake. Mistakes lead to a violation of the rules for reward and punishment.

AVOID FAMILY BIAS
Be aware that [*metsuke* overseers] should deeply know and consider the background [of the people they are observing], including the right or wrong doings of their father, mother, brothers and other relatives, and they should not make superficial judgements.

Commentator two
This is because a *metsuke* overseer may favour someone related to him or alternatively may underplay any relations in an act of humility. Therefore, [when you are investigating someone] deal with other people [with whom you do not have a personal connection] and not with your own family members.

ARRIVE LATE TO AN INVESTIGATION
It is a principle to arrive late to an investigation where a judgment *has* to be made. However, this depends on the situation.

Commentator two

[*Metsuke* overseers] should come late to investigate a matter because if they come early and observe the proceedings with their own eyes, then even a small matter cannot be ignored. It is not beneficial to give weight to the smallest accusation. However, this will depend on the situation.

LISTEN TO BOTH SIDES

In all matters, even issues concerning common people, [overseers] should first listen to both sides before they make a judgement and should not make judgement without careful consideration.

Commentator two

If a judgement is made by listening to only one side, the case will be prejudiced against the other and may result in the wrongful conviction of an innocent person.

TREAT ALL RANKS EQUALLY

Someone who has broken the law should be judged the same whether they are of high or low rank. If the person is high ranking, know that their [unlawful] actions should not be condoned. It is best to value the good deeds [of a person] and to discuss any negative ones in as light a manner as possible – this is done to protect the reputation of the *samurai* in question. It is a state of excellence to adhere to the righteous path.

Commentator two

Military laws will fail unless those who violate them are convicted, regardless of social status. That being said, it is a primary principle to speak more of good deeds and less of bad ones; this will help promote fewer criminals. You must stick to the righteous path and show no favouritism in anything.

Issui-sensei says

Remember, keep the following four principles in mind at all times:

1. *kan* 観 – observation
2. *bun* 聞 – listening
3. *ken* 監 – supervision
4. *setsu* 節 – discipline

This is what everyone in all positions should keep in mind.

Yokome (横目) covert observers perform the same job [as *metsuke*] and report back to the general, but they do this without informing other *samurai* that they are also a form of overseer. They even make judgements on the *metsuke* themselves.

CHAPTER FIFTEEN

物見之事[91]
Monomi no koto

SCOUTS

Commentator one

This title can also be written with the ideograms 斥候. The first ideogram, 斥, means 'degrees' and the second, 候, means 'look' – together they should be read as *monomi*.[92]

Commentator two

The ideograms 斥候 [which are normally read as *sekkō*] should be read as *monomi*.

[Lord Takeda Shingen's poems state:]

軍ニハ物見ナクテハ大将之石ヲ抱テ淵ニイルナリ

*If it were not for monomi scouts, the lord would kill himself
by jumping into deep water with a heavy stone in his arms.*

一戦ニ日取リサシノソキ物見ヲカケテカ子テ計ヘ

*For battle, set aside divination for dates and direction and instead send
monomi scouts before you make any plans and consider everything.*

---

91 The Koga transcription uses the ideograms 斥候, which are normally read as *sekkō*, but the document here is saying they should be read as *monomi*. This suggests that when reading old manuscripts this combination of ideograms should always be read in this way.

92 The first ideogram has multiple meanings. It is possibly understood as 'to look on with degrees of standard' – i.e. to observe with measured judgement.

Issui-sensei says

[Scouting] should be undertaken by a *kachi-gashira* – captain of warriors on foot. The position of *kachi-gashira* is not described here.

According to old ways, [a scouting group led by a] *kachi-gashira* is called *ō-monomi* and one without a leader is called *ko-monomi*. [However be aware that] some groups led by a *kachi-gashira* are called *ko-monomi*.[93]

大物見

Ō-monomi

LARGE SCOUTING GROUPS

One *kashira* captain creates a formation to fully observe the enemy. They may sometimes enter into combat.

中物見

Chū-monomi

MIDDLE-SIZED SCOUTING GROUPS

This is thirty to fifty people who venture out to get close to the enemy to observe them. Sometimes they may enter into a skirmish.

小物見

Ko-monomi

SMALL SCOUTING GROUPS

This is one or two people who venture out to discover the status of the enemy.

Basically, every *samurai* should know the way of *monomi* scouting. To do this job requires knowledge of the battlefield and the principles of warfare. It is possible that any *samurai* could be ordered to perform *monomi* scouting by the general, so all *samurai* should learn and know this subject.

---

93 'Old ways' implies that this method of naming groups was outdated at the time of writing. The version that comes after this statement is the updated version.

Commentator one

The principles of the battlefield are known as *sho chū go no sandan* 初中後ノ 三段 – the three phases of a battlefield.[94]

1. *zabi* 座備 – formations
2. *gyōretsu* 行列 – to form up
3. *kassenba* 合戦場 – the killing fields[95]

Commentator two

Overall, *monomi* scouting involves not only scouting and understanding the status of the enemy in a confrontation, but also using [the wisdom of] those who are experienced in all matters to speculate on the pros and cons of a situation from a military standpoint. If they do not examine *budō* – the path of the *samurai* – [scouts] may miss a chance to attack or overlook some other advantage. At the siege of Ōsaka, the warriors Ban Dan'emon and Yoneda Kenmotsu [who were in the castle] performed a night raid on Hachisuka Awa no Kami's troops [who were outside the castle]. Prior to this event, experienced people had informed [those outside the castle] that the bridge at the gate named Honchōguchi was not drawn back, [which indicated that it was going] to be used as a starting point for enemy night attacks [and so the besiegers were able to anticipate the night raids]. Therefore, any person performing as a scout, regardless of their position, should be resourceful and uncover such [insights] by considering the military ways of the *samurai* (*budō*).

MOVING OUT AND RETURNING

When moving out of a camp or position, make sure that your appearance is that of a normal *samurai* so that you do not stand out.

The points below are on how to move out and return [when performing as a scout].

---

94 These are three distinct stages: phase one is the static start of a position, phase two is the movement phase and phase three is the actual start of conflict. This division is reflected in the name *sho chū go*, which means 'the beginning, the middle and the end'.

95 i.e. the battleground. 'Killing fields' has been used here to show that combat is in action.

千鳥カケ

Chidorigake

Zig-zag riding

This should be employed so as to have a wider view of the area.

ヲクレ帰[96]

Okure-gaeri

The coward's return

The coward's return is not good, as it means that your weak side is shown to the enemy.[97]

キヲイ帰[98]

Kioi-gaeri

The competitive return

The competitive return is positive as you can deal with the enemy when attacked.

Commentator two

After moving out to scout, the *okure-gaeri* coward's return is disliked as it entails returning by turning to the right. The preferable way of returning is by turning to the left, which is called *kioi-gaeri* – the competitive return. It is advisable to ride in a wide zig-zag manner on the way out, in order to discover ambushes and understand topography.

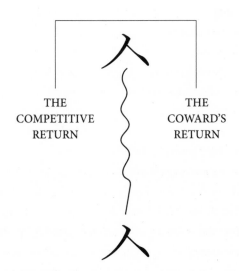

THE COMPETITIVE RETURN

THE COWARD'S RETURN

---

96 The Koga transcription uses the ideograms 後帰.

97 This sentence is implied – 敵受悪シ.

98 The Koga transcription uses the ideograms 競帰.

A poem by Gamō Genzaemon:

テキ間之道見ニ行ト念ヲ入レ一筋ハカリ見テハ帰リソ

When scouting within the area between you and the enemy, try to carefully observe all but do not observe only along a single and straight direction.

SIGNALLING BACK TO YOUR ALLIES

When on a *monomi* scouting mission, there is a way of signalling among your allies by riding your horse in a certain fashion. This will enable you to signal three hazards:

1. *fukuhei* 覆兵 – a group waiting to attack
2. *fuse* 伏 – samurai who are hiding
3. *kamari* 陰 – a mixture of *dōshin* and *ashigaru* troops

[The signal to be given for each of these] should be arranged before setting out.

Monomi scouts should pay special attention to the following among other things:

- mountains
- woods
- narrow paths
- deep rice fields
- bushes
- valleys
- deep grass fields
- behind river banks

Commentator two

[At the siege of Ōsaka] the warrior Sugihara Hitachinosuke Chikanori performed *aizu no monomi* – scouts who send back signals. This was done in the area of Imafuku when the famous general Uesugi Kagekatsu tried to save the warrior Satake Yoshinobu.

ENCOUNTERING ENEMY SCOUTS

When encountering enemy scouts, whether in a case of single combat or two versus one, it is desirable to dismount from your horse and drive your horse towards the enemy immediately. This is a tradition for an encounter on a narrow path.

Commentator one

You should release your horse towards the enemy because it is difficult to fight on horseback on a narrow path. Dismount from your horse quicker than the enemy and set it onto the enemy so that the horses will fight with each other, then kill the enemy by taking advantage of this.

Commentator two

If on a narrow path, you should dismount quicker than the enemy and drive your horse towards them so that it will make the enemy horse rear up on its hind legs, causing the rider to fall.

PUTTING YOUR MISSION FIRST

When performing as a *monomi* scout, do not fight for your own fame and achievement. There is an important way to talk in this situation.

At the start of a battle scouts from each side sometimes come forward into no man's land and cannot help but engage with each other in combat. This fighting is discussed in the scroll *Ippei Yōkō* and is called *hare no kōmyō* – an auspicious achievement.

Commentator one

Address [enemy scouts] thus: 'As we are engaged in this important mission today, let us have combat after we return from this mission. We now know each other's banners [so we may find each other again].'

Commentator two

At the battle of Sekigahara, on the fifteenth day of the ninth month, the warriors Sawai Saemon, Sofue Hōsai and Mori Kageyu from the Kantō side ventured out on a scouting mission where they came across the warriors Tsuda Kosaburō and Inui Jirōbei. When they were about to enter into a spear fight, Hōsai rode in between the two sides and said: 'Both our groups have been assigned important tasks so I am not sure that we should fight for our own achievement and put our task to the side. It is a natural state of mind for *bushi* warriors to wish to fight each other when in battle [but now is not the time to do so].' Both sides were impressed by this and parted. This action was possible because Hōsai was an experienced warrior.

助物見

Suke-monomi
ASSISTANT SCOUTS

Hon-monomi (本物見) main scouts are [sometimes] assisted by two people and these three should scout together. The main scout should take the middle route while the other two take the flanks.

As shown in the drawing below, assistant scouts should follow the main scout while also moving in from the sides [as shown in the crossover points]. If they detect an ambush, they should signal this to the main scout. Main scouts move deeply forward, while assistant scouts do not go as deep. If they were to go in deeper then they would undermine the prestige of the main scout.

ASSISTANT MAIN ASSISTANT

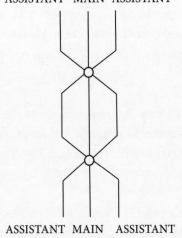

ASSISTANT MAIN   ASSISTANT

繫物見

Kakari-monomi

SUPPORTING THE SCOUTS

This is also called *okuri-ashigaru* (送足軽), meaning to send out foot soldiers to protect the main scouts, or *mukae-zonae* (迎備), to receive defence.

Commentator two

Okuri-ashigaru is when *monomi* scouts are sent out in an emergency with an additional unit of *ashigaru* foot soldiers to protect them. *Mukae-zonae* is when it is necessary to send *ashigaru* foot soldiers to hold back the enemy so that scouts can return safely.

信之物見

Shin no monomi

SURVEY SCOUTS

This means to estimate the number and prowess of the enemy, the size of the province and the number of properties within. This should be done by *bugyō* or *monogashira* commanders, but regardless of how high or low their positions are, this type of scout surveys the manners, customs, language and various other things in addition. This is known as *shin*.

Commentator two

These scouts are of great importance. Make sure to choose *samurai* for this task who are thoughtful, resourceful and wise, but also brave and careful. At the siege of Ōsaka, Shinkun [Lord Tokugawa Ieyasu] sent the warrior Watanabe Zusho to perform this type of scouting mission. He observed everything with care and even went so far as to bring back the measurements of the bamboo bundle shields [that the enemy had created].

深之物見.[99]

Fuka no monomi

DEEP-VENTURING SCOUTS

This is to scout deep inside a distant enemy province. These scouts move 3–5 *ri* inside the enemy land to estimate the size of the enemy army and other aspects.

継物見

Tsunagi-monomi

RELAY SCOUTS

This is to scout and relay information.

飛脚物見

Hikyaku-monomi

FAST SCOUTS

This is to travel the highways of an enemy province over multiple nights and by travelling overnight.[100]

The above selection of points gives an outline of *monomi* scouting. Choose appropriate people for these missions, such as experienced older people or people of courage and wisdom.

POINTS TO KEEP IN MIND FOR MONOMI SCOUTS

- [When observing an enemy] procession, the estimation used should be one mounted warrior for each *ken* in distance when counting.
- For two warriors on foot, it is also 1 *ken* of distance when counting.
- In a procession with a double column, there will 120 mounted warriors for each *chō* of distance or 240 warriors on foot for each *chō* of distance.
- Be aware that when they are in a circular formation, the actual number is

---

99 The first ideogram in the title of this article can also be pronounced *shin*. However, this would then be the same phonetically as the preceding article title, which would be confusing. Therefore, we have given the alternative transliteration for the second title.

100 The text could mean to ride throughout the night or to ride for several days and stay overnight in certain locations. Either way, it is to travel fast through enemy territory.

always larger [than it looks], but when in a square formation the number is always smaller than it looks.

- When on a height, enemy numbers look larger.
- When in a low place, enemy numbers look smaller.
- When in an open place, enemy numbers look smaller.
- When in a narrow place, enemy numbers look larger.
- At night fence posts look like human beings, but [unlike humans] fence posts are of a uniform height and do not move.
- At night fire looks higher. If you observe fire and you see it as part way up the mountain, know that it will actually be lower than it appears.
- At night fire always looks closer [than it actually is].

Keep the above in mind during your observations.

Tradition says that when you get a glimpse at a warrior passing by when you are in a narrow area, focus on the colour of his horse and his banner. If you try to observe too many details, you will always fail.

There is a way called *yōjinhi* – deceptive fire. Do not make a fuss when you see such fires, as these are fuses that have been lit and left on tree branches or so on by the enemy.

Commentator two

Yōjinhi is the same as the way called *shirushi noroshi* in the scroll *Ippei Yōkō*. It is a precautionary measure taken by the enemy to make it look as if they have forces in position.

Issui-sensei says

Tradition says that to get an army across a river, move half the number to a hill and have the rest cross the river. The people left in the higher place are meant to attract attention.

Commentator one

'A hill' does not have to be an actual hill. It can be any position where they attract attention.

Commentator two

When the enemy wishes to cross a river, they sometimes try to lure your forces to a mountainside or higher place or another such area by sending a unit as a decoy, when in actual fact they are crossing a river. Also they will divide their forces [at the river] so as to have troops defend them while crossing over.

Issui-sensei says

Tradition says that to make an evaluation, bring together all information on the province, people and places, and look for any inconsistences that may indicate that the enemy has forces in hiding.

Commentator two

Details on comparison are transmitted in the scroll *Dakkō [Shinobi] no Maki*.

WAYS TO TELL THAT AN ENEMY THAT HAS TAKEN UP A POSITION IS ACTUALLY GOING TO RETREAT

- The *konida* baggage train unit will appear unsettled.
- There are many musketeers positioned in the enemy vanguard.
- The flags are not moving even though the troops appear to be getting ready to advance.

WAYS TO TELL THAT THE ENEMY IS TAKING UP A POSITION

- There is an accumulation of goods.
- Many warriors are moving about scouting and riding around.
- Mounted warriors are dismounting from their horses.
- Flags and pole arms are propped up in position.
- Warriors are seen here and there building earthworks or fences.

Commentator two

Inexperienced people can easily make mistakes when trying to work out whether the enemy is taking up a position or not. For example, at the siege of Ōsaka the enemy built a formation facing the position of Sir Kazusanosuke Tadateru [a son of Tokugawa Ieyasu]. *Monomi* scouts were sent to observe the enemy and they reported that the enemy was of a large number and that a battle would break out the next day. However, the enemy moved back to their side that night. This mistake occurred because the scouts were inexperienced and not competent.

WAYS TO TELL THAT COMBAT IS ABOUT TO START

- Scouts are frequently sent out.
- Horses are neighing.
- There is movement within the flags.
- The *chi* of earth is rising with frequency.
- *Ashigaru* foot soldiers can be seen at the front.

If the above are observed, battle will without doubt commence. Also, when a battle is about to start, a messenger who has been sent from the command group to the vanguard will not return [to the command group]. Be aware that this is a sign that a battle is starting.

Commentator two
Details on this matter are transmitted in the scroll *Ippei Yōkō*.

WAYS TO TELL THAT THE ENEMY IS ATTACKING

- The formations remain quiet.
- The flags move forward.
- More space is created between the first and second units.
- Each unit assembles.

There are traditions about *seiki* (勢気) energy and *chi*.

WAYS TO TELL THAT THE ENEMY IS RETREATING

- Their formations are dissolving.
- *Ashigaru* foot soldiers are not in order.
- Flags are moving [from their position] and forming up together.
- Weapons are being held in a casual manner.
- Forward forces are moving to the rear – this is always a sign of retreat.

WAYS TO TELL WHETHER A RETREATING ENEMY IS STRONG OR WEAK

- A strong enemy [may] gather together in a lower place, whereas a weak enemy will retreat up to a height and move in a fragmented formation.[101]
- Be aware that strong enemies will reassemble after a rout.

WAYS TO TELL WHETHER A RETREATING ENEMY HAS LEFT A FORCE IN HIDING

- If there is a village or somewhere advantageous to hide but the enemy retreats away from it, know that there are hidden forces in that place.
- If the enemy moves and sticks to mountains or woods, know that there is no separate force hiding in that position.

UNDERSTANDING DIFFERENT TYPES OF FIRE

野火

Nobi

Field signal fires

These are fires that burn in a low and wide area. They look the same as when farmers burn mountainsides.

燼火[102]

Hōka

Tactical and signal fires

[When observing from a distance,] you can tell if a fire has been set by the allies, because the rising smoke is thinner at the front [of the enemy] but thicker at the rear [of the enemy]. If the fire has been set by the enemy, the smoke will be strong at the front and lesser at the rear. This is done so that they can retreat under the smokescreen.[103]

---

101 They will not be in a single group; they will divide their troops so that the whole army cannot be annihilated.

102 放火 in the Koga transcription. This can mean either a signal fire or a tactical fire.

103 This text is not entirely clear, but it appears to suggest that allies set fires behind the enemy to blockade them, whereas the enemy sets fires between them and the allies to create a barrier to aid their escape.

Commentator one

If the enemy sets a fire and retreats, know that the fire will be intense at the beginning. Conversely, if your allies set a fire and attack, know that it will be slow at the beginning but will increase in intensity later on.

Commentator two

Hōka is also called *hōsui* (燧燵). The first ideogram, 燧, means to raise a fire signal on a mountain top, and is a way of signalling in the daytime. The second ideogram, 燵, is to raise fire as a signal at nighttime. This is mentioned in the *Records of the Grand Historian* [by Sima Qian].

Issui-sensei says

Tradition says that the skill of *tsukebi* (付火) setting fires involves lighting fires in multiple locations. Once you have done this, attack immediately when [enemy] soldiers will be in great confusion.

地焼
Jiyaki
Ground burning

This is to burn the area around a castle to create space [and clear the land]. Ground burning is also done when taking up a position. In most cases it is done when defending a castle.

[When observing an enemy position,] tradition says not to confuse ground burning with *kaji* (火事) accidental fires. If it is an accidental fire, you will notice that the fire starts at a single point and the [enemy] troops fall into confusion.

自焼
Jiyaki
Self-burning

This is to burn to aid tactics. Such fires can be mistaken for accidental fires, but *jiyaki* fires occur in unlikely places such as where there is no wind.

Tradition says that *jiyaki* can be used to deceive the enemy: [the enemy] may mistake it as a normal fire, which will draw them in for the kill. With this type of fire, you will see fire burning in two or three places, but people will appear unconcerned. You will not hear raised voices, and the flanking units will not be in disarray.

焼働

Yakibataraki

Burning the retreat before entering into combat

This is to burn behind your own army, ships, bridges or castles. Understand that this is a death-defying measure.

Commentator two

One example of the skill of *yakibataraki* occurred when the general Uesugi Kenshin approached and attacked a mountainside castle owned by Hōjō Ujiyashu. During the approach Uesugi Kenshin burned bridges along the river Ochi.

焼退

Yakinoki

Burning in retreat

This is to burn in front of your own army and retreat under a cover of smoke.

Apart from the above points [which are points that scouts should know], there are other elements to consider concerning flags and combat, but it is acceptable [for scouts] not to know such things.

Commentator one

The articles up to this point relate to scouting done by *kachi-gashira* commanders of warriors on foot and other such warriors. The following points relate to scouting by *karō* – senior counsellors. When discussing ancient times, remember that the famous warrior Musashibō [Benkei] ventured out on a scouting mission.

THE IMPORTANCE OF SCOUTING

Basically, *monomi* scouting is essential in warfare. If a scout reports back even one false word, this could cause a serious problem. Scouting is a key to determining victory and defeat and provides the foundation for tactics and any changes that need to be made.

Commentator two

At the siege of Ōsaka, [Lord Tokugawa Ieyasu] sent the warrior Honda Izumo no kami to observe the river and asked him about the current. He reported that the current was too strong to cross. On hearing this, the lord became angry, saying that he was not like his father but acted like a girl instead. Izumo no kami was regretful about this and was later killed in battle.[104]

Issui-sensei says

In ancient times, during the Genpei War (1180–1185) Minamoto no Yoshitsune went to the west and [before him] Musashibō Benkei ventured out to scout as one would expect in such a critical situation.

物見定法五箇之習

Monomi jōhō goka no narai

THE FIVE BASIC METHODS OF SCOUTING

1. *shinmi* 真見 – survey scouting
2. *kimi* 奇見 – scouting to discover irregularities
3. *seimi* 勢見 – scouting to observe the status of the enemy forces
4. *kemi* 気見 – scouting to observe *chi*
5. *sonaemi* 備見 – scouting to discover the enemy formation

Although these methods have been mentioned previously and are listed here as standards, there are another five categories of scouting that come from ancient times:

---

104 This is a theme in the text. There are specific ways to report to a commander so that the report does not damage the morale of the troops.

1. *naga no monomi* 長物見 – scouting for an extended period of time
2. *chisoku no monomi* 遅速物見 – scouting for detailed information
3. *tan no monomi* 短之物見 – short-term scouting
4. *machi no monomi* 待物見 – waiting and observing
5. *kake no monomi* 懸物見 – scouting that includes combat

It is essential to pay full attention and take note of any signs of change.

Commentator one

Naga-monomi – scouting for an extended period of time – is to observe matters over time. When in an enemy province, such scouts observe everything that is found in and around the area and along the streets [as they travel].

Chisoku no monomi – scouting for detailed information – is to investigate every detail about the target, taking as much time as possible. Such scouts [focus on the target itself and] do not have to pay much attention to the route or area on the way.

Tan no monomi – short-term scouting – is to look and judge at speed.

Shinmi is the same as the scouting previously mentioned [and means survey scouting].

The *ki* in *kimi* – scouting to discover irregularities – means irregularity in the sense of whether the enemy is employing regular or irregular [tactics]. This form of scouting involves looking for a change in the enemy.

Seimi – scouting to observe the status of the enemy forces – is to look at the energy (勢見) of the enemy forces.

Kemi – scouting to observe *chi* – is to look at the *chi* (気見) of the enemy.

Sonaemi – scouting to discover the enemy formation – is to ascertain whether the enemy formation is substantial or insubstantial.

Commentator two

According to the *Three Strategies*, when neither the beginning nor the end is visible no one is able to gain a full understanding. This is a primary principle for *monomi* scouts.

CHAPTER SIXTEEN

陣場奉行之事
Jinba-bugyō no koto

BATTLE CAMP CONSTRUCTION COMMANDERS

Two of these are required.

Like *fushin-bugyō* construction commanders, *jinba-bugyō* battle camp construction commanders need to be able to assess what is required [of the proposed construction]. One tradition says that they should know and discern the relative strengths of both the enemy and the allied forces.

They should know the following subjects in detail:

- *toride* 取出 – external fortresses
- *tsukejiro* 付城 – tactical fortifications [built near enemy castles]
- *koya* 小屋 – huts and quarters
- *ikusaba* 軍場 – battlefields

Commentator one

The term *toride* originally means 'to be outside of' [so remember that these external fortresses are for forces to move out towards the enemy]. Such fortresses [do not have to be massive, but] can work with a single moat instead of three layers of defence.

Ikusaba here means to deal with the footing situation on a battlefield.

Commentator two

Details are in the scroll *Shirotori Koyatori no Maki*.

Issui-sensei says

Use the traditional elements listed below and take advantage of topography:

- upstream and downstream
- riversides
- the colour of stones – as water is found below them[105]
- mountains and valleys
- if the number of people is large or small
- deep rice paddies
- distances
- vantage points
- positions where ambushes may be laid

Commentator one

'Vantage point' here means a place from which the enemy can observe your troops. If the enemy does have a good view over your troops, construct screens to obscure the view.

MOVING POSITION

If it is required that you have to move position, first the *taishō* should make sure the position is secure and then should investigate at nighttime. [The battle camp construction commander] will require the *fushin-bugyō* construction commander to accompany him so they can discuss the matter.

Commentator two

You should move position when you conclude that your current location is not advantageous for a castle attack or for a confrontation with the enemy in its position.

---

105 The point here is you can discover if there is water in the area by the colour of the bottom of stones.

CALCULATING THE NUMBER OF WARRIORS

First consider the number of your allies, then investigate the topography of the area the enemy will advance into.

When calculating mounted warriors, remember:

- A 3 *ken* square is required for four mounted warriors.
- A 1 *chō* square can contain 1,600 mounted warriors.[106]

[Further to this, when just looking at a line of 1 *chō*:]

- On the front face of a 1 *chō* square there will be twenty-six mounted warriors.[107]

When calculating warriors on foot, remember:

- A 1 *ken* square can contain six warriors on foot.
- The front row for a 1 *chō* line will have 360 warriors on foot.
- A 1 *chō* square can contain 21,600 warriors on foot.[108]

The above calculation is a way from old customs and should be modified according to the topography. The *jinba-bugyō* battle camp construction commander should evaluate all pros and cons and report to the six *bugyō* commanders. They in turn call for the four *bugyō* who discuss the matter and then give orders to the *fushin-bugyō* construction commander.

---

106 There are twenty 3 *ken* squares in the length of 1 *chō*, meaning that there are eighty mounted warriors in a single 1 *chō* line. A 1 *chō* square contains 400 squares of 3 *ken* (20 × 20), which explains why the total number of mounted warriors inside that area is 1,600 (400 × 4).

107 This is confusing, as the preceding point appears to tell us that eighty mounted warriors can fit across a 1 *chō* front line. However, here it uses the word *omote*, which means 'front-facing' in this context. So it could be that the 'twenty-six mounted warriors' referred to here are the ones *right* at the front, and then the remaining warriors out of the total of eighty are just behind, but still within a front line (or, strictly speaking, a front band) that is 60 *ken* (1 *chō*) wide and 3 *ken* deep.

108 There are sixty 1 *ken* squares along a front line of 1 *chō*. Therefore, the front row holds 360 warriors (60 × 6). This figure is then multiplied by the sixty 1 *ken* rows in a 1 *chō* square to give the total number of warriors in a 1 *chō* square as 21,600 (60 × 360).

Commentator one

The front line of a battle formation will have twenty-four mounted warriors for 1 *chō* in distance and these will be led by two *kashira* captains. This adds up to twenty-six in total.

TAKING ACCOUNT OF DIRECTIONS

The following is a teaching concerning direction. This is an essential point to be considered, so take account of [the directions of] the sun, moon, wind, rain, woods, villages and the like.

Commentator one

Concerning the sun: it is bad to face the sun in combat. Also it is desirable to have the warmth of the sun [on your back].

   Concerning the moon: when the moon does not cast a shadow, the enemy will infiltrate in secret.[109]

   Concerning the wind: consider upwind and downwind.

   Concerning rain: consider whether it is heavy or gentle.

   Concerning woods and forests: check wooded areas to see whether the enemy has taken advantage of them.

四奉行之事
Yon bugyō no koto

THE FOUR COMMANDERS

Those in this position should listen and discuss, judging everything for all kinds of positions. They deal with matters concerning:

---

109 This is referring either to making sure that the battle camp is designed in such a way that there are no dark areas created by moon shadow or simply to taking account of whether the moon is bright or not. When the moon is bright it casts a shadow and so this is *not* a good time to infiltrate.

- *kanjōnin* 勘定人 – accountants
- *fuchikata-bugyō* 扶持方奉行 – fief administrators
- *fushinkata* 普請方 – matters of construction
- *ninsoku ika* 人足以下 – the management and operation of labourers
- *daidokorokata* 臺所方 – accounting
- *kingin* 金銀 – finances (gold and silver)

Be aware that this position is important, as the four *bugyō* calculate the resources of the *taishō* and manage the *samurai*. For example, they calculate the total amount of gold and silver and fief distribution. Accountants work under them so they can estimate and discuss such matters.

Once a battle starts, hoards of gold, silver, rice and money will be required. If you do not plan carefully before you start, you will often become bogged down with troubles. The four *bugyō* should never forget this.

At a battle site, [the four *bugyō*] should help the command group, the vanguard or other places where the situation is critical; they are considered as *uki-musha* floating warriors who serve and assist a general. When defending a castle [against a siege], these four commanders should take turns to move to each position to give instructions for the correct operation of all *samurai*.

Commentator one

People in this position are required to make estimates based on a full understanding of all processes, from the beginning through to the end.

普請奉行之事
Fushin-bugyō no koto

CONSTRUCTION COMMANDERS

Two of these are required.

There are no special comments for this position. They should carry out all orders for construction both quickly and reliably. There should be separate group leaders for each unit and subordinate officers should also be appointed to ensure that everything is done in an organized way, as good organization is the criterion by which the achievements of a *fushin-bugyō* construction commander are measured.

Points on constructing huts and camp quarters: do this as soon as possible upon the order given by the general. If the general demands those in this position to give him an estimate on such a construction, there is something called *dai-koyatori* (大小屋取), which is rough estimation for the construction of huts. This has been passed down from ancient times. Use this to work out the numbers involved. This is transmitted in another scroll.

陣場ノ三見

Jinba no sanken

THE THREE POINTS TO CONSIDER WHEN CREATING POSITIONS

1. *i* 井 – wells
2. *mizumichi* 水通 – watercourses
3. *setchin* 雪隠 – toilets

These are transmitted in the scroll *Kōketsu*.

堀ノ習
Hori no narai

TEACHINGS ON TYPES OF MOAT

外堀

Sotobori

OUTER MOAT

Commentator two

This is a moat built around an outer enclosure.

内堀
Uchibori
INNER MOAT

Commentator two
This is a moat built around an inner enclosure

用心掘
Yōjinbori
ADDITIONAL MOATS

Commentator one
These are moats dug for extra caution. It is preferable to have water within them, but if it is a dry moat it should have a ridged mound on the inside and a fence on the mound itself.

片薬研掘
Katayagenbori
ANGLED MOAT

Commentator two
One side of this type of moat is dug vertically; the other side is steeply angled.

両薬研
Ryōyagenbori
V-SHAPED MOAT

Commentator two
This is angled equally on both sides [in a V-shape]. Make sure to dig deeply.

柵堀
Sakubori
RIDGED MOAT

Commentator one

This contains ridged mounds on the inside; it is not to be filled with water.

畦堀
Azebori
PATHWAY MOAT

Commentator one

This is used for marshes and it should be terraced. Create many ridgeways within it.

袋堀
Fukurobori
DEAD-END MOAT

Commentator one

This is to be constructed beside a mountain.

Commentator two

This is to be constructed with a mountainside at one end [of the moat] and to be well-constructed on the inside of the moat itself.

搔上堀
Kakiagebori
BANK AND DITCH

Commentator one

This is 1 *ken* 2 *shaku* wide and 1 *shaku* deep. Have sand scattered [inside it] or soak the base with water so that the earth will be flat [and will show footprints]. This is done to know if there have been any spies [infiltrating] in the area.

Commentator two

This is 1 *ken* 2 *shaku* wide and 1 *shaku* deep. Have sand scattered [inside it] or soak the base with water so that earth will become flat. However, this type of moat does not have stone walls but just an earthen bank [which is built using the soil dug out of the moat]. Sand is then laid evenly and raked, mainly for the purpose of checking for *shinobi* or deserting warriors.

土居敷之事
Doishiki no koto

CONSTRUCTION OF EARTHEN MOUNDS

Measurements for earthen mounds:
- For a height of 3 *ken*, the thickness should be 8 *ken*.
- For a height of 2 *ken*, the thickness should be 6 *ken*.

In the case of a hardened earth mound, the thickness for a height of 3 *ken* should be 6 *ken*, not 8 *ken*.

For a *tsuiji* wall:[110]
- If it is 1 *ken* in height, it should have grassy mound at the base.
- A *tsuiji* wall built on the inside of a moat should have pebbles and broken roof tiles mixed in with the soil.[111]

A *tsuiji* wall with fence:
- [The base] should be 1 *shaku* and 2 or 3 *sun* high and 3 *shaku* wide.

Various types of wood can be used for fences. Such walls can also be called *chirifusegi* – protection against dust.

---

110 A wall made of a mixture of mud and clay between wooden frames (similar to wattle and daub).

111 The roof tiles are often layered to an almost brick-style formation.

Commentator one

A 1 *ken tsuiji* wall should have inside it a grass earth mound up to half of its height.

As previously mentioned, a *tsuiji* wall should be built in a moat if the moat is wide. This is because a wide moat will generate waves and the waves will damage stone walls. This is called a *namiwari* (波ワリ) – wave breaker.

柵振様之事
Saku furiyō no koto

CONSTRUCTION OF FENCES

Fences should rise 7 *shaku* 5 *sun* above the ground, and should have a connecting beam across them 5 *sun* below the pointed tips of the posts. The posts should be positioned at intervals of 4 *sun*.

Commentator two

One theory states that fences made of logs are called *saku* (柵), whereas fences made of square wood are called *shaku* (尺).

仮柵
Karisaku
TEMPORARY FENCES

These should be 7 *shaku* and 2 or 3 *sun* high, with an interval between posts of 4 *sun* 5 *bu*. They have three horizontal beams [linking them], the highest of which should be 5 *sun* below the pointed tips of posts. [The middle beam] should be tied 5 *sun* below [the top one] on the outside [of the fence]. The lowest beam should be 5 *sun* from the ground and tied on the inside. All joints should be tied from the outside.

Commentator one

These are 7 *shaku* high, with intervals [between the vertical posts] of 4 [*sun*].

蚤柵

Sōsaku[112]

QUICK FENCES

These are hastily built fences for temporary use. Posts are secured in the ground at intervals of 1 *ken* with intervening vertical posts not being fixed in the ground [but lashed to the cross-beams].

葛柵

Kazura-saku

VINE FENCES[113]

These are made of thin bamboo, Japanese bush clover and the like. There should be three wooden posts for each *ken* in length and two horizontal beams tied [across the posts]. Fences made of Japanese wisteria are strong enough to stop horses crossing [through them]. This is a tactic for nighttime use.

一代柵

Ichidai-saku

SHORT-TERM FENCES

There is one beam at the top and one beam at the bottom.[114]

末代柵

Matsudai-saku

LONG-TERM FENCES

These are hedges or thorny barriers of trifoliate orange trees,[115] which are supported with robust posts.

---

112 The text gives two readings for this; the other is *hayasaku*.
113 Fences made from thin plant material.
114 This may also be interpreted as meaning there are two beams at the lower part.
115 *Citrus trifoliate.*

述柵木

Nobesakugi

FENCES FOR BANNER POLES

These are 8 *shaku* 5 *sun* high [in total] and built with four vertical posts of Chinese sumac[116] which have five horizontal beams of chestnut wood tied onto them. Build these fences on both sides of the gate of a battle camp and attach flags, banners and small markers to them. The intervals should be 5 *sun* between vertical posts and 1 *shaku* between horizontal beams. The construction should consist of four posts and five beams tied together and be 6 *shaku* in height.[117]

Commentator one

Construct a fence of four vertical and five horizontal [posts] by tying them up in this way. Small flags should be tied on with strings.

虎落結作法
Mogari yui sahō

HOW TO SECURE AND CONSTRUCT FENCES

[The following points explain different types of fences and other forms of obstruction.]

菱虎落

Hishi-mogari

DIAMOND-SHAPED SPIKED FENCES

Constructing diamond-shaped *mogari* fences: each diamond [as shown in the

---

116 *Rhus javanica.*

117 The text mentions two different heights. We have assumed the 8 *shaku* 5 *sun* measurement is the height of the fence and flags combined. However, grammatically it sounds as if the posts are 8 *shaku* high. It is not clear.

image below] should have sides that are about 4 or 5 *sun*. This type of fence is 7–9 *shaku* high, or even up to 1 *jō*. It has five horizontal beams tied together on the inside. Pieces of bamboo should be assembled just as a *kimono* is overlapped at the front. All pieces of bamboo should be equal in height and sharply pointed at the top.

Tradition says that to build huts in an area of 500 *ken* requires 10,000 pieces of bamboo.

[?]虎落[118]

Kata-mogari
FENCES ALONG A WALKWAY
These are bamboo fences built halfway up an earthen hill [fort]. Put supports in place and secure the fence with large stones at the base.

Commentator one
For example, have *mushabashiri* pathways [along the earthen hill] between the castle wall and the moat. The pathways should be 2 *ken* [in width]. Secure the fences with Japanese loquat canes in the middle of the pathway, dividing the space. The 1 *ken* wide path to the front of the divide will then become the *mushabashiri* – the warrior's walkway.

Commentator two
Kata-mogari fences are built halfway up the bank of an earthworks and supported with Japanese loquat canes. These fences should be at a high point on the mound. The length can vary.

---

118 Archaic ideogram.

猿虎落

Saru-mogari

MONKEY FENCES

Use bamboo without splitting it in two. Bind the canes together and erect the fence. It should have five horizontal beams.

笹垣

Sasa-gaki

THIN BAMBOO FENCES

These should be 5 or 6 *shaku* high and built by binding [thin bamboo] together. Posts should be put at intervals of 5 *sun* 4 or 5 *bu*. Three to five horizontal beams should be used. This is a type of tied fence to be built around the entire circumference of a battle camp, inside of which there are moats and *tsuiji* walls.

猪垣

Shishi-gaki

WILD BOAR FENCES

Split bamboo down its length, tie it up and alternate them. Have the bamboo with the rounded surface on the inner side and the cut surface on the outer side.

水虎落

Mizu-mogari

SPIKED FENCES IN WATER

Fix this kind of fence into the middle of the waterbed of a shallow moat around a castle. It should be 3 *shaku* 8 *sun* high and have sharpened tips like arrows. Use *saikachi* (皂角)[119] wood to weigh it down; this also makes the water murky.

行馬縄

Gyōmanawa

TRIP ROPES

This is to stretch ropes along a route where night attacks or spies are likely to come. Furthermore, guards should be positioned nearby. The ropes should be

---

119 *Gleditsia japonica.*

stretched at a height of three fingers below the kneecap,[120] and positioned in a staggered way. At a position 3 *shaku* in front of each rope, dig a hole 2 *shaku* wide and 2 *shaku* deep.

Commentator one

Each rope should be 1.5 *ken* long. Any longer than that and they are not effective, as they sag in the middle. The space between ropes should be 2 *shaku*.

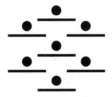

Commentator two

The space between the ropes should be 1 *shaku* 5 *sun* and multiple ropes should be set out. The length of the rope should be between 1 and 1.5 *ken*. If it is longer it is not effective as it sags in the middle.

乱杭

Rangui

SPIKES

These should be made of logs that reach waist height and arranged in groups of five. The length of the [spiked area] depends on the defensive qualities of

---

120 *Sanri* (三里) – a specific part of the body in Chinese medicine.

the ground, whereas the depth of the area should be 3 or 4 *ken* [so that people cannot pass through].

逆茂木
Sakamogi
THORNY BRANCHES
These consist of double fences with thorny branches of the Japanese honey locust plant[121] tied between them. You can also use *karatachi* thorny branches.[122]

竹把之作法
Taketaba no sahō
CONSTRUCTING BAMBOO BUNDLES
Bamboo bundles should be constructed and attached to a framework. They should be about 5 *shaku* high and [multiple bundles placed together against a frame should measure] 1 *ken* across. The bundles themselves should be 2 *shaku* or 2 *shaku* 5 *sun* in circumference and they should be secured tightly to the frame.

Commentator one
Place the bamboo bundles onto this frame and secure them. Also, attach *yuminawa* ropes for your bow here.

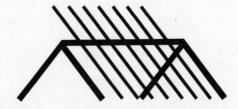

Commentator two
[The drawing below shows an example of the kind of bamboo bundle that should be placed against the frame.]

---

121 *Gleditsia japonica.*
122 *Poncirus trifoliate.*

陥穴[123]

Otoshiana

PITFALL TRAPS

Places where *otoshiana* pitfall traps should be created:

- narrow paths
- steep areas of ascent
- place where landslides are likely to take place

Place caltrops or spikes in the traps and make the soil look old, then seed plants, grasses or greenery on top of them.

Tradition says to make the soil look old by sprinkling it with water in which rice has been washed. Plant vegetable seeds such as Japanese radish or even plant cuttings for this purpose.

持竹把

Mochi-taketaba

MOBILE BAMBOO BUNDLES

These should be 3 *shaku* or 3 *shaku* 5 *sun* in circumference and 6 or 7 *shaku* in length. Position a stick of loquat wood [to help each bundle stand up] or build something like a saddle rack and rest [the bamboo bundle against it.]

---

123 The Tōkyō transcription uses only the first ideogram.

Tradition says it should be longer if the enemy is close and shorter if they are distant.[124]

Commentator two
Use Japanese loquat wood for the handle, or as previously mentioned, use a saddle rack [to stand them against] – this saddle rack is called an *ushi*.

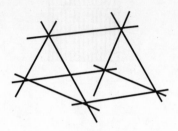

Commentator three
In another school they use the willow [boards] that are 1 *sun* thick, 1 *shaku* 2 *sun* wide and 2 *shaku* 5 *sun* high. Chain mail is positioned [as a skirt] at the lower end [of the shield] and is the same as that used on armour for *sane* (小ネ) plates. At 8 *sun* from the top of the willow board, build a viewing port [in the shield] and 1 *shaku* down from this viewing port position a horizontal bar [on the inside] to serve as a handle.[125]

仕寄竹束
Shiyori-taketaba

BAMBOO SIEGE WALLS

Construct three posts per 1 *ken* of distance with three horizontal beams tied

---

124 Most likely this is referring to the length of the supporting stick so that the angle changes.
125 This is a small handheld shield with a viewing port and chain mail skirt.

onto them. Put bamboo bundles onto the framework. This should be done late at night under the supervision of the *ashigaru-daishō* foot soldier commander.

To use such siege walls there are two phases of positioning to be considered:
1. moving forward to dig holes
2. bringing the siege wall forward and driving the *hikae no ki* support stakes in place

Fifty people are engaged in this process:
- Ten *doritsu no ban* – trench guards
- Ten *chūshin no mono* – observers who report
- Ten *shinobi no mono* – infiltrators
- Five people for the *kuruma nawa* [shown in the diagram below] – do this for each [side], so this adds up to ten people in total
- Ten *ban no mono* – guards

Arrange the siege walls appropriately and create a gate or door in a space set between them. The door should also be made of bamboo which has been tied together. Secure it tightly with bolts and build a guardhouse.

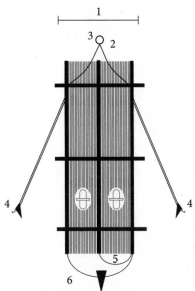

Positions numbered in the image:
1. rope stretched out to the front
2. *kuruma nawa* – rope with ring
3. *taimatsu* – torch
4. *hikae no ki* – pegs for support
5. *doritsu* – trenches
6. *maenawa* – front rope

Create gun ports by knocking a spike or something similar through [the walls].

When advancing with this [equipment], move out of the trenches and stretch a rope to the front [number one in the diagram. Do this to mark out the area of construction] and then move forward and erect it at that point. Lower torches [down the other side] with the rope [number two in the diagram].

The pathway [trench] used to advance the siege walls should be dug in a zig-zag manner. *Shinobi* infiltrators are essential in a siege. The depth of the trench should be 4 or 5 *shaku*. Dig like this and tighten your siege. It is constructed in a zig-zag manner so as to defend against musket fire.

土俵ヲ積事

Dohyō wo tsumu koto

SANDBAG CONSTRUCTIONS[126]

Sandbags should be piled in the style of *mendoriba* (メン鳥羽) – overlapping like the wings of a hen.[127] This [way of piling sandbags] is also called *funatsumi* (舟ツミ) – stacking on ships.

The zig-zag trench [shown below] is used to move the temporary walls [forward during a siege].

---

126 Large rice bags filled with earth.

127 The sandbags overlap in the same fashion as the bricks in a brick wall.

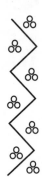

仕寄竹把ウシ縄之事

Shiyori taketaba ushinawa no koto

TRIANGULAR MOBILE SHIELD

This is also a bamboo bundle and should be constructed as shown in the image below. If pushed in any direction, it will not fall over [but will 'roll']. Therefore, roll it towards the enemy while hiding behind it as you approach [a siege].[128]

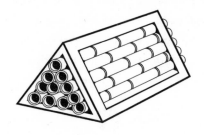

井楼臺之事

Seirōdai no koto

SANDBAGS AS A FOUNDATION FOR *SEIRŌ* – WATCH TOWERS

This concerns how to construct and add height to a watchtower. The base should be made by piling up sandbags.

---

128 The image here is an embellishment. The original is simply a three-dimensional triangle.

CHAPTER SEVENTEEN

儒者
Jusha

CONFUCIANISTS

Any number of Confucianists is acceptable.

They perform the same function on the battlefield as they do in normal times. They stay close to the general (*shō*) and talk about the Way, but also they 'smooth' or correct a general's malice or insanity by explaining to him various examples of ancient sages and their deeds – just as in normal times.

They discuss the right and wrong of every matter and should not hesitate or be afraid to say such things even to a general. Needless to say, they should transmit and pursue the truth of all things. They also assess enemy letters of reconciliation, appeals for surrender and the like.

本道外科
Hondō geka

PHYSICIANS AND SURGEONS

Numerous physicians and surgeons are required.

They should be proficient in administering various medicines to cure every disease. There are things to be orally transmitted on the following three points.

HOW TO INFORM SOMEONE OF THE SERIOUSNESS OF THEIR ILLNESS AND CONDITION

Commentator two
When you talk to officials or other such people, you should talk relatively seriously, telling them they are tolerating a disease or injury well.

HOW TO INFORM SOMEONE OF THE SERIOUSNESS OF THEIR INJURY

Commentator two
Talk lightly to those who are injured, but talk seriously to others [about the injured person].

A PHYSICIAN SHOULD NOT FIGHT TO GAIN HIS OWN ACHIEVEMENTS

Commentator two
Basically, [physicians and surgeons] should not fight for their own interest, unless a battle gets so out of control that even the general himself has to fight.

Issui-sensei says
It is a tradition to mark the *hara-obi* stomach band of the injured.

Commentator two
This is done as a caution so that people will not loosen [their *hara-obi*] without cause.

Issui-sensei says
[Physicians and surgeons] should also be aware that they may have to join consultations or assessments where the general may ask them about the following points:

- *tenri* 天利 – astrology
- *gunki* 軍氣 – the *chi* of battle
- *enki* 煙氣 – *chi* within smoke

Commentator two

Details are mentioned in the scrolls *Gunki Yōhō* and *Gunshū Yōhō*. Be aware that whether to use or not use [such areas of knowledge] depends on the situation.

軍配者
Gunbaisha

ESOTERIC TACTICIANS

A multiple number of these are required.

These people understand the manners and customs of warfare and conduct rituals in connection to weapons and tools.

People in this position observe any changes in the early morning. Specifically, they observe *chi* and time, perceive if the wind is for or against the army and conduct rituals of good luck and evil luck. They also take charge of astrological subjects.

Commentator two

Details on how to determine the following are mentioned in the scroll *Gunbai Yōhō*:

- *hidori* 日取 – date
- *tokidori* 時取 – time
- *kokyo* 孤虚 – negative and positive directions
- *ōsō* 王相 – the five phases of strength and their connection to the seasons
- *unki* 運気 – divination and luck
- *tenmon* 天文 – astrology
- *jikken* 実検 – head inspections

- *yaire* 矢入 – ritual arrow shooting
- *kachidoki* 勝鬨 – war cries
- *bugu no seihō* 武具ノ制法 – rituals for military gear
- *hifu* 秘符 – secret talismans
- *jumon* 呪文 – spells

間者
Kanja

SPIES

Numerous spies are required.

They discreetly infiltrate the enemy and secretly report back to their allies. Also they discover enemy tactics and deceive the enemy general to benefit the allies. In ancient times this role did not exist in Japan. However, during the Genpei War (1180–1185) local people were used for guidance; this is called *kyōdō* and is mentioned later. The name [of *kanja*] appears to have existed as late as the Kenmu period (1334–1336), around the time of the battle of Akasaka castle fought by Kusunoki Masashige.

According to the traditions from some Chinese writings, the *gokan* – five types of spy – were used.

Commentator two

There are five types of spy and these are described below. Spies investigate, explore and get to know information about the enemy. In Japan they are called *shinobi no mono*.[129] The spy can be used to find out detailed information about the enemy before a battle starts.

---

129 The main text has separate sections for *kanja* and *shinobi no mono* – *shinobi no mono* being covered after *kanja*. However, the commentator here uses *shinobi no mono* to mean *kanja*. The two are close in terms of their duties. However, as explained in the *Dakkō Shinobi no Maki*, there are slight differences.

The ideogram for *kan* 間 [from *kanja*] is alternatively represented as:

- *chō* 諜 – this is found in the *Zuo Zhuan* classic
- *saisaku* 作細[130]
- *yūtei* 遊偵

During the time of the Chu Dynasty in China, Chen Ping had a spy infiltrate the army of the Chu to obtain information. Know that spies will give no benefit if they are not used well; therefore, know how they were used in the above episode. Spies cannot be usefully employed without a certain level of ingenious wisdom. Gold and silver should not be spared [but should be spent liberally on spying].

Sun Tzu says:

> *Hostile armies may face each other for years, striving for the victory that is decided in a single day. This being so, to remain in ignorance of the enemy's condition simply because one begrudges the outlay of a hundred ounces of silver in honours and emoluments is the height of inhumanity.*

If you love [and would not part with] even a small amount of your fortune and do not know how much the people in your army are struggling, this is not considered benevolence. However, if you spend hoards of gold [on the use of spies] to find out information about the enemy, securing victory by providing contingencies for your allies and taking hold of every advantage, then the people in your army will not suffer from a prolonged war. Also, if taxes are reduced farmers will not resent the ruler and your forces will be substantial and will not be defeated by the enemy who is trying to expose your gaps. Generally, spies (*kan*) require a massive investment in gold and silver so as to yield a good knowledge of the enemy in order to complete a swift victory.

---

130 The ideograms are reversed in the *Bansenshūkai* manual (*The Book of Ninja*).

五間

Gokan

THE FIVE TYPES OF SPY

1

因口ノ間

Inkō no kan

Local spies

This is to use local people by listening to their words.

Commentator two

Local spies are also called *kyōkan* (郷間), and these *kyōkan* are local spies in the enemy province. You should approach people in villages with lies and give them gold, silver and money. Use them to assess whether [the enemy] is substantial or insubstantial, strong or weak. When you intend to make war against the enemy, then beforehand you should become familiar with local residents in such enemy provinces. Do this in peacetime by making them feel that they owe you something, so you can gain information on the military status of the enemy, the behaviour of the lord and other such matters. You can even identify the abilities of generals, their personal achievements and the braveness of individuals.

2

内良ノ間

Nairyō no kan

Internal spies

This is to tempt and use a close [enemy] retainer or somebody else close to the enemy lord. This is very important indeed.

Commentator two

Internal spies become friendly with the close retainers of the enemy lord. Bribe them heavily to discover information on their area. Also, bribe and convert: those who have a grudge against the [enemy] lord and who are enthusiastic for profit; those who are very talented but have lost their position because of some issue and, having left their employment, have fallen on hard times; or those who are not truly loyal and are in fact dishonest and always duplicitous. Do this so that they will divulge to you their secrets. This is how internal spies work.

3
反徳ノ間
Hantoku no kan
Converted spies
This is to make use of an enemy spy. It is a god-like and complete way.

Commentator two
When the enemy sends spies to your side to discover your tactics, pretend not to know that they have entered and treat them as if you are unaware of their intent even though you actually do know their real objectives. Use them for the benefit of your own side. This is called *hankan* – the converted spy.

When enemy spies have entered, you can deliberately feed them false information, while hiding the truth, to make them believe your falsehoods. Mislead them to gain benefit for your own side.

In the old days, Mōri Motonari found a blind spy working [against him] for his enemy, Sue Harukata. [Mōri Motonari] used him as a *hankan* converted spy so that he could finally defeat Sue Harukata. Also, Chen Ping of the Han Dynasty used spies from Chu to create discord between Xian Yu and Fan Zeng. This is all part of the skill of *hankan* – the converted spy. Furthermore, when an enemy spy (*kan*) scouts around your position, you might bribe him to work for your side instead. This is another technique of *hankan*.

4
死長ノ間
Shichō no kan
Doomed spies
These provide much benefit. Send them to the enemy to divulge something that benefits your own side.

Commentator two

They are also called *shikan* – the doomed spy.

Annotations on the *Art of War* say that *hankan* converted spies approach the enemy, but in the end are killed by them.[131] This is a technique to put spies under heavy obligation to undertake a secret mission that has a one in ten thousand chance of success.

To destroy the enemy, give your spy one specific [enemy] name, so as to trap [and ruin that person]. Have your spy tell [this name] to an enemy spy so that the enemy spy will report it to his master. If the enemy general takes it as true [it will be of great benefit]. However, if he does not believe it, then he will think your spy has lied and will have him killed and you will gain no benefit. This is an example of *shikan* – the doomed spy.

Also, if [your spy] stays on the enemy side, pretending to change sides and work as a converted spy, he should work discreetly to undermine enemy tactics and secretly communicate back to your side. If the enemy discovers this, the spy will be immediately killed. This is also an example of *shikan* – the doomed spy.

In modern days, at the siege of Ōsaka, the warrior Obata Kanbei Kagenori pretended to take the side of Hideyori and got into the castle. He attended conferences and disrupted the enemy tactics. This is another example of *shikan* – the doomed spy.

Yet another example comes from ancient times when Kusunoki Masashige attacked Akasaka castle and he sent Onchi Sakon to infiltrate the castle during daytime. This is a skill which is bound to result in death, as it has a one in ten thousand chance of success.

[In China] Li Yiji was sent as a *shikan* doomed spy from the Han Dynasty to the camp of the Qi Dynasty.

In modern times Ishida Mitsunari sent the warrior Kaganoi Yahachi to the area of Kantō to complete his plan to kill Mizuno Izumi no kami – this was as an assassin (刺客).

---

131 The meaning here could be that an enemy spy is converted and sent back to the enemy to carry out a mission on your behalf that will almost certainly result in the spy's death. So a converted spy becomes a doomed spy.

In ancient times in the Yan Dynasty, Jing Ke and Qi Wuyang were sent to kill Qin Shi Huang. They were assassins, but this is also a type of *kanja* spy.

5
天生ノ間
Tensei no kan
Surviving spies
This concerns those who infiltrate the enemy and complete their covert missions with excellence.

Commentator two
Choose those who look stupid on the outside but who are bright on the inside; those who are ill-shaped but wise-minded make resourceful spies. They should enter the enemy forces by disguising themselves, insinuate themselves by using [enemy] interests to know their situation and tactics, then bring back such information and report. They should associate themselves with those working for the administrators who control everything and know fully the [enemy's] secret plans. By doing this they can inform their side about such matters.

These are called *seikan* – surviving spies (生間).

Issui-sensei says
The above are *gokan* – the five types of spy. They should be used according to the situation.

Commentator two
The above are called *gokan* – the five types of spy – and are used in military families (兵家).

Sun Tzu says:

> It is only the enlightened ruler and the wise general who will use the highest intelligence of the army for purposes of spying and thereby they achieve great results.

Details are mentioned in the *Art of War* in the chapter 'The use of spies'.

忍之者
Shinobi no mono

INFILTRATORS

Numerous infiltrators are required.

These are military intelligence agents (情役). They act independently and are considered as *ikko no shinobi* – single operators.[132] Alternatively, they can be called *dakkō no shinobi*. All [leaders] need their own *shinobi* operatives. Their work is concerned with the deepest secrets of the *taishō*'s mind and his inner heart.[133]

Commentator one
Dakkō no shinobi is transmitted in our *shinobi* scrolls. It is key that the *taishō* considers all phases [when he uses *shinobi*], moving through *sho chū go* – the beginning, the middle and the end.

Commentator two
In our school, the skills of *shinobi* soldiers are transmitted in our *shinobi* scrolls.

SHINOBI TRADITIONS AND SKILLS
The following are traditions and skills of the *shinobi*.

---

132 The Tōkyō transcription uses the ideograms 一固ノ忍, whereas the Koga transcription uses 一己ノ忍.

133 This statement is somewhat ambiguous. It can be taken to mean that *shinobi* need to discover the deepest secrets of the enemy *taishō*'s mind, but that they also need to know how their own *taishō* is thinking so that they can do what he would want them to do. When working behind enemy lines, *shinobi* are often unable to communicate with their *taishō*, so they need to be able to 'read' his mind when planning their next move.

如常ニシテ人ノ詞可聞知事

Tsune no gotoku nishite hito no kotoba wo kikishiru koto

Listen to people talk while behaving as normal

國村里他人ヲ禁スル所ニ取入事

Kuni mura sato tanin wo kinzuru tokoro ni toriiru koto

Infiltrate a province, village, settlement or place where other people are forbidden to enter

国ノ士ヲ積ル人ヲ以テ可知事

Kuni no samurai wo tsumoru hito wo motte shiru beki koto

Estimate and know the number of *samurai* of a province by using people

Commentator one

These people include *geisha*, people of the arts,[134] and *rōnin*, master-less *samurai*.

家數小屋數可積知事

Iekazu koyakazu tsumori shiru beki koto

Estimate and know the number of houses or camp huts

行列人數可積知事

Gyōretsu ninju tsumori shiru beki koto

Estimate and know the number of people in a procession

Commentator one

This is to get an idea of the overall number involved.

---

134 *Geisha* in this context is a person of the arts. *Geisha* has many connotations other than the one with which we associate the term today. In fact, at the time that the commentator was writing, the kind of female entertainer we think of when we hear the term *geisha* would have been known as a *geiko*, and other terms, also *geisha* was the domain of men. Understand that *geisha* does not mean the same as it does today.

宮寺ニ行取入ベキ事
Kyūji ni iki toriiru beki koto
Insinuate oneself into temples or shrines

Commentator one
This is done by making donations.

家人ノ眠リタルヲ可知事
Kajin no nemuri taru wo shiru beki koto
Know if people in a house are asleep

Commentator one
There are tools for this.

家へ夜可忍入事
Ie e yoru shinobi iru koto
Infiltrate houses at night

Commentator one
Do this through deception.

塀ノリ様之事
Hei noriyō no koto
Climb walls

Commentator one
Do this by using a *kaginawa* grappling hook and *daishō* swords [as a stepping off point].

垣クヽリヤウノ事付乗様
Kaki kukuriyō no koto tsuketari noriyō no koto
Get through and cross over fences

Commentator one

Use straw mats [to place over the fence].

沼越之事
Numagoe no koto
Cross over marshes

Commentator one

For this use wooden frames. Use *hō* wood,[135] then use cattail or bamboo [on the frame surface] and cross over [the marsh].

夜火見様之事
Yoru hi miyō no koto
Observe lights at night

Commentator one

[Create a horizon with something like a fan and use it to observe the light.] When the light ascends, that means it is moving away; when it descends, that means it is approaching. Also, lights look closer and higher in the darkness but thinner and farther away in the moonlight.

人ノ金銀持タルヲ可知事
Hito no kingin mochitaru wo shirubeki koto
Know how much gold and silver people have

Commentator one

Do this by deluding and enticing them with objects.

家ノ窓忍様之事
Ie no mado shinobiyō no koto
Break in through windows [or openings]

---

135 *Magnolia obovate.*

Commentator one

Place an object against the window shutter and lift it. Alternatively, cut through with tools.

塀築地破様之事

Hei tsuiji yaburiyō no koto

Break through outside walls and plaster walls

Commentator one

There are tools transmitted for this purpose.

鍵縄作様之事

Kaginawa tsukuriyō no koto

Create a grappling hook

Commentator one

Use bamboo cylinders in addition [to the hook].

東西知様之事

Tōzai shiriyō no koto

Discover the direction

Commentator one

Seed leaves grow and point north and south. Also use star constellations, topography and the like.

門戸シメヤウノ事

Monko shimeyō no koto

Secure doors and gates

Commentator one

There are traditions on how to use the grappling hook for this.

人家ヱ可入時ノ事

Jinka e iru beki toki no koto

Know when to infiltrate a house

Commentator one

Be it during night, day or twilight.

色ヲ替利ヲ可取事

Iro wo kae ri wo toru beki koto

Take advantage of something by changing the approach

Commentator one

Obtain something by seeking other 'pathways'.

目付ノ道草結フ事

Metsuke no michi kusa musubu koto

Make markings by tying grass

Commentator one

Tie grass at every fork in the road.

犬ヲ用事并犬ノ真似用ル事

Inu wo mochiiru koto narabini inu no mane mochiiru koto

[Understand] the use of dogs and imitating a dog

Commentator one

At the time of infiltration use the oral tradition called *satoinu* – local dogs. [*Shinobi*] sometimes disguise themselves as a merchant, farmer or various other kinds of people.[136]

---

136 The term 'dog' is also used to mean various forms of *shinobi* or infiltrator. In Natori-Ryū, the term can mean various types of spy as well as the actual animal itself.

闇キ時火ヲ用ル事
Kuraki toki hi wo mochiiru koto
Know how to use fire when it is dark

Commentator one
Know how to carry fire and tools.

深ク忍テ早ク引取事
Fukaku shinbite hayaku hikitoru koto
Infiltrate deeply but exit quickly

Commentator one
If [an exit strategy] is prolonged, it can cause trouble.

胴火ノ事
Dōnohi no koto
Use the *dōnohi* – ember-carrying cylinder
Details of this are in another writing.

Commentator one
There is both the tool and the recipe to consider.

上ヲ動シ地ニ不思議ナシテ人ノ心ヲ取ル事
Ue wo ugokashi chi ni fushigi nashite hito no kokoro wo toru koto
Draw people's attention away by making something move at a height or by showing something mysterious on the ground

Commentator one
Very few people can focus on two directions at once.

The above teachings can be applied to everything. Know that appearing normal is essential for *shinobi*.

In the Takeda clan of Koshū, they used thieves called *suppa* as *shinobi*, but [*shinobi*] are also called *Kōka-mono* – men of *Kōka*. The term *shinobi no mono* was established in Japan. It is said that all of these [types of people] communicate well among themselves to gain information. There are teachings to be secretly transmitted and they are called: *mumon no ikkan*, the gateless gate, and *shinchi no hō*, the art of knowing people's minds. These are the deepest secrets of the *shinobi*.

CHAPTER EIGHTEEN

筭勘者
Sankanja

ACCOUNTANTS

Numerous accountants are required.

They administer the accounts in warfare. They are in charge of revenue and expenditure for construction and rations, as well as the financial incomings and outgoings of the entire army.

They work with various officials on the accounts. However, there are many teachings on calculation, which are not mentioned here as it would take too long. Even mentioning a part of their skills would not be enough, as it is difficult to master the profession without fully pursuing the path. Accountants should always try to commit themselves to the way of accounting and have discernment on all matters.

Commentator two
Accountants sometimes take part in a council of war when it is related to such issues as:

- estimation of the area when building a castle and barracks
- information on distances and topography of mountains, rivers, seas, land, etc.
- assessing the pros and cons of different modes of transport, such as transport by cart, or going by sea
- deciding on the ways of collecting tax and ensuring clarity in details
- calculating the gain and loss of gold, silver, rice and money; also construction costs or anything else that requires calculation

右筆
Yūhitsu

SECRETARIES

Numerous secretaries are required.

They should always know the various customs and manners of writing.

The following list outlines specific duties of secretaries:

白帋之事
Hakushi no koto
THE WAY OF WHITE PAPER

This is mentioned in the *Kōketsu* scroll. [It is the way of writing and sending letters.]

首札書様之事
Kubifuda kakiyō no koto
HOW TO WRITE TAGS FOR DECAPITATED HEADS

- For heads of the upper class, write in *shin* – block style.
- For heads of the middle class, write in *sō* – cursive.
- For heads of the lowest class, write in *kana* – phonetic markers.

If both the decapitated enemy and the ally who killed him are generals (*shō*), then writing should go on both sides of the tag. If the enemy is a general and the ally is an ordinary *samurai*, the writing should go on the front of the tag.

Commentator one

These tags are 4 *sun* long.

Commentator two

When an allied *samurai* has killed an enemy general, write the name of the enemy general on the front of the tag in block style and the name of the *samurai* on the same side below it, but in cursive style. If a general of your side has killed an enemy general, write the name of the enemy general on the front and the allied general on the reverse.

首桶ニ書付様
Kubioke ni kakitsuke yō
HOW TO WRITE ON A HEAD CONTAINER

Write the name on the lid. Sometimes a *sutra* is written on the side of the cylinder. Draw a swastika pattern on the inside on the lid.[137] Sometimes the name of the *samurai* who has killed the person [is placed under the lid]. To be orally transmitted.

Commentator two

A *sutra* or *indō* is a Buddhist scripture that leads the soul of the deceased person to the pure land of Buddha. It should be written by a monk.

首帳書様之事
Kubichō kakiyō no koto
HOW TO WRITE IN THE BOOK OF HEADS

Write the date, place and description of the head. The following is the form it should take.

According to tradition insert the number of the head, from head number one to head number thirteen; after that, just write the name.

Record the following:

- era and year – e.g. Tenbun (insert number of year)[138]
- month
- day

---

137 The Koga transcription states that this should be on top of the lid.
138 Japanese dates consist of the era name and the year – for example, Tenbun 1 (equivalent to 1532).

- time
- taken during the battle of (insert name)
- the name of the province
- the name of the place within the province
- notes on the decapitation

Here are some examples of recording in the book of heads.

Example one
The following heads were taken by the *oumamawari* – mounted guards to the *taishō*.[139]

Commentator two
The term *oumamawari* is equivalent to *gokinju* – esquires of the lord.

[Example continued]

Number one: head, one in number (insert name and title of the deceased), killed by (insert name and title of the man who made the kill) – killed by spear.

Number two: head, one in number (insert name and title of the deceased), killed by (insert name and title of the man who made the kill) – killed by great sword.

Number three: head, one in number (insert name and title of the deceased), killed by (insert name and title of the man who made the kill) – they were [initially] captured alive.

Example two
[The following heads were taken by] the members of the group led by (insert commander's name).

Number one: head, one in number (insert name and title of the deceased), killed by (insert name and title of the man who made the kill) – killed by spear.

---

139 御馬廻.

Number two: head, one in number (insert name and title of the deceased), killed by (insert name and title of the man who made the kill) – killed by great sword.

Number three: head, one in number (insert name and title of the deceased), killed by (insert name and title of the man who made the kill) – they were [initially] captured alive.

Example three
[The following heads were taken by] the members of the group led by (insert commander's name).

Head, one in number (insert name and title of the deceased), killed by (insert name) who is a member of the group led by (insert commander's name).

Head, one in number (insert name and title of the deceased), killed by (insert name) who is a member of the group led by (insert commander's name).

Apart from the above, [the record] should also state that there are countless soldiers captured, killed or driven away. In one method of writing, write the number of those captured, then record the total number of the heads [actually counted] in units of hundreds, and then state that the number of those simply killed was countless. You should use the full height of the paper and attach extra sheets if needed.[140]

Commentator two
At the siege of Ōsaka, the warrior Matsuura Yaemon, under the command of Kimura Nagato no kami, and the warrior Asabe Seibei, under the command of Hotta Zusho, both took heads. Toyotomi Hideyori's secretary, Shirai Jin'emon, was in charge of the book of heads at this time. Matsuura approached with a decapitated head and claimed to be the first to take an enemy head. Shirai did not write this distinction down, but simply recorded it as 'one head by Matsuura Yaemon'. When Asabe brought in his captured head, Shirai decided that it was he who had actually taken the first head, even before Matsuura had

---

140 The use of paper and formal styles of folding is a detailed subject. Here it means to have the paper in landscape orientation and write vertically from right to left. When there is no space left, add an extra sheet to the left.

taken his, because Asabe took his head farther away than Matsuura and so it took him longer to return from that place. As the evidence was clear, Matsuura was proven to be the second. Shirai said to Matsuura that it was an old custom that secretaries wait for the other heads to arrive before they proclaim which head is the first.

過去帳

Kakochō

HOW TO WRITE IN THE BUDDHIST DEATH REGISTER

Those allies who are killed should be recorded in the *kakochō* – Buddhist death register. The following details should be noted: year, month, day, hour, name of battle and place.

[Here are some example entries.]

(Title and name of the deceased) was killed but also killed an enemy at the same time.

(Title and name of the deceased) was killed in close combat (*kumi*) with the enemy.

(Title and name of the deceased) was killed in combat (*tatakai*) with the enemy.

(Title and name of the deceased) was killed from spear fighting (*yariai*) with the enemy.

(Title and name of the deceased) was killed while leading an attack.

In the above, if the enemy's name is known, it should also be recorded. Someone who left behind a great exploit should have their exploit written down [in the style of the list above]. Each group can have its own record.

手負帳

Teoichō

HOW TO WRITE IN THE BOOK OF THE INJURED

As in the above, record those allies injured with the date [year, month, day, time] as follows.

(Title and name of the injured) received two wounds, struck with a great sword during a battle with (name of enemy), wound received in the middle of the forehead on the helmet and the breastplate. Continued to cut and kill his enemy in the end.

(Title and name of the injured) fought with several people, suffered (insert number of) spear wounds on (insert parts of the body).

(Title and name of the injured) fought on horseback with (insert number of enemies) and received (insert number of) spear wounds on (insert parts of the body) and also received (insert number of) great-sword wounds on (insert parts of the body).

(Title and name of the injured) received (insert number of) great-sword wounds to (insert parts of the body) from an assailant to the rear while pinning down an enemy and trying to decapitate him.

感状之書様

Kanjō no kakiyō

HOW TO WRITE APPRECIATION LETTERS

Although there are important points when writing, all will depend on what the general desires.

上

Jō

Upper level

- *murui no kōmyō* 無類高名 – unparalleled achievement
- *batsugun no hataraki* 抜群働 – fighting above and beyond the masses
- *eiyū no bushi* 英雄武士 – heroic warrior
- *wasuregataki hataraki* 難忘働 – unforgettable achievement

中

Chū

Middle level

- *ikki tōsen no hataraki* 一騎當千働 – mighty warrior who can match 1,000 men
- *hirui no hataraki* 非類働 – achievement without bounds
- *me wo odorokasu hataraki* 驚目働 – a glorious achievement to behold
- *hitori no hataraki wo motte* 以一人働 – a single-handed achievement (insert accomplishment)

下

Ge

Lower level

- *shinmyō no hataraki* 神妙働 – a blessed achievement
- *kaigaishiki hataraki* 戒々敷働 – an achievement of competence
- *kitoku no hataraki* 奇特働 – an achievement beyond the norm
- *kidai no hataraki* 希代働 – a rare achievement for our age

Ideograms recommended for use [in such letters] include:

- *itarite* 至 – extremely
- *hataraki* 働 – fight
- *kokorozashi* 志 – ambition
- *chūkō* 忠功 – loyal achievement
- *kokoroire* 心入 – attention
- *gechi* 下知 – orders
- *sashizu* 指圖 – instructions
- *yū* 勇 – courage
- *tezei* 手勢 – forces or troops
- *tebiki* 手引 – guidance
- *shingari* 殿 – rear guard
- *tsuyoshi* 強 – powerful
- *funkotsu* 粉骨 – dedication
- *chūsetsu* 忠節 – faithfulness

As well as including the ideograms above, letters should contain well-written sentences in accordance with the achievement. Be aware that giving a letter of appreciation that does not match the achievement is the fault of the general.

矢文書様
Yabumi kakiyō
HOW TO WRITE A LETTER ATTACHED TO AN ARROW
This should be written in a circular manner from the binding at the bottom of the feathers. The name of the recipient should be written within the fletchings. It should not have an arrowhead.

Commentator two
It should be written in a circular manner so that it is easy to read and will not become worn.

Commentator three
It is not acceptable to write your name in short form when writing letters during a campaign as this brings disgrace to your name.[141]

[This is the end of the list of tasks for *yūhitsu* (右筆) secretaries].

---

141 This is known as a *katana* (片名), meaning 'an incomplete name' (note that it has no connection to the sword of the same name). It is considered ill-mannered to drop a section of your name in such a formal context.

CHAPTER NINETEEN

出家之事
Shukke no koto

MONKS

The number of monks required is not definite.

During a campaign, monks perform Buddhist memorial services for the dead just as they do at normal times. However, the way of performing the service is not the same as normal. It is always the case that when *samurai* are killed on the battlefield, the grief of the fathers or sons will cause the army to become demoralized. In such a case, the monks should perform a service in a way that encourages the fathers or sons to have as little grief as possible.

Since ancient times, monks have been sent to the enemy side to aid in negotiations and reconciliation. However, the enemy may often suspect that this is a ruse and capture the monks and interrogate them by torture. They will speak out fully when physically tortured. If monks can manage to separate themselves from death and have a correct mind, they will understand the Way and make correct judgements.

When an excellent enemy warrior has been killed, his head may be sent back to the enemy once it has been inspected. In ancient times, the head of Kusunoki Masashige was sent back.

If a head is sent back to you from the enemy, have a monk (*shukke*) accept it and do the following. Construct curtains with bamboo posts. Have loop holes in the *tenno* – the top section of the curtain – and observe the head through the holes. Regarding the arrow placed on the lid of the head container, know that this should be snapped in half and thrown away. [The arrow] may be returned [to the enemy] if the situation demands it.

Apart from the above, there are no special comments.

Commentator two
There are three virtues in sending a head back:
1. The enemy will grieve and be discouraged.
2. It shows respect to the enemy.
3. The enemy will be distracted.

There are rules for this and details are mentioned in the scroll *Gunbai Yōhō*.

山伏之事
Yamabushi no koto

MOUNTAIN HERMITS[142]

The number of *yamabushi* required is not definite.

They perform services to the gods during a campaign, as well as performing incantations for those *samurai* who would like prayer service. Sometimes [real *yamabushi*] are used as *kanja* spies, because fake *yamabushi* can be easily detected. Therefore, if there are any who are willing, use these *yamabushi* [as spies]. Apart from the above, there are no more comments for these.

---

142 'Those who dwell in the mountains.' People who follow ascetic lives and who concentrate on elements of the Shingon faith. The name is known in the West.

太鼓打之事
Taikouchi no koto

DRUMMERS

The number of drummers required is not definite.

They should focus on drumming so as to move the army forward. If the situation becomes pressing, they will be eager to fight but they should hold themselves back. The way of drumming is mentioned in another scroll. They should drum according to the general's desire, but there are set rules for this [and the following must be considered].

[The following are the different ways and beats of drumming.]

初中後之三段
Shochūgo no sandan
The concept of *sho chū go* – beginning, middle and end[143]

九字
Kuji
The ritual of *kuji*

引軍
Hikiikusa
Withdrawing an army

---

143 The three phases of the start of combat.

掛軍
Kakariikusa
Attacking with an army

城責
Shirozeme
Attacking a castle

舟軍
Funaikusa
Ship battles – 'consider the wind'

There are set rules for each of the above situations.

貝吹之事
Kaifuki no koto

CONCH SHELL TRUMPETERS

The number of conch shell trumpeters required is not definite.

They should always practise playing with extreme diligence. When a battle becomes intense, conch shells should always sound out.

The name of the parts and how to construct conch shells are written in another scroll.

A conch shell blow should continue without interruption. It should start quietly and become more powerful as it goes. The sound should not become weaker towards the end – this is called *okure goe* – the coward's voice. However, this does not apply in the case of signals.

Methods on use should be discussed as needs arise. However, teachings from ancient ways are listed below and [involve conch shells being used to] accompany drums.

九字吹事
Kuji fuku koto
Accompanying the ritual of *kuji*

OOOO)))))

七五三之事
Shichigosan no koto
The principle of seven-five-three

)))))))OOOOO)))

ハナシ吹[144]
Hanashi fuki
Long notes

ユリ吹[145]
Yuri fuki
Vibrato blows

---

144 放吹 in the Koga transcription.
145 揺吹 in the Koga transcription.

Details are mentioned in another scroll and are not to be written here. It is a principle not to use the word *fuku*, meaning 'blow', but instead to use the word *tatsuru*, meaning 'perform'.[146]

In some cases apprentice *yamabushi* may be used as conch shell trumpeters. How to sound [the conch shell] is to be taught through practical experience.

鐘之役
Kane no yaku

GONG RINGERS

The number of gong ringers required is not definite.

They are [used in] the same [way] as drummers and conch shell trumpeters. [How to ring the gong] should be decided according to the occasion. Drawings are in another scroll.

Gongs are used mostly to pull back [troops] during battle, whereas drums are used for advancing.

Tradition says that gongs should be avoided in ship battles. In fact, they should not be rung at all.

Commentator two

Ringing gongs is strictly avoided on a ship because when [you are on] water the *chi* is of the element of *in* and if you add the energy of *in* [from a metal gong] to the element of *in* [already present in water] it will dampen the spirit of the advance [by leading to doubly negative *chi*].

---

146 Some of the names and terms in the text actually use the base ideogram for *fuku*, even though it says to avoid this word. The point is that the word *tatsuru* should be used instead of *fuku* in formal situations.

金穿
Kanahori

MINERS

Miners are sometimes used to dig towards a mountain castle. People within the castle should be aware of this and should bury [large] earthenware pots within the grounds of the castle. When tunnelling close to the fortifications, dig with spades instead of hoes. Miners are proficient at digging castle foundations and moats, and also siege constructions and water conduits. They are employed above all for trenches.

[Other positions undertaken on a military campaign]

The following people should be taken to a battle. Use those who are quick rather than those who are good.

- *hakuraku* 白楽 – horse experts
- *daiku* 大工 – carpenters
- *kaji* 鍛冶 – blacksmiths
- *yashi* 矢師 – fletchers
- *yumihiki* 弓引 – bowyers
- *tsurusashi* 弦差 – stringers
- *sakan* 左官 – plasterers
- *eshi* 繪師 – painters

猿楽
Sarugaku

THEATRICAL PERFORMERS

They should always be taken to war as they have certain uses.

Commentator two

When the soldiers of Chu became resolute [in their defence], Zhang Liang [their enemy] played a Chu song on the flute to break their spirit. Also, Sakai Saemon used to dance the *ebi-sukuimai* – the comical shrimp-scooping dance [to confound the enemy]. Use such tactics when you cannot think of any other plan.

ヒジリ / 川原者[147]
Hijiri[148] / kawaramono

OUTCASTS

They clean human and horse corpses during a campaign. Generally, they also clean all places within the castle compound.

I think that these people are dispensable as tasks of this nature can be dealt with by anyone if needs arise.

The above categories are the kinds of people who should be taken on a campaign and used according to their position. An ancient teaching says: 'A good general uses people correctly and does not rid himself of anyone.'

---

147 屠者 and 河原者 in the Koga transcription.

148 *Hijiri* is a versatile word. It can be used to refer to a saint, a high-level monk, an unofficial monk who does not belong to a temple, a hermit monk or an itinerant merchant. However, the Tōkyō transcription is in phonetics and the Koga transcription implies a butcher of animals.

CHAPTER TWENTY

AN OUTLINE OF HIGH-RANKING MILITARY POSITIONS[149]

上
将
軍
JŌ-SHŌGUN

君 KUN
臣 SHIN

主 SHU
将 SHŌ

右
将
軍
U-SHŌGUN

左
将
軍
SA-SHŌGUN

國
子
KOKUSHI

下
将
軍
KA-SHŌGUN

中
将
軍
CHŪ-SHŌGUN

副
将
軍
FUKU-SHŌGUN

鑒
軍
KANGUN

---

149 This chapter was originally positioned at the start of the first scroll of *Heieki Yōhō*. However, it has now been moved to the end of the second scroll (see Introduction). Note that *sa* (left) and *u* (right) are the orientations from the point of view of the *jō-shōgun*.

[The following is an explanation of the positions shown in the previous illustration.]

主 将[150]
Shushō

THE LORD AND HIGH-RANKING RETAINER – PART ONE

Commentator one

The term *shu* here means *jō-shōgun*, which is the main military leader, whereas the term *shō* means a general of a troop (一隊). The full term *shushō* used here should be considered as *jō-shōgun* – the supreme leader of a force.

君 臣
Kunshin

THE LORD AND HIGH-RANKING RETAINER – PART TWO

Commentator one

The term *kun* refers to a lord, while *shin* refers to generals and high-ranking retainers, such as the rank of *samurai-daishō*. However, this position is not at the level of *jō-shōgun* – the supreme leader.

The first human emperor, Emperor Jimmu, appointed Michinoomi no mikoto as his military tactician on the day he departed for a military expedition to the east and conquered the barbarians. This custom of appointment started with Yamato Takeru no mikoto and since then a general (*shōsui*) has been sent on all military expeditions.

---

150 This article and the article after require a considerable amount of explanation and are expanded upon in later volumes.

The *Gunbōryō* document[151] says [the order of ranks is]:
- *dai-shōgun* 大将軍 – supreme military commander
- *fuku-shōgun* 副将軍 – deputy *shōgun*
- *gungen* 軍鑒 – military supervisors
- *gunsō* 軍曹 – senior military officers

An army that consists of more than 10,000 soldiers requires:
- one *shōgun* – military commander
- one *fuku-shōgun* – deputy *shōgun*
- two *gungen* – military supervisors
- four *gunsō* – senior military officers
- four *rokuji* – secretaries

For an army of 5,000–9,000, reduce:
- the number of *fuku-shōgun* above by one
- the number of *gungen* above by one *gungen*
- the number of *rokuji* above by two

For an army of 3,000–4,000, reduce:
- the number of *gunsō* above by two

Each example above represents an *ichigun* – a single division.

A *sangun* – the whole force[152] – requires:
- one *dai-shōgun* – supreme military commander
- three *shōgun* – military commanders
- four *fuku-shōgun* – deputy *shōgun*
- four *gungen* – military supervisors
- ten *gunsō* – senior military officers
- eight *rokuji* – secretaries

---

151 軍防令, 'Statute on military defence', a chapter from a collection of ancient statutes written in the eighth century.

152 *Sangun* (三軍), literally 'three armies', but means the entire force.

The *Three Strategies* says that the methods of a lord-general (*shushō*) are aimed at commanding the hearts of heroes.

國子
Kokushi

PRINCES

[This is a prince to an emperor or the son of a *jō-shōgun* – the supreme leader.]

鑒軍

Kangun

MILITARY SERVICE OF A PRINCE

Commentator one

As well as princes of the emperor, this includes the sons of the *jō-shōgun* himself. Their military service is called *kangun* (監軍).

Princes of an emperor, who can also be called *taishi* (太子) or *kashi* (家子), attend an army when war occurs. This service is also called *kankoku* (鑒國) and is a position just below that of *jō-shōgun*.

上将軍
Jō-shōgun

THE SUPREME LEADER

Commentator two

[An explanation of the image on page 242.]

Shu (主) has the same meaning as *kun* (君), while *shō* (将) is equivalent to *shin* (臣). If [the top two sets of ideogram pairs in the previous illustration are] read together horizontally, they make [the two terms of] *shukun* (主君) and *shōshin* (将臣) [when reading from right to left].

The first term is *shukun* [when read horizontally from right to left] and refers to the emperor of the land or it can also mean the military leader (*kubō*) when used in reference to a whole country (*tenka*). The leader of a province is called a *taishu* (太守), or the term *kokushu* (国主) can be used.

The second term when read horizontally [from right to left] is *shōshin* (将臣) and this means left and right ministers [of the court]. The concept of *shōshin* is equivalent to the common term *tairō* (大老), which is a great counsellor who aids the military leader (*kubō*).

In a provincial administration, the term *karō* is used for a senior counsellor.

Sa-shōgun, u-shōgun, fuku-shōgun, chū-shōgun and *ka-shōgun* are the terms used to represent generals of the army. The entire army (*sangun*) is divided into three [and each division is led by one of the following]:

- *jō-shōgun* – the military commander
- *sa-shōgun* – *shōgun* of the left
- *u-shōgun* – *shōgun* of the right

Jō-shōgun is the *shukun* overall lord [as seen to the right of the image] and he commands with the aid of the *shōgun* of the left and the *shōgun* of the right.

左将軍
Sa-shōgun

SHŌGUN OF THE LEFT

Commentator one

This is a position for [a high-ranking] retainer to undertake. Although *sa-shōgun* is above the position of *fuku-shōgun*, the *sa-shōgun* cannot assume the role of the *taishō* lord-commander when the original lord-commander is absent.

右将軍
U-shōgun

SHŌGUN OF THE RIGHT

Commentator one

Those generals who have reached their position as a result of their excellent abilities are called *shō* (将), while those who command people through wisdom and intelligence are called *sui* (帥). Also, according to the Chinese encyclopedia *Jibutsu Kigen* (事物記原), generals are called *tayū* (大夫) when residing within their province but are called *shōgun* (将軍) when in an army. In the *Zuo Zhuan* (春秋左傳), they are called *gensui* (元帥).

副将軍
Fuku-shōgun

DEPUTY *SHŌGUN*

He will act as *jō-shōgun* when the *jō-shōgun* is absent.

Commentator two

The *fuku-shōgun* (deputy *shōgun*) does not take command alone [but assists those who command].

中将軍
Chū-shōgun

MIDDLE *SHŌGUN*

They will act as *fuku-shōgun* (deputy *shōgun*) if needs arise.

下将軍
Ka-shōgun

LOWER *SHŌGUN*

They will act as *chū-shōgun* if needs arise.

Commentator one
- *fuku-shōgun* – deputy *shōgun*
- *chū-shōgun* – middle *shōgun*
- *ka-shōgun* – lower *shōgun*

Generally, the above positions are occupied by relatives or those with the same family name as the *jō-shōgun* because they will act in the interests of the *jō-shōgun* if needs arise.

Concerning battles: the above [various types of *shōgun*] should follow as retainers [to the main military leader]. Examples of these are the following warriors:
- Yoshisuke[153] who served Yoshisada[154]

---

153 Nitta Wakiya Yoshisuke, brother to Nitta Yoshisada.
154 Nitta Yoshisada.

- Tadayoshi[155] who served Takauji[156]

When appointing military personnel, the *jō-shōgun* is sometimes referred to as *kongai* (闇外). This term is the same as *shōgun*. There are specific ways and manners to follow in such cases. The *shōgun* of the left and right are also called *hen* (編) and the *fuku-shōgun* may be known as *hi* (裨).

Issui-sensei says

The above lists are generals of troops and they follow the orders of the lord (*kun*). At the battle of Kamakura (1333), Nitta Yoshisada was appointed as a commander (*sui*) of the entire army with Ōdate Jirō Muneuji as *shōgun* of the left and Eda Saburō Yukiyoshi as *shōgun* of the right. At the same time, the warrior Horiguchi Saburō Sadamitsu was the *jō-shōgun*, while the warrior Ōshima Sanuki no kami Moriyuki was the deputy *shōgun*. Their force of more than 507,000 people was led forward over Kewaizaka hill by the warriors Horiguchi, Yamana, Iwamatsu, Ōida, Momonoi, Satomi, Toriyama and Nukata. However, Nitta Yoshisada had superiority above all of the generals and had command of the entire army.

Commentator one

The above information is found in volume ten of the *Taiheiki* war chronicle and is an example of how a *sangun* – a full military force – is governed here in Japan. The word *sangun* is often used to represent the entire army. One full division is constructed of 12,500 people and three full divisions consist of 37,500 in total. However, it seems that in many cases, *sangun* simply means a large force but does not have to represent a specific number.

Yoshisada was regarded as the lord (*shukun*) by the generals as they received orders from him.

Commentator two

[As commander in chief,] Yoshisada had the clans of Horiguchi, Yamana,

---

155 Ashikaga Tadayoshi, half-brother of Ashikaga Takauji.
156 Ashikaga Takauji.

Iwamatsu, Ōida, Momonoi, Satomi, Toriyama and Nukata with him in support and he led the 507,000 people when he advanced over the hill of Kewaizaka.

将帥之縁起
Shōsui no engi

THE ORIGIN OF *SHŌSUI* GENERALS [AND OTHER TERMS FOR COMMANDERS]

The *Shokugen-shō* (職原抄) manual says that the position of general is of grave importance. Whether in the past or the present, they command armies who advance into foreign countries.

In our country generals are said to have originated in the age of the gods. The deity Amaterasu Ōmikami wished to send her heavenly descendants to Nakatsu-kuni in Toyoashihara.[157] These descendants were the deities Futsunushi no kami, who is now the god of Katori shrine, and Kenraishin, who is now the god of Kashima shrine. They are said to have subjugated those who did not obey [and thus these gods became generals].

臣
Shin

HIGH-RANKING MINISTER-GENERALS

There are two minister-generals, one of the right and one of the left. However, the number of senior counsellors (*karō*) is not definite.

---

157 This is a mythical place that represents the whole of Japan.

Commentator two

In the imperial court (朝廷) [the position of *shin* consists of] left and right ministers, while in the military government (公方) the following three positions are taken up by minister-generals (*shin*):

- *shitsuji* 執事 – administrative controller
- *kanrei* 管領 – *shōgunal* deputy
- *tairō* 大老 – great counsellor

Issui-sensei says

Ministers (*shin*) are in a position to administer to the nation. They deal with life-or-death situations for the whole nation (*sharyō*), and they also consider the rise or fall of the nation itself. With full awareness of the way of benevolence, which contains the Five Precepts of the Sage,[158] [minsters] should hold loyalty as a principle and upon orders from the lord, they should lead the army, move out to war and achieve victory.

Commentator two

In the term *sharyō* used above, *sha* means 'gods of the land'. He who holds the power of a state should worship the *sha* and celebrate rituals [in their honour]. The second part, *ryō*, means 'gods of the harvest'. Ancient lords were first given lands by the emperor and would go back to the land to build shrines to celebrate both the gods of land and of the harvest, which all the people of the land worshipped for the security of the populace. Thus, *sharyō* represents the foundation of a state, and is considered to be the state itself.

For an army it is not enough to win multiple battles in a row. For ultimate success, it needs to be victorious over the *entire* campaign. [In ancient China] during the Chu–Han contention – a war which lasted for eight years – Emperor Gaozu of Han lost every battle until he defeated Xiang Ji at the battle of Gaixia, which firmly established his dynasty. Another example of this principle is provided by Shinkun [the lord Tokugawa Ieyasu], who successfully came to power over the whole country by the end [of his struggles].

---

158 五常: (1) 仁 benevolence, (2) 義 righteousness, (3) 礼 courtesy, (4) 智 wisdom, (5) 信 fidelity.

CHAPTER TWENTY-ONE

臣道
Shindō

THE WAY OF THE MINISTER-GENERAL

[Seven articles on teachings from ancient China on correctly serving a lord]

ARTICLE ONE

The Chengzi (程子) brothers, who were great Confucian scholars during the Song Dynasty, say that minister-generals (*shin*) should serve the lord by fully devoting themselves to the path of loyalty and that they should do this in everything without even a hint of selfishness. If your mind and body are fully devoted to the subject of loyalty but the lord still does not take heed [of your advice], remember that it may be the case that the lord is blind to such ideas and that it does not mean that you yourself are unrighteous. It is not the correct way for a minister-general (*shin*) to blindly follow or flatter the lord just in order to secure more land.

Commentator two

To blindly follow or flatter should be avoided not only by minster-generals (*shin*) but also by ordinary *samurai*.

ARTICLE TWO

Yang (楊氏) of Qui Shan said that if high-ranking retainers advise their lord to control the people with strict punishment or advise him in a way that goes beyond *budō* military ways,[159] it should be considered as an attempt to force the lord to discard benevolence and righteousness. If the lord is manipulated into setting aside his benevolence and righteousness and is without mercy, he will not be able to win the hearts of the people. If this happens [the people] will always move against the lord, and then how can he maintain his dignity? Therefore, [minister-generals] should only suggest ways to the lord that keep him on a righteous path.

Commentator one

During times of turbulence govern with the principle of the civilian (*bun*), while in peacetime rule with the principle of the military (*bu*). Minster-generals should never forget for a single moment the concept of *bunbu* – civil and military ways. It is a mistake for a minister-general (*shin*) to advise a lord (*kun*) solely from a military point of view.

There are many examples of this. [Records pertaining to] Minamoto no Yoshitsune and Nitta Yoshisada show what happens when a *taishō* does not have an appropriate mindset, is unaware of the righteous way and does not consider benevolence. Examples closer to our times are Oda Nobunaga, Uesugi Kenshin, Takeda Shingen and others.

ARTICLE THREE

According to Hu Yin (致堂), high-ranking retainers who have loyalty for their lord and receive love from him should not be concerned in any way for their own safety, but instead should dedicate themselves to ensuring that the lord does not make any mistakes. It is not the path of high-ranking retainers only to pursue their own personal advancement and to turn a blind eye to the lord's mistakes. However, although it is of primary importance on the path of high-ranking retainers to correct a lord's mistakes, I think that they should not remonstrate with the lord on a subject that is beyond the scope of their duties. Remember, it is not correct to remonstrate outside of one's own areas of responsibility.

Wu Feng Hu Hong said that a retainer should maintain correctness by continually observing benevolence and righteousness. As long as he is

---

159 i.e. to exert military force over the populace.

benevolent and righteous, he will not be at fault. If he remonstrates with the lord, he should do so by maintaining his position on the righteous path and restraining the lord from his personal desires. He should point out political mistakes, uncover treacherous retainers and have them removed, and so on. Also keep in mind that situations often end badly [for retainers when they] go against their lord. In all, ensure that the lord follows the Way and treats his retainers honourably.

Commentator one

Hu Yin said that high-ranking retainers should not think of their own safety; they should think only of their loyalty. It is not the path of high-ranking retainers to consider only their own prosperity and to neglect the straying of the lord into unrighteousness. In ancient times, good retainers would die to admonish their lords. How could retainers of our times forget loyalty in pursuit of their own interest?

If you yourself are not righteous, yet you remonstrate with the lord, know that this is not the correct path. If you are without honour, there can be no righteousness.

An old poem says:

いつはりを人にはいひて遺ぬべき心のとはばなにと答えん
You may tell a lie to others, but what would you answer
if you questioned yourself?[160]

In older times [in China] there was a position called *kangikan* (諫議官), a counsellor of caution, but any [high-ranking retainer] – even if they do not hold that specific position – should admonish the lord whenever needed but only in a way that the lord will accept. If you admonish too bluntly a lord who is not on the correct path, the lord will not only rebuke such a statement but he may make you pay for it with your life. Be aware of this.

---

160 i.e. if you honestly question your own motives, you will know if you are lying for your own benefit.

To manage others, you first need to manage yourself. When reproaching a lord, avoid highlighting only his faults. This is without any doubt a mistake. If you follow the way of honesty and benevolence, you will enable your lord to see his shame for himself. This is the way of loyal retainers.

ARTICLE FOUR

Luo Yu Zhang (羅豫章) said that honesty and loyalty must remain the main principles of high-ranking retainers when they serve their lord. If they are honest there will be no mistakes and if they are loyal they will accumulate no grudges against them. The two aspects [of honesty and loyalty] function like the two hands of a human. If one is disproportionately favoured over the other, difficulty will follow. If a retainer is more honest than loyal, he will sound harsh without realizing it. If he is more loyal than honest, he will demonstrate a lack of bravery.

Furthermore, Zhu Xi (朱氏) said that someone who wants to correct his lord should first correct himself. He also said that it is the duty of a prime minister to discover good men and have them serve the lord. You cannot retain those [who are capable] without you yourself showing modesty in your dealings with others.

Commentator one

There is no benefit in having a horse that can run 1,000 leagues if you do not also have a rider with the skill to handle it – this teaching should be applied to senior ministers (*saishō*).[161] Senior ministers are sometimes classified as counsellors (*sangi*), and for this position a general (*shin*) or someone higher than fourth rank [at court] is required. Of course, they must also be competent; these people should be assigned by official order. They should deliberate and decide the policies within the court. When on a military campaign, such a position is taken up by the secretariat (*yūhitsu*).

Wei Liao Zi (尉繚子) said that if excellent horses are ridden with the whip, distant roads can be travelled. If men of worth and men of rank unite, the path towards correct governance is illuminated.

---

161 i.e. talented people need talented leaders.

ARTICLE FIVE

Lu Jiuyuan (陸象山) said that if the lord is failing to govern properly or is making errors of judgement, do not directly admonish him; instead, try to guide the lord's mind to take the [correct] path. Unless the lord has achieved a correct state of mind, if you do try to remonstrate with him over one or two mistakes, then further, and irrevocable, misfortune will inevitably arise. [However,] once the lord achieves a correct state of mind, he will naturally stop making errors.

Commentator one

If a foundation is established, the Way will be complete. If a foundation is not established, there will be a lack of control. If you advise the lord on benevolence, virtue, righteousness and the Way with due respect, he will naturally end up following the righteous path, even if he appears unrighteous from time to time. Conversely, if his *honshin* – true mind – is not correct, the lord will end up becoming corrupt, even if he sometimes appears righteous.

ARTICLE SIX

Xu Heng (許衡) said that if you get too close to the lord as a high-ranking retainer (*shin*), it will undoubtedly cause mistakes to occur. Simply follow the correct path and earnestly endeavour to fulfil your duties while serving the lord and maintain a proper distance from him. This does not mean you should estrange yourself from the lord.

If you find someone who is capable, have him serve the lord; or hire others who are accomplished and bring them into the lord's clan. Do not think highly of yourself for this and do not announce to others that it was your doing. Instead, tell people that it was a decision made by the lord. Similarly, if you successfully dismiss an evil man or denounce a criminal, do not claim this as a personal achievement; instead, say that it was the lord's will. No matter what reward or reduction of punishment has been determined, consider the matter as having been decided by the lord and view your role as being simply to execute what the lord has decided. If you take credit for the decision, it will undoubtedly lead you to become too assertive and to have more enemies and it will make the lord [look] incapable. Is this the way a loyal retainer should be?

Consider this: although the moon and stars reflect the light of the sun,[162] the moon is at its fullest illumination when it is furthest from the sun, something which happens on the fourteenth and fifteenth day, halfway through the lunar month. For [the first] five or six days of the month and for the same period at the end of the month, the moon is closer [to the sun] and is darker. This analogy applies to the relationship between a lord and his retainers. It is a basic principle to keep in mind. Know that [retainers] should reflect [the lord's] light by keeping at a distance from the source. Since ancient times, there have been instances where [retainers] got too close to the lord and abused power through the lord's good grace but failed to obtain victory; in this way they ruined themselves. This may appear to be the fault of the lord, but it is actually the fault of the retainer.

Commentator one

If the lord and high-ranking retainers are too close, it will automatically lead to over-familiarity. If they keep their proper distance, the dignity of the lord will be enhanced. This does not mean to have less loyalty.

Recruit worthy people who will extol the lord's moral virtues and will persuade people to follow his example. This method should not be revealed as [a retainer's] own achievement.

Forget personal benefit and value loyalty instead. Dismiss anything evil in an instant and conduct reward or reduction of punishment with the same ethos. However, [a retainer may sometimes have to commit dark deeds] under his own name so as not to tarnish the name of the lord.

If the sun, the moon and stars cross in close proximity, [the moon and the stars] lose the light that they emit. How could humans alone not consider [and act upon] this fundamental principle? As well as high-ranking retainers, some *samurai* without title brag about their closeness to the lord, work every day and push themselves higher, supported by the lord's authority. This may have positive short-term outcomes, but will end in destruction. By not thinking of the clan, these people ruin themselves. Some may hold a grudge against the lord for this, but you must understand that the lord is totally without fault and

---

162 This predates the modern astronomical understanding that stars emit their own light.

that they have ruined themselves by following such a way. Be very careful about this matter.

Commentator two

The moon and stars have no light in themselves but shine with the aid of the sun. However, they lose their ability to reflect light when they come too close to the sun itself. Be aware that the way of the lord and his retainers demonstrates this principle.

ARTICLE SEVEN

Sun Tzu (孫子) said that high-ranking retainers, even if they advance against and defeat the enemy and successfully ruin [the enemy] country, should do so without coveting fame. If they retreat, they should not do this with fear of going against the lord's will; instead, they should concentrate on making the decision most likely to lead to success in the situation at hand. If you judge it is best to attack, even if the lord's order is not to fight, you should advance. The principle is thus: if you are assigned the role of a general, sometimes [it is best to] not follow the orders of the lord.

In the *Zuo Zhuan* (左氏傳), it says that King Fugai (夫槩) stated that ministers may act in righteousness without waiting for an order. I say that this is because righteousness is the primary factor. Those who have no righteousness and become too proud of their own achievements think little of the lord's orders and are considered as rebellious retainers.

Commentator one

Sun Tzu says: 'The general should advance without coveting fame and retreat without fearing disgrace.' This is exactly what loyalty in warfare is and also demonstrates how a general may act without orders from the lord. This is *hasha no daidō* (伯者ノ大道) – the great path of the conqueror.

Issui-sensei says

The above are principles for high-ranking retainers. It is what people in ancient times have said. Be fully aware of them.

Commentator one

The above seven articles are the loyal ways of various Confucians and are not unreasonable. It is said that on occasion someone who has been assigned as a general (*shō*) does not have to adhere to the order of the lord.

This reflects the common saying:

義ヲ見テセザル［ハ勇無ナリ］

To see that which is correct but not follow it through displays a lack of courage.

How could those of integrity not value this concept?

臣可慎十箇条

Shin Tsutsushimubeki Jikkajō

TEN ARTICLES THAT HIGH-RANKING RETAINERS SHOULD VALUE

ARTICLE ONE

神道可敬事

Shindō uyamaubeki koto

RESPECT THE PATH OF THE GODS

Commentator one

Gods are displeased if they are shown disrespect.

It is said that the message from the gods is thus:

豈非正直一旦依怙終蒙日月憐上神敬ナクシテ下疑

*Honesty may not reward you with immediate benefit, but know that
it will be cherished by the sun and moon in the end.*

Commentator two

The gods reside within an honest man. According to the gods, honesty does not bring temporary and immediate personal rewards, but is celebrated by the sun and moon in the end. Generals (*shin*) do not have to visit shrines and make wishes, but only need to keep honesty in mind, question themselves as to whether they are faithful or not and keep themselves from evil intention. If the superior are unbelieving, the inferior will be even more so. If a state is governed with honesty, what can go awry? If the mind engages with *makoto no michi* (誠ノ道), the path of honesty, the gods will protect you even if you do not pray. This is the way you should conduct government.

ARTICLE TWO

軍禮可正事

Gunrei tadasubeki koto

MAINTAIN PROPER MILITARY DISCIPLINE

Commentator one

A poem states:

竹の屋も松の心を人として上に下を智人は人なる

Even a construction made of bamboo should have a heart of pine and those of a high position should show the way for those below.[163]

Sun Tzu talked about the concept of *sanrei goshin* (三令五申).[164] This is the practice of giving an order three times but informing the recipients [of the details] five times. It is the fault of a general not to instil correct military discipline.

The *Record of the Great Historian* says: 'When a ruler's personal conduct is correct, discipline will be maintained without orders needing to be issued. If the ruler's personal conduct is not correct, orders may be issued but they will not be followed.

---

163 This poem has been translated more to display its meaning and is not a direct translation. It implies that lower people should still maintain higher principles.

164 *Sān lìng wǔ shēn* in the original Chinese.

Commentator two

If high-ranking retainers do not have a proper understanding of the noble and the humble, laws will not be correct. Therefore, courtesy should always be maintained. If military regulations (令) are not proper, serious defeat will follow. Sun Tzu mentions [the importance of] repeating an order. Be aware that if military discipline is not properly conducted, it is the general's fault.

The concept of *rei* (礼), meaning 'courtesy', reflects heavenly principle and consolidates human affairs, whereas *rei* (令), meaning 'regulations and discipline', is derived from law and ethics.

Commentator three

This article is about conducting and following rules that have been followed since ancient times.

ARTICLE THREE

誇身事

Mi wo hokoru koto

BEWARE OF SELF-PRIDE

Commentator one

This concerns overvaluing one's own wealth and self-respect.

There is an old saying about the poor man who does not flatter and the rich man who is not too proud.

Commentator two

As minister-generals (*shin*) govern a nation, everyone respects them. This causes them to forget what they actually are before they are aware they have forgotten. They will think little not only of the humble but also of the noble and high ranking. This will arouse resentment in the people and set others against them, causing them ruin in the end. There are a number of examples of this both in Japan and China.

ARTICLE FOUR
不可軽事事
Koto wo karonzu bekarazaru kotom
DO NOT THINK LITTLE OF THINGS

Commentator one
A poem states:

庭に生るちりぢり草の露にもひとつも月のやどらぬはなし
*On all the blades of grass in a garden, there is not one dewdrop
that does not reflect the moon.*

Do not think of small things as unimportant and do not fear important things.

Commentator two
Fire starts with a tiny spark and massive riverbanks collapse because of minute holes. Do not disregard small matters. During a campaign even a tiny issue can cause a catastrophic defeat. If it is not 'nipped in the bud', it will grow into a disaster that needs 'cutting down with an axe'.

ARTICLE FIVE
依怙贔屓不可致事
Eko hiiki itasu bekarazaru koto
DO NOT PLAY FAVOURITES

Commentator one

財宝害身　金玉棘道也
Treasure leads to ruin and globes of gold make a path difficult to tread.

Commentator two
The ideograms representing selfishness, 依怙, mean 'to indulge your heart's

desire' and the ideograms for favouritism, 贔屓, can mean 'to lose treasures'.[165] If generals (*shin*) indulge themselves, they may be drawn to show preference to certain people or may accept bribes of large amounts of money. With this, they may reward those who have not achieved or punish those who are innocent. In such a situation, their men will quit them and the state will become insubstantial [and defenceless]. This should be avoided.

ARTICLE SIX
不可耽利欲事
Riyoku ni fukeru bekarazaru koto
DO NOT WALLOW IN GREED

Commentator one
Consider this as similar to how the warriors Nagasaka [Chōkan] and Atobe [Katsusuke] ruined the reign of Takeda Katsuyori. Remember, treasure leads to ruin and globes of gold make a path difficult to tread.

Commentator two
Even the masses should be careful not to indulge themselves in greed. However, this point is especially significant for generals (*shin*).

When disputes occurred concerning the lineage of [Uesugi] Kenshin, [the province of Echigo] was attacked by forces from Kōshū and encountered serious difficulties. As a result, the warriors Naoe and Yamashiro [from the Echigo forces] devised a plan to bribe the warriors Nakasaka Chōkan and Atobe Ōinosuke Katsusuke [as described by commentator one above]. This action was taken to prevent [the Takeda forces] from attacking Echigo. The prowess of the Takeda family began to diminish and this led to the fall of the clan, which ended with the twenty-seventh heir, Takeda Katsuyori. This was due to greed.

An old *kyōka* (satirical verse) says:

---

165 To have favourites results in losing things of actual benefit.

アハレヤナ国ヲ寂滅セシコトハ越後ノカネノヒキナリナリ

*Alas, what ruined the Takeda family in the end was bribes
given with the money of Echigo.*

ARTICLE SEVEN

賞罰必信事

Shōbatsu kanarazu shinjiru koto

ALWAYS BE TRUTHFUL WITH REWARD AND PUNISHMENT

Commentator one

Rewards do not imply favour, and punishments do not imply disfavour.

As an example, an old poem states:

父ハうつ母ハいだきてかなしめる　心いかにと子ハ思ふらん

*A father hits his child and a mother laments with the child in her arms.
Surely the child will wonder what their intentions are?*

If soldiers and servants lose their faith in reward and punishment, they will have much doubt in mind. Si Ma Fa said that rewards should not be delayed beyond an appropriate time, as it is best that people quickly profit from correctness, and that punishment should be dealt out immediately, for it is best that the people quickly observe the harm of doing that which is not good.

Commentator two

Give reward without delay; punishment can be postponed.[166] Give people the benefit of the doubt when rewarding and punishing: if there is any doubt, give reward but withhold punishment. Reward and punishment do not depend on high or low status, but are the very foundation of authority and the constitution of a state.

---

166 Some of the teachings and commentators advocate delayed punishment, whereas others state that it should be given immediately. This depends on the situation and the source.

ARTICLE EIGHT

不可驚事事

Koto ni odoroku bekarazaru koto

DO NOT BE STARTLED OR HAVE FEAR OF ANYTHING

Commentator one

To be startled betrays a lack of preparation.

Commentator two

Being startled indicates that you are coward. Even if hit by thousands of lightning strikes, do not be alarmed. Stand firm like a gigantic mountain.

When faced with a critical battle, do not go pale; the amount of colour in your cheeks shows your level of courage. Know that if a person is not kind, no good can come of it. Keep in mind that kind people are courageous, but courageous warriors are not always kind.

ARTICLE NINE

好色可遠慮事

Kōshoku enryo subeki koto

REFRAIN FROM LUST

Commentator one

This pertains to the love of both men and women.

It is said that homosexuality defeats the wisdom of the aged and lust [with women] leads to [detrimental] conversations. Inspired by his love for the daughter of [Suwa] Yorishige, [a Takeda family member named] Takeda Yoshinobu killed Takeda Shingen.[167]

Commentator two

Warnings against lust have been given since ancient times. Lust with men is called *harō* (破老) and lust with women is called *hazetsu* (破舌), either of

---

167 It is believed that the general Takeda Shingen died of natural causes, so this most likely comes from a reference in the *Kōyō Gunkan* manual to an attempted assassination.

which can lead to the fall of a nation. In ancient China, King Zhou of Shang indulged in pleasure with Daji. Emperor Xuanzong of Tang was infatuated by Yang Guifei. In Japan, Nitta Yoshisada was fascinated by Kōtō no Naishi, while Imagawa Ujimasa overindulged in a homosexual relationship with Miura Uemon, which reduced [the clan's] prestige. This resulted in the ruin of the state and the individuals concerned, and all because of lust. There are numerous examples in Japan and China. Both generals and other *samurai* should refrain from this, reminding themselves that state and castle could be ruined if the king is captivated by a glamorous woman.

ARTICLE TEN

酒楽不可過事

Shuraku sugosu bekarazaru koto

DO NOT OVERINDULGE IN DRINKING AND PLEASURE-MAKING

Commentator one

With alcohol, allow someone to become drunk to observe their nature (性).
With pleasure, allow someone to indulge in pleasure to observe their mind (心).[168]

The *Record of the Great Historian* says that drinking to the utmost ends in combat and indulging in pleasure to the utmost ends in sorrow.

Commentator two

The *Record of the Great Historian* says that there is a way to see the nature (性) [of a person] by allowing that person to get drunk and a way to see their mind (心) by offering them pleasure. A ruler who indulges excessively in alcohol and pleasure will misuse their authority and bring grief to their domain. Be very careful to maintain control. Confucius warns that even if you drink alcohol with no limit, you should not allow yourself to become muddled by it.

---

168 Two very close concepts: the first is your innate character and the second is your thoughts.

Issui-sensei says

All *samurai* should keep the above ten articles in mind. However, this is especially important for high-ranking retainers above all people, who should have extreme respect for these points and never fail to observe them.

Heigu Yōhō

IMPORTANT WAYS ON
MILITARY TOOLS

CHAPTER TWENTY-TWO

ANNOTATIONS ON THE IDEOGRAMS USED IN THE TITLE OF THIS SCROLL[169]

兵

Hei

SOLDIER

In ancient times the ideogram *hei* (兵) stood for *heiki* (兵器), which means 'weapons'. This ideogram is also found in the term *gohei* (五兵) – five types of weapons. These weapons are:[170]

1. *yumi* 弓 – bow
2. *hoko* 殳 – halberd
3. *bō* 矛 – spear
4. *ka* 戈 – halberd with horizontal blade attached
5. *geki* 戟 – halberd with blades to both sides (one curved up, the other angled downwards)

In the present day, the ideogram 兵 appears in various terms that refer to *samurai* (士). Words that contain this ideogram include:

- *heishū* 兵衆
- *heisotsu* 兵卒
- *gunpei* 軍兵
- *kōhei* 甲兵[171]

169 Due to repetition between the two commentators, their annotations have been combined in this section.

170 This is a duplication of the lists given in the scroll *Heika Jōdan*.

171 These four terms are almost interchangeable and all broadly mean '*samurai*'.

Furthermore, know that in battle warriors (武夫) go to battle with weapons (兵), which is how the ideogram for *hei* (兵) has come to mean 'warrior' [i.e. those who use weapons in war].

Whereas in China there are five types of soldiers with weapons,[172] in Japan the weapons in use today are:

- *yumiya* 弓矢 – bows and arrows
- *tachi* 太刀 – great swords
- *naginata* 長刀 – halberds

Since conflict is settled with the five basic weapons, *bushi* warriors are called *hei* in military terms.

具

Gu

GEAR

At present, the ideogram *gu* (具) means equipment used by soldiers (兵士) and such equipment is known as *heiki* (兵器) weapons. In short, *heiki* is equivalent to *hyōjō* (兵杖) and both mean 'military equipment'.

The ideogram *gu* (具) is also read as *tsubusa*, meaning 'specifics', or *sonawaru* meaning 'to be equipped with'. Thus, in this context it means 'gear'.

要

Yō

IMPORTANT

This is also read as *kaname* in the *kun*[173] reading and means 'pivot'. According to the *Xiao Jing* document: 'Ancient kings had perfect virtue and followed *yōdō* – the path of principles.' The annotations for this document say that this [path of *yōdō*] is the deepest truth.

The word *yō* implies something that is small, but [remember that a pivot, though small,] brings the whole together. Thus, ten books within our

---

172 This can be read either as five types of soldier or five types of weapon, so it could refer either to units of soldiers specializing in use of a certain weapon or the specific weapons themselves.

173 Japanese can be read in two ways: *kun* is the Japanese reading and *on* is a Chinese-derived reading.

school use the ideograms 要法 (*yōhō*) within their titles, which signify their pivotal importance.

法

Hō

PRINCIPLES

The ideogram *hō* (法) represents a path or rules on a certain subject. Here undesirable rules are omitted and good ones are recorded. This ideogram is also used in such words as *hatto* (法度), meaning 'regulations', and *hōshiki* (法式), meaning 'methods and systems'.

Overall, the last two ideograms in the term *yōhō* mean 'to transmit essential principles' [and in the case of this scroll refer to] military equipment used by warriors. Therefore, this [document] is named *Heigu Yōhō* – 'Important ways on military tools'.

INTRODUCTION BY
COMMENTATOR ONE[174]

Heihō, the military path, is *the* great path that protects and supports the world and is the very essence of supreme peace. The Yellow Emperor in China and the great deity Amaterasu Ōmikami in Japan both highly appreciated this idea. To assist the emperor in the upper echelons and also to benefit the people at the bottom end of the spectrum, there have been numerous excellent generals in Japan and China who settled rebellions and defeated vicious armies. Their reputation has crossed the generations to the present day. Examples [of great

---

174 This is the first of two introductions, written by commentator one and commentator two respectively. The first is in *kanbun*, a form that combines elements of Chinese and Japanese. While the two introductions overlap in numerous respects, a comparison of the language of the original texts shows that one was not copied from the other. This suggests that the teachings of different branch schools were broadly the same.

generals] include: Tai Kung Wang, Zhang Liang, Sun Tzu, Wu Zi, Han Xin, Zhūgě Liàng, [Minamoto no] Yoshiie, [Minamoto no] Yoshitsune, [Kusunoki] Masashige and [Takeda] Shingen. Without military virtues how can a state be governed and how can the world be settled. As Sun Tzu stated, 'The art of war is of vital importance to the state.'

Today there are still quite a few schools in existence that are tributaries of [the original source of] military ways (*heihō* 兵法) and they transmit military skills (*gunjutsu* 軍術) to the world. Examples of such schools include: Kōshū-Ryū, Hōjō-Ryū, Ōuchi-Ryū, Yamanoi-Ryū and Ogasawara-Ryū. These schools cover different versions of *heihō* and differ in many details from one another, but in essence they all contain the four principles of:

1. *kenbō* 権謀 – strategies
2. *keisei* 形勢 – situational analysis
3. *inyō* 陰陽 – the esoteric subject of *yin* and *yang*
4. *gikō* 技巧 – practical skills

These principles can be encapsulated in just one word, *rinkiōhen* (臨機応変), which means to be flexible according to the situation.

However, many stupid generals and ignorant *samurai* of today do not understand that the military arts (*heihō*) are used to govern a state and bring peace to the world. Instead they distort the arts of *heihō* into the ways of brutality and viciousness. Alas, how could they be more incorrect? Even after understanding the outline of the fourteen points of deception, the five constant factors, the seven considerations and the use of spies in Sun Tzu's [*Art of War*], it is still not easy to discuss *heidō* – the way of the soldier.[175]

Someone once asked the following question:

> *Since our school is referred to as Kusunoki-Ryū, we have transmitted more than twenty writings, starting from the scroll Heigu Yōhō all the way to Kōketsu no Maki at the end. But consider this, the introduction to the document Shichisho Kōgi*

---

175 The first chapter of Sun Tzu's *Art of War* outlines fourteen areas where deception is used; it also contains the five constant factors and the seven considerations. The use of spies is found in the thirteenth chapter.

(七書講義) – Lectures on the Seven Military Classics – says that there were originally 182 schools in the reign of the Han Dynasty, which were refined into thirty-five schools. Later these thirty-five schools were studied, discussed and classified into four different kinds. In the Tang Dynasty, thirty-three lineages maintained the writings and traditions that are found in the sixth chapter inside the document known as the Si Ku Quan Shu (四庫全書) – Complete Library of the Four Treasuries. Compared to these extremely extensive Chinese documents, the writings transmitted within our school comprise a mere one tenth of the original teachings and thus I wonder, how could such a comparatively small number of manuals manage to transmit the deepest secrets of military techniques (軍術之奧義)?

The answer to that question is as follows.

As these proverbs state:

千里之行モ一歩ヨリ起

A journey of a thousand miles begins with a single step.

岷江之觴ヲ濫ルモ楚入リ無底

At the source of the river Mingjian you can float only a small cup,
but as it enters the territory of Chu it becomes extremely deep.

These proverbs allude to a path that begins in minuteness but which extends to the colossal and starts from the lowest point but reaches the greatest of heights. [Consider the legend of] Zhang Liang: he was given one scroll that was enough to make him into a master who served a king. Know from this that it is wrong to think that reading vast amounts makes you a scholar and also remember that each person has their own way to follow.[176] The ways to follow are found in the concept of *shinōkōshō* (士農工商), the four ways of:

---

176 Reading a tremendous amount does not make you an expert. It is by studying and understanding the core principles that you become an intellectual.

1. *samurai*
2. farmers
3. artisans
4. merchants

Samurai should protect the state with *heihō* military ways, farmers should farm, artisans should build mansions, and merchants should buy and sell in markets. This is the way they should be. Farmers who do not farm, artisans who do not carve and merchants who do not trade will become useless people of pleasure. A *samurai* who does not study military ways is just as worthless. *Samurai* are in a position to protect these other three types of people, so they should not shirk from governing a state, settling turbulence or giving commands.

This scroll, which is named *Heigu Yōhō*, is one of the first to be transmitted in our school. This is because *samurai* should always study and train in the use of bows and arrows, horses, spears and swords.[177] *Samurai* should know the names of the parts of their equipment and furthermore, since people are not often trained in the donning of armour [these days, they may] not remember such part names correctly. This is the reason why this scroll is transmitted and learned in the first stages of study.

INTRODUCTION BY COMMENTATOR TWO

Heidō, the way of the soldier, came into being when weapons were created during the reign of the Emperor Fuxi, and [warfare] was spread across the world during the reign of the Yellow Emperor[178] when he slew a rebellious retainer

---

177 Due to publishing constraints, this scroll has appeared in the second volume instead of the first. Originally, it was one of the first two scrolls of the school. In this series, it has been moved to fourth position.

178 A Chinese legendary figure said to have reigned from 2510 to 2448 BC.

in the desert of Zhuolu. In Japan, the Emperor Jimmu extended his military power all over the country with the tactical help of the warriors Michinoomi no mikoto and Umashimaji no mikoto. In China, there have been those who were excellent at tactics, such as Tai Kung Wang, Zhang Liang, Han Xin, Wolong, Sun Tzu, Wu Zi and Li Zing. In our country, excellent tacticians include Ōe no Koretoki,[179] Minamoto no Yoshiie and Minamoto no Yoshitsune. Other examples include the warrior Kusunoki Masashige from our middle ages, as well as the modern figures Takeda Shingen, Uesugi Kenshin, Yamamoto Shigenori, Obata Kagenori and Hōjō Ujinaga. Thus military skills (*gunjutsu*) have continued to improve and are trained within society.

Today there are a lot of schools that are descended [from those ancient tacticians], such as Hōjō-Ryū, Kōshū-Ryū and many others. Each of these schools' teachings are based on ancient Chinese ways (天官) and they also include the art known as *jōsei* (城制), the principles of castles. However, some schools focus on the subject of military formations but have less to say about wearing armour, while others are precise about the subject of *inyō*, which is *yin–yang* theory, but are more vague about [military] prowess. The ancient master of our school, lamenting this incompleteness, studied various schools. Having identified each school's deficiencies, he supplemented the areas that were lacking and established this school, which is now named Kusunoki-Ryū. Although there are so many military schools that can be studied, they each have the same overriding principle (理), which can be broken down into the following four [areas]:

1. *kenbō* 権謀 – strategies
2. *keisei* 形勢 – situational analysis
3. *inyō* 陰陽 – the esoteric subject of *yin* and *yang*
4. *gikō* 技巧 – practical skills

Remember, the essence of the above can be represented by just one word, which is *rinkiōhen* (臨機応変) – meaning to be flexible according to the situation.

---

179 An aristocrat and scholar who lived from 888 to 963 and is reputed to have compiled the document *Kinetsushū*.

CHAPTER TWENTY-THREE

EARLY ARMOUR

Commentator one

In ancient times, armour was made of the hide of the rhinoceros[180] as iron was not yet used.

Commentator two

The word *rinkō* (鱗甲) means 'the scales of fish and the shells of turtles', which protect these creatures from water and waves, just as *yoroi* (甲) armour is worn by soldiers to protect them from spears, arrows and bullets.

A SHORT HISTORY OF ARMOUR

The *Kigen* (記原) document [which dates to the second century BC] mentions *ikō* (衣甲) armour, and the *Mozi* (墨子) document and the *Taibaiyinjing* (大白陰経) manual say that armour should be made by cutting it from leather. Furthermore, the *Guanzi* (管子) text quotes an episode from the *Inner Scripture of the Yellow Emperor*[181] about a person named Gen'nyo[182] who advised the emperor that he too should be equipped with armour.

The *Kikkōshū* (拮抗集) book says that armour originated when Gautama [the Buddha] gave sermons about the way of Buddhahood on Vulture Peak Mountain. This is because the Four Heavenly Kings were equipped with six

---

180 Probably a reference back to archaic times in mainland Asia.

181 黄帝内傳 in the original text, the ideograms differ slightly from the original Chinese.

182 Possibly Jiutian Xuannu, the goddess of war, sexuality and longevity in Chinese mythology.

tools to protect them from obstacles and hindrances and were used to expel all demons.

As can be seen, armour began to spread all over the three nations from these times.

Commentator one

The previously mentioned *Jibutsu Kigen* manual consists of eleven volumes written by Sentō (銭塘),[183] and was expanded on by Hu Wen Huan (胡文). Broadly, it shows the origins of things in the three realms of heaven, earth and man.

The word *ikō* used earlier implies 'clothes of iron' and is similar to the term *kaii* (戒衣), which means 'to be equipped'. The *Shiben* (世本) manual is similar to the famous writing named the *Record of the Grand Historian*, while the *Kikkoshū* book is a secret writing concerning the origins of various things.

The Four Devas mentioned previously are the Four Heavenly Kings who are:

1. Tamonten (多聞天) [– connected to the north]
2. Zōchōten (増長天) [– connected to the south]
3. Kōmokuten (広目天) [– connected to the west]
4. Jikokuten (持国天) [– connected to the east]

Commentator two

Concerning the points mentioned previously: the *Kikkōshū* manual is a Japanese writing, while the Four Devas are the Guardians of the East, North, South and West. The three nations mentioned refer to India, China and Japan.

Issui-sensei says

One theory says that in our country [armour] came into use when the Empress Jingū departed to invade three kingdoms inside of Korea. These three kingdoms were Silla, Paekche and Koryo.

Commentator one

Empress Jingū was the fifteenth sovereign and her personal name was

---

183 Pronunciation unknown; therefore, a Japanese version has been used here.

Okinagatarashihime. She was a great-granddaughter of Emperor Kaika and the daughter of Okinagaōji. She was also the mother of Emperor Ōjin. She suppressed these three Korean kingdoms in response to an imperial order given by her predecessor, Emperor Chūai.

Commentator two
The three Korean kingdoms mentioned in the text above are also called Mahan, Jinhan and Byeonhan and are confederacies in present-day Chōsen [Korea].

Issui-sensei says
According to another theory, armour [as we know it today] had not been used [in the invasion of Korea mentioned above], but instead they only had *haramaki*-style body armour [which is an early version with lacing up the back]. It is also said that in Japan, armour (*gusoku*) was first made with cattle leather in the Miyazaki district in the province of Hyūga and that it spread from there.

Commentator one
The four elements of *yoroi* armour are:[184]
1. *minamoto* 源 – black thread
2. taira 平 – purple thread
3. *fujiwara* 藤原 – the five colours (五音)
4. *tachibana* 橘 – green with a darker graduation towards the top (萌黄匂)

Commentator two
In the reign of the first emperor, Jinmu, armour (*gusoku*) was made from 2,000 head of cattle and they used leather from either the neck area or from the knee.

One theory says that armour originated in the Miyazaki district of Hyūga province, where they made it from cattle leather, and that it spread from there all over the country.

Issui-sensei says
The reason why many armourers existed in Nanto [that is to say Nara] in the

---

184 These elements represent the four main houses of *samurai* history.

period of Jiryaku 3 (1067), which was during the reign of Emperor Go-Reizei, is that a man called Ban Shirō Sukekane from the Ban family saw leather armour from Hyūga and created a set of armour called *goʾon-odoshi* (五音威) – armour with lacing of five colours. This is when armour was first produced in Nara.

Sukekane had three sons: Iwai was the eldest; then came Sakonji, who died young; and the third son was Banda. The descendants of Iwai and Banda have passed down the tradition [of armour construction] all the way to the present day. This is the origin of armour construction in Yamato.[185]

Commentator one

Emperor Go-Reizei (1025–1068), mentioned in the above text, was the seventieth emperor. His personal name was Chikahito and he was the first son of Emperor Go-Suzaku.

Commentator two

The man called Ban Shiro Sukekane [mentioned previously] held the position of *hokumen no shi* – protector in the north.[186]

The term *goʾon-odoshi* means 'lacing of the five colours' – these are:

1. *ao* 青 – blue
2. *ki* 黄 – yellow
3. *aka* 赤 – red
4. *shiro* 白 – white
5. *kuro* 黒 – black

The family name Banda (伴田) then branched off into Haruta (張田) and now has become Haruta (春田). The family of the son called Iwai forged base iron [for armour], while the Banda line dealt with the lacing and threads used to connect the armour. Other branches of the Banda family include Umebara (梅原), Samado (狭間戸) and Wakito (脇外).

---

185 An alternative name for Nara.

186 *Samurai* of the north (北面ノ士). This was a bodyguard positioned in a room to the north of the emperor, which was a prestigious position.

鎧甲
Gaikō

DIFFERENT FORMS OF ARMOUR

The two ideograms used in the title for this section [are 鎧 and 甲] and both mean the same thing – armour. The second ideogram, 甲, is commonly read as *kabuto* – helmet. However, you should know that this is a *huge* mistake. [You must understand that the meaning of the ideograms can change depending on the context. For example,] someone who conquerors an entire land is called a *tenka no kōsha* (天下ノ甲者) – the greatest warrior under heaven. However, the *kō* from *kōsha* (甲者), meaning 'warrior', does not have the same meaning as the *kō* in the word *kōotsu* (甲乙), which means 'superior and inferior', but it does have the same sense as the *kō* in *katchū* (甲冑) – this means armour (甲) and helmet (冑) together. The word *kōotsu*, 'superior and inferior', originated under the Emperor Wu of Han and referred to curtains called *kōchō* (甲帳). The *chō* ideogram means 'curtains' and *kōchō* means curtains made from superior (*kō*) material. On the other hand, *otsuchō* (乙帳) curtains were made from inferior (*otsu*) material. [Therefore, the combined term *kōotsu* means 'inferior and superior'.][187]

---

187 The point here is that the first ideogram, 甲, means 'armour' and the second ideogram, 冑, means 'helmet', so the complete term means 'armour and helmet'. When people see the first ideogram, 甲, on its own, they mistake it for 'helmet'. But if that were correct then when the two ideograms were used together they would read as 'helmet and helmet', which would not make sense. This sentence is proving the author's point that the ideogram 甲 cannot be read as *kabuto* helmet but must *only* be armour in the context of military gear. Today this reading is a common mistake, one that may have been passed down from the seventeenth century. The explanation about the curtains shows that in another context the same ideogram, 甲, has no connection to armour but actually means 'higher grade' or 'superior'. It would appear that people even in the writer's day mixed the two up. In short, the ideogram 甲 means either 'armour' or 'superior', depending on the context.

Commentator two

The first ideogram of the [title of the main text is] *gai* (鎧), which means 'armour made of iron', while the second ideogram, *kō* (甲), means 'armour made of leather'. Separately, they should *both* be read as *yoroi* [the common name for armour]. Therefore, *both* ideograms mean armour and so it is a devastating mistake to read the second ideogram, 甲, as *kabuto* – helmet.

[The following common saying is also a mistake.] The phrase *tenka no kō* (天下ノ甲) – 'the greatest [person] under heaven'[188] – is used to describe an excellent person, and here the ideogram 甲 means 'excellence' [or 'the highest quality']. [Perhaps the reason for the ideogram's incorrect use to mean 'helmet' is that] a helmet is worn on the highest point [of a warrior]. The use of *kō* in this phrase does not mean helmet but is actually from the use of exquisite curtains in China. Thus, the ideogram in question 甲 does not hold the same connotations as when it is used in *katchū* (甲冑), armour and helmet. [When the *samurai*] Hachiman Tarō Yoshiie attacked the area of Ōshū, he established a system of priority seating [for his men]. It consisted of superior positions [甲] and inferior positions [乙]. Those warriors who had made achievements in the wars were allowed to take 'superior' seats, while those who had not achieved had to take 'inferior' seats. Thus the ideograms [mentioned in the main text] always refer to 'superior and inferior'.[189]

---

188 Possible transcription error as the final ideogram is missing.

189 This section is complex and requires an understanding or explanation of the context and grammar used for each case when referring to the ideogram 甲. In short, the ideogram 甲 can mean (1) 'armour' or (2) 'superior', but it does *not* mean helmet. Even the *samurai* of Natori's time made this mistake and now it has entered common parlance. The arguments above show how this came about. The commentator is saying that the mistake is becoming common.

CHAPTER TWENTY-FOUR

HELMET: FRONT VIEW

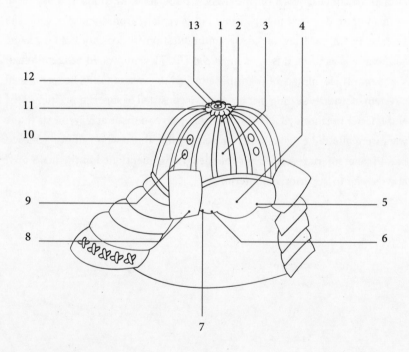

1
息出之金物
Ikidashi no kanamono
Ring around the air vent

2

天邊

Tehen

Upper part of the helmet

Alternative ideograms for this are *tenketsu* (天穴).

3

正面

Shōmen

Front of the helmet bowl

This is also called *makkō* (真向).

4

見上ノ板

Miage no ita

Inside of the peak

5

ハブサキ

Habusaki

Both sides of the underneath of the peak

6

内兜

Uchikabuto

Area around the base of the peak and the inner helmet

7

忍ノ緒付鐶

Shinobi no otsuke no kan

Rings for the helmet cord

The rings are on the inside and are not shown in this image.

8

吹返

Fukikaeshi[190]

Helmet wings

These are situated on both sides.

9

星下ノ穴

Hoshishita no ana

Holes below the helmet studs

10

星

Hoshi

Studs or rivets

11

八幡座

Hachimanza

Seat of the god Hachiman

[The multi-layered ring structure around the air vent]

12

上玉

Agedama

Securing ring for the *hachimanza*

13

天空

Tenkū

Top vent

This is also called the *ikidashi no ana* (息出之穴).

---

190 Often casually referred to as *fukigaeshi*.

内張
Uchibari
Inner lining[191]

This is not visible in the illustration.

HELMET – SIDE VIEW

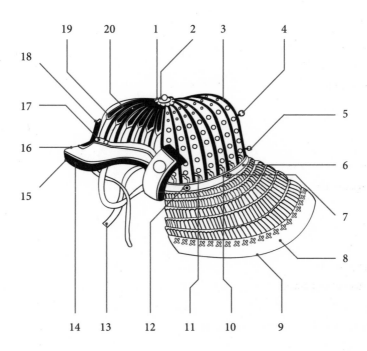

1

濃菊

Jōgiku
First chrysanthemum ring[192]

---

191 Sometimes called *ukebari*.
192 This and the following term are unknown. However, they both imply a flower-like

2

透菊

Sukashigiku

Second chrysanthemum ring

3

筋金

Sujigane

Reinforcement ridges

4

甲照鐶

Kōshō no kan

Rear ring

5

母衣付鐶

Horotsuke no kan

Ring for the *horo* cape

6

鉢付板

Hachizukeita

Connecting band

7

死去鋲

Shikyo no byo

Rivets on the connecting plate[193]

---

arrangement, leading us to conclude that they are a part of the *hachimanza* ring structure that surrounds the air vent at the top of the helmet.

193 Number 7 and number 10 are similar but the text does not explain the difference between them. They use the same two ideograms but in reverse, which has connotations of life and death. Number 7 is the rivet in this case and number 10 appears to be either the

8

菱綴板

Hishitoji no ita

Cross-stitched plate

9

肩摺

Katazuri

Shoulder-touching edge

10

去死

Koshi

Border of the connecting plate

11

檜垣

Higaki[194]

Decorative 'boundary'

12

鉢付金物

Hachitsuke no kanamono

Connecting rivet for the helmet bowl

13

忍緒

Shinobi no o

Cord

---

whole construction or a base for the rivet. Unclear at present.

194 Small decorative plates at the base of each section of the helmet bowl.

14
眉庇
Mabisashi
Peak

15
見上板
Miage no ita
Underside of the peak

16
雨走
Amabashiri
Convex camber of the peak

17
三光鋲
Sankō no byō
The three rivets at the front

18
鍬角本
Kuwa tsunomoto
Base for helmet crest

Commentator one
This is also called the *oharaitate* (ヲハライ立) – the square-cross-sectioned crest horn.

19
剣頭
Kengashira
Tip of the decorative 'sword blade' plates

20

鎬垂

Shinodare

Decorative 'sword blade' plates

EXPLANATIONS OF PARTS
OF THE HELMET

天空之事

Tenkū no koto

THE [HOLE TOWARDS THE] HEAVENS AND THE SKY

This is also called the *ikidashi no ana* – the ventilation hole. Some helmets do not have these, however most will. When you handle [the helmet] in normal times, do not put your fingers in the hole. It is commonly said that the *tenkū* is where the 98,000 gods of war enter and leave. Therefore, it should be valued highly.

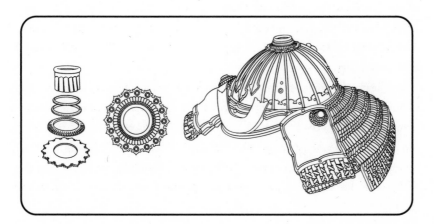

Commentator one

The above statement [concerning the gods of war] is a common proverb. Concerning the point about the gods of war entering and leaving through the hole, know that the following is a warning to those who have doubts [about whether they should or should not put their fingers in the hole].

[Three reasons for not putting your finger in the helmet vent:]
1. Your finger may become stuck.
2. Oil from your fingers left around the hole will cause degradation.
3. [The warrior is in the highest tier of society,] the helmet is the highest point of the warrior and the *tenkū* vent is the highest point of the helmet. [Therefore, it would be disrespectful to put your finger in the hole.]

It is for these three reasons that you should not put your finger in the hole when handling a helmet.

Commentator two

Avoid putting your finger in the hole, because your finger may get stuck. Also, grease from your finger will cause the iron to rust. Furthermore, as the *tenkū* hole is at the top of the helmet, it is revered as the place where the gods of war reside. The god of war is the deity Miwa Daimyōjin (三輪大明神), who is also known as Ōnamuchi no mikoto (大己貴命). The manifestation of this god is a snake with 98,000 scales, which is where the expression 'the 98,000 gods of war' comes from.

Sometimes secret correspondence and also normal letters can be hidden inside the *tenkū* hole, so remember that it is important to examine the inside when inspecting people at checkpoints and other such places. Also, it is an old custom that when [someone] is defeated in battle and he is going to cut his own stomach, he first removes his helmet by putting his finger into the *tenkū* hole. Furthermore, you can rest and stand your helmet crest inside the hole.[195]

---

195 This sentence is theoretical and may not represent the actual teaching. The sentence is lacking in detail. It should be considered as a possibility.

Issui-sensei says

According to tradition, the *tenkū* hole is there as an escape vent for air, which can become trapped during battle. Thus, the *tenkū* vent hole should be in a beneficial position. There are secret traditions on this in the *Kōketsu* scroll.

Commentator one

On a battlefield, certain things can be placed within this vent; there are oral traditions on this point. Be aware of such benefits and that in the military skills (軍術) of our school there are different points to consider according to the person and the battle or situation – these things should be kept secret.

Commentator two

The secret traditions on the beneficial places should be transmitted orally when teaching moves to the higher levels.

息出之金物之事

Ikidashi no kanamono no koto
RING AROUND THE AIR VENT
There is no other meaning attached to this. The air vent has to have a metal ring around it.

Commentator two

Remember, the gods dwell within an honest person.

上玉之事

Agedama no koto
DECORATIVE RING FOR THE *HACHIMANZA* – SEAT OF HACHIMAN
Most [helmets] have these, but some do not – especially many older helmets. If a feature offers no practical benefits, then sometimes there is no need for it to be added.

八幡座之事

Hachimanza no koto

SEAT OF HACHIMAN[196]

This is the base upon which the *agedama* decorative rim rests. As the gods of war enter and leave through the *tenkū* hole, the *agedama* decorative rim is commonly understood to represent a sacred boundary[197] between [humans and the] gods, which is why this base is called the *hachimanza* – the seat of the god Hachiman. It is also said that this section [of the helmet] has been used on gear since the days of Hachiman Tarō Yoshiie in ancient times, which may be another explanation for its name. Know that ancient helmets and those helmets called *kōraihachi* (高麗鉢) do not have this section. No matter which explanation [of the name's origin] is true, this part is for decorative purposes only and has no practical benefit. For this reason, have it constructed in any fashion that you wish [see examples below].

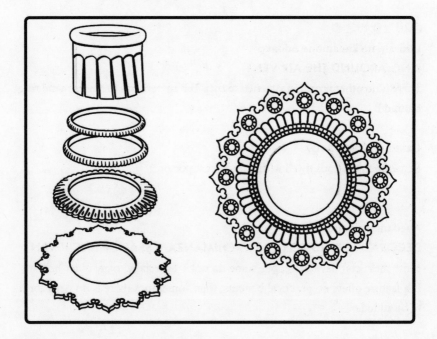

---

196 Hachiman (八幡) – sacred guardian of warriors.
197 *Igaki* (囲垣) – a fence used in Shintō shrines to separate the worldly from the holy.

Commentator one

[Another theory is that the name derives from] Emperor Ōjin, who had the alternative name Hachiman-ōi after the god that *bushi* warriors revere.

The Hachiman Tarō Yoshiie mentioned previously was of the seventh generation of the Seiwa Genji clan. His father was Iyo no kami Minamoto no Yoriyoshi, who was the general of defence for the northern lands.[198] Hachiman Tarō Yoshiie inherited military scrolls, which he gave to Mutsu no kami Ōe. [Furthermore, Hachiman Tarō Yoshiie] was also called Genta. After his coming-of-age ceremony, he obtained his adult name, Hachiman Tarō, and was given the position of *shōshii* – senior fourth rank of the imperial court. He died in 1105[199] on the eighteenth day of the eighth month at the age of sixty-seven. His mother was the daughter of Kazusa no suke Taira no Naokata who was an ancestor of the Hōjō clan.

星之事
Hoshi no koto
STUDS OR RIVETS[200]

There are four of these and they are set in the four directions. They are used for when you wish to tie a headband around the helmet. However, some helmets do not have them. The *hoshishita no ana* are the holes below these studs. They have a decorative function, as coloured threads can be passed through them; they are also called *shōzoku no ana* – holes for attire.[201]

Commentator one

These studs are also called *shiten no hoshi* (四天ノ星) – studs for all four directions or heaven. Wearing a headband around the helmet is a sign of

---

198 鎮守府将軍.

199 This is recorded as Chōji 2; however, it is believed that he in fact died in Kasho 1, which was 1106.

200 These are named *hoshi*, which literally means 'stars'. However, throughout this series the term will be translated as 'studs or rivets'.

201 These four holes found around a Japanese helmet once held decorative cords. However, this practice fell out of fashion.

courage. The studs also have a practical use; they protect the holes below them from great-sword blows.[202]

At the battle of Mikatagahara, the warrior Honda Heihachi went to battle in a *kara no kashira*-style helmet[203] and there he rallied the army, which was in rout. In those days such helmets were rare.

A satirical poem states:

イエヤスニスギタルモノガ二ツ有リ　カラノカシラニ本田平八

Tokugawa Ieyasu has two things that are more than he deserves:
the first is a kara no kashira *helmet and the second is Honda Heihachi.*

甲照之鐶之事

Kōshō no kan no koto

SECURING RING ON THE REAR OF THE HELMET

This is used to attach the *agemaki*[204] coloured cord. In ancient times there was only *eboshi*-style protection; proper helmets were invented at an unknown but later date. The *agemaki* decorative cord is attached to represent the cord that was once used on *eboshi* caps. These days it is also called *kasajirushi no kan* (笠印ノ環) – the ring for an identifying mark on a helmet. This came about when someone removed his identification mark from his sleeve and attached it to this ring so that his allies could identify him when he was the first to attack during a battle.

Commentator one

In the rebellion of Taira no Masakado, from the first day to the fourteenth day of the second month of Jōhei 3 (934),[205] the warrior Masakado instructed his men [to use this ring on the rear of the helmet to attach their identification mark]. At this rebellion 197 people died together. [Another theory states that] the person [who first fixed his sleeve identification mark to the ring of his

---

202 These four small studs around the helmet stop sword blows from cutting straight down and removing the decorative threads that once were fitted to Japanese helmets as described in the text.

203 唐ノ頭, a helmet with large horns and long hair attached.

204 A coloured cord attached to the rear of the helmet in a decorative knot.

205 Correctly, Jōhei 5.

helmet] was actually [Fujiwara] Tawara no tōta Hidesato [who was the enemy of the above-mentioned warrior Masakado].

Concerning the *agemaki* cord: the *agemaki* is a braided cord that originated in ancient times when someone called Ōtomo no Satehiko went to Korea and returned with a Chinese man called [illegible text], who was in his service. This same man Ōtomo no Satehiko returned to Korea six times but settled in Hakatazu in Chikuzen [in Japan]. Here he engaged in braiding cord, a craft that became known as *touchi* – Chinese braiding. Local women learned the skill and started to produce cords. An alternative story says that there was a man around Karatachi in Hachijō [Kyōto] whose name was Tagui no Kiyo. He served the local governor and when the governor went to Chikushi [in Japan] he lived in the [town of] Hakata, where he married a woman who braided cord. After ten years they went back to Kyōto and started a prosperous business and became wealthy. This was recorded in a writing called *Kodama* (小玉).

AGEMAKI

Commentator two

[An alternative theory concerning the helmet rings is that] the 'someone' in this account was actually the warrior Tawara no tōta Hidesato. On the first days of the second month of Jōhei 3,[206] when Sōma Masakado was suppressed, [Tawara no tōta Hidesato] took his sleeve identification mark and attached it to the ring [on his helmet].

---

206 Correctly, Jōhei 5.

Issui-sensei says

Tradition says that this ring is used for identifying marks when in mountains and forests and for nighttime battles.

Commentator two

In mountains or forests do not carry banners, as they will get stuck on branches. Instead use *kasajirushi* (笠印) helmet marks for identification. Neither should banners be carried in night battles, because they cannot be seen in the darkness.

吹返之事

Fukikaeshi no koto

WINGS

These are simply extensions of the *hachitsuke no ita*, the helmet bowl rim, and there is nothing more to be said on this. Sometimes they carry the clan crest.

Tradition says that those who shoot arrows should not have such wings [on their helmet].

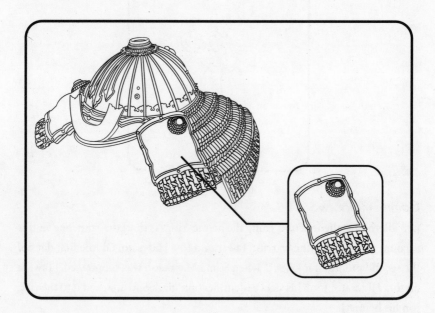

Commentator one

Sometimes the right wing is hinged or some helmets do not have any wings; this is for when shooting arrows. In *kyūdō*, the way of archery, there are other teachings for the shooting of arrows and you should follow the teachings you consider best. [If in doubt] follow the teachings you prefer. Also, it appears that in ancient times when archers performed *tōya* (遠矢), shooting arrows over a distance, or *hareya* (晴矢), ceremonial shooting,[207] they would take off their helmet and attach it to the *takahimo* cord on their armour.[208]

Concerning the *hachitsuke* helmet bowl rim: the top part of this band is also called the *koshimaki no ita* – the plate that secures the neck protection to the helmet.

Commentator two

Fukikaeshi helmet wings are meant to enhance your spirits. Generally, anything jutting outwards is considered to be positive. Larger helmet wings are no better than smaller ones, but some people may consider larger ones to show higher levels of spirit and, therefore, to be more positive. It is desirable to cut out and fold the first *shikoro* neck plate so as to make a helmet wing with a square end. Some people say that helmet wings are not good, as the wings get in the way when you are drawing a bow, but this is not a convincing argument. If the front crest is of the *kazuno-kuwagata* style,[209] it will not interfere with the bow string [as it is angled so that it is out of the way].

角本之事

Tsunomoto no koto

CREST HORN

This nail-like implement is called the *tsunomoto*. Those with a square cross-section are called *oharai-tsunomoto* (御祓角本).

---

207 This term no longer exists. It translates literally as 'special occasion shooting'.

208 This cord is incorrectly considered to be at the shoulder. However, Natori-Ryū says only that it is on the right side of the body.

209 鹿角鍬形, deer-horn crests, which point directly upwards and thus do not interfere with the bow string.

Commentator one

After Prince Shōtoku had subjugated the Moriya clan, he paid his respects at a great shrine and invited the gods to reside within him. Since that time [the base spike to hold the helmet crest] has been called the *oharaiasadate* – the hemp purification front crest horn.[210] Also, the prince created a helmet crest in the form of a statue of the god Bishamon and used this on his helmet. As a result, sometimes on old figurines of the deity Bishamon you can still see marks[211] that show that they were once put onto crest horns. [Take note that] sometimes old Buddhist statues have holes that fit onto horns [so that they can be used as helmet crests].

Helmet crests are often compared to animal horns and that is why the word *tsunomoto*[212] – the fixing horn – is used.

眉庇之事
Mabisashi no koto
PEAK

Some peaks are large and some are small, but people in the past said that it was better to have a shorter peak because too long a peak would drop down and cover your eyes when fighting and, as helmets are heavy, air would become trapped. That being said, too short a peak can also be a problem when you are besieging the enemy and coming under intense arrow and musket fire and you want to tilt your head forwards [to use your peak for protection].

A longer peak will not let you see ahead, which forces you to raise your head, an action that is considered excellent in a warrior. This is called *ikubimusha* (猪首武者), the boar-necked warrior[213] – you should know that this is a state to be commended.

---

210 A hemp purification tool was used in shrines to clean away negativity and promote a connection to the divine. The prince would have used such a tool to perform his ritual of spiritual cleansing and so, to represent this purity, he renamed the base horn that holds the crest. After this he used a statue of the god Bishamon as the front crest on his helmet. This shows his connection with divinity and his level of purification.

211 Most likely, these are small holes on the underside of the figure where it has been pushed onto the crest horn.

212 A compound word of 'base' (本) and 'horn' (角).

213 i.e. stout and with the head tilted slightly back.

My humble suggestion is thus: as it is hard to decide between the two lengths because each has its advantages and disadvantages, it is best to use the positives of both and choose [a peak length] that is between the two.

Tradition says that it is desirable to paint the inside of the peak cinnabar red.

Commentator one

[The inside of the peak] should be painted this colour to improve your complexion. It is beneficial to paint this in the colour of *terra rosa*.[214]

Sometimes there are leather reinforcement sections called *chikaragawa* (力革), which support the ring for the helmet strap. It is best to make a round hole [in the lining] for the ring [to pass through] so that the helmet strap can be attached.

At each end of the peak there is a section called the *habusaki* (ハブサキ). In the writing *Hōgen Monogatari*[215] it was recorded that the warrior Chinzei Hachirō Tametomo was shot by the enemy, [and that the arrow] hit this section around the peak and left a scar on his forehead. The arrow that hit him was shot by the warrior Kamata Hyōe Masakiyo.

Be careful, sometimes the word *hatsuburi* (半首), the faceguard, is used instead of *habusaki* (ハブサキ), the section below the peak. Be aware of this mistake and do not repeat it.

In one *nōh* play, Lord Kiso Yoshinaka looked behind him [while he was retreating] to see where the warrior Kanehira was. Just then an arrow hit him and lodged under his *uchikabuto* – the area between the peak and the inner helmet. This was because Lord Kiso had his face positioned upwards.

Consider the phrase:

人ニ内兜ヲ見ラレタル
For the inside of your helmet has been seen by others.

This is an expression meaning total defeat by the enemy. If the inside of your helmet is visible, it means that you are about to be decapitated.

---

214 Theorized, as the ideograms are unknown.
215 保元物語.

Commentator two

Our ancient master thought that the helmet peak had disadvantages if it was [too] long or [too] short, and therefore recommended a medium-length peak. This length is called *hizume-gata* (馬爪形) – hoof-shaped. Normally, the peak serves to shield your eyes from sunlight so that you can take better aim.

Because you cannot eat or drink whenever you like when on a battlefield, you will become tired and look pale, but if the inside of your helmet peak is coloured red you will appear to have a better complexion.

内張之事

Uchibari no koto

INSIDE LINING

If the lining is of linen or cotton, then have it made with two layers and fine stitching.[216] Also, it is considered good if you apply gold leaf below this lining as this is meant to protect against the sunlight.

Commentator one

This is also known as *ukebari* (ウケ張) – the floating lining.

Commentator two

Alternatively, [it can be said that the lining of] the helmet is called the *urabari* (裏張), the back lining, while [the lining of] the armour is called the *ukebari* (浮張), the floating lining.

Gold has coldness as a property and so it will keep heat away from the inside of the helmet. If a helmet gets warmer, iron or lead bullets can pierce it more easily [because the metal is at a higher temperature]. Layering gold leaf on the inside will firstly prevent degradation, but will also [help to] stop arrows or bullets penetrating.

---

216 This means that the material is stitched throughout, across the entire face of the lining.

綴之事

Shikoro no koto

REAR NECK PLATES

Both *manjū* (幔中) neck plates that are curved outwards and *hineno* (日根野) neck plates that are curved slightly inwards consist of upper, middle and lower sections. However, there is also a type called *wake-shikoro* (分ケ錣), which is divided into multiple sections, and another called *yosesugake* (寄簀懸), which has small gaps in the lacing of the plates. This is the style known as *nuinobe* (縫延).

Tradition says that those [helmets] that have been called *sanmai-kabuto* (三枚兜), three-layered, or *gomai-kabuto* (五枚兜), five-layered, since ancient times are so named to specify the number of neck plates that are attached. [The lowest of these plates is called the] *katazuri no ita* (肩摺ノ板), the shoulder-touching plate. This name does not imply any practical benefit; it just means that it brushes the top of the shoulder.

Commentator one

Concerning the *hineno*-style neck plate, which curves slightly inwards: the *samurai* Hineno Oribe, who lived during the reign of Lord Hideyoshi, had unparalleled expertise [in this area and thus it is named after him].

Concerning the *katazuri no ita* shoulder-touching plate: it has no extra benefit to record, but it is so called because it touches the shoulder – this is simply the lowest plate.

Commentator two

The *manjū* style of neck plate, which curves outwards, has a rounded shape, whereas the *hineno* style has an inward warping.[217]

Concerning the *manjū* style, which curves outwards: the top [plate] is most rounded, the middle less rounded, and the bottom least rounded of all.

Concerning the *hineno* style, which has a slight inward curve: the top plate is most warped, the middle less warped and the bottom least warped of all.

---

217 On the helmet, the lower neck plate is either curved slightly outwards or in the second style, curved slightly inwards. However, in either case the curve is very subtle.

Know that in both styles the bottom neck plates look very similar but you can distinguish between them by observing the *katazuri no ita* shoulder-touching plate.

Concerning the *wake-shikoro* style, which is divided into multiple sections: this uses the technique of having three separate plates just like the tassets of armour.[218]

Concerning the *yosesugake* style described previously: this has bindings like reed screens as it has lashings spaced out in a few places.

忍之緒付之鐶之事
Shinobi no otsuke no kan no koto
RINGS SECURING POINTS FOR THE HELMET STRAP

There may be either three attaching points, which is called *mitsu-tsuke* (三ツ付), or four, which is called *yotsu-tsuke* (四ツ付). There is no significant difference between the two, but in our school only three rings are used.

Commentator one

There are seven ways to secure this cord. Use the way called *mihoyagake* (三保屋カケ), and remember that three rings is best.

Commentator two

Three attaching rings are preferable, as this [makes the strap] easier to rig.

The cord should be made of bleached ramie and the length should be 7 *shaku* 9 *sun* for a helmet with four attching points and 7 *shaku* 2 *sun* for one with three attaching points – all of which are on the inside of the helmet. The way of securing it should be transmitted orally. There is a knot called *mihoya-musubi* (三保屋結), which is said to be beneficial to use.

Issui-sensei says

There are numerous parts [of a helmet] other than those listed above, but there is no benefit [in recording] them all here so they have been omitted.

---

218 Neck plates can consist of three or five layers that go all the way around the back of the armour in a single piece covering the neck; or, as in the style described here, they can be divided vertically into separate right, middle and left protective flaps.

CHAPTER TWENTY-FIVE

STYLES OF HELMET DECORATION

八方白

Happōjiro

GOLD BOWL SECTIONS IN EIGHT DIRECTIONS

On the top of some *samurai* helmets, you may see the helmet bowl plates divided into eight gold sections running vertically down the bowl from the vent at the top.[219]

Commentator one

This style can have eight *shinadare* [small sculpted areas that look like straight swords around the helmet] in all eight directions.

---

219 This sentence has been greatly expanded to make it understandable in English. However, the meaning remains the same.

SHINADARE

Commentator two

This is classified as a *yō no kabuto* (陽之冑), helmet of the light, because gold is of the element *yō* and represents the sun, which illuminates all eight directions. That is where the name of this style comes from: *happōjiro* means 'covering all eight directions'.

One definition of a *happōjiro* helmet is one where the *shinadare* sword-like decorations are made of gold. All *happōjiro*-style helmets have *kumogata* rim decorations around them. Helmets with studs (*hoshikabuto*) and those with *ryūzu* dragon carvings should be worn in combination with the style of armour that has *unohana odoshi* (卯花威) white lacings.

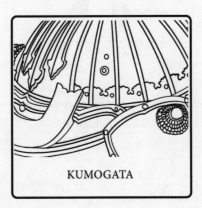

KUMOGATA

四方白

Shihōjiro

SILVER BOWL SECTIONS IN FOUR DIRECTIONS

This has silver sections [running vertically around the helmet bowl] in four directions.

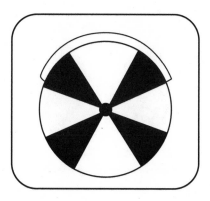

Commentator one

This style of helmet also has *shinadare* sword-like features embossed on each section.

Commentator two

This is classified as an *in no kabuto* (陰之冑), helmet of the dark, because silver is of the element *in* and represents the moon. The moon lights the four directions, thus it is named *shihōjiro* – silver lines of the four directions.

As well as having four lines, a *shihōjiro*-style helmet also has a *kuwagata* crest and *kumogata* rim decorations in all four areas. Those front crests of the *kuwagata* style should not be used by anyone except the *taishō* commander. This type of helmet should be worn in combination with armour that has exclusively black lacings.

二方白

Nihōjiro

GOLD OR SILVER BOWL SECTIONS IN TWO DIRECTIONS

This has lines of the helmet bowl plated in gold and/or silver.

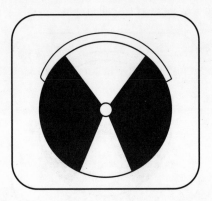

Commentator one

One theory says that this style of helmet may also have small *shinadare* sword-like features embossed on two sections [of the helmet bowl]. This appears to be a reasonable assumption.

Commentator two

This style of helmet has a harmonious balance of the elements of *in* and *yō*. [Another way to achieve this balance would be to] combine the *happōjiro* eight-sectioned style and the *shihōjiro* four-sectioned style to make twelve gold or silver plate sections. However, twelve is a weak number (虚) and therefore this style is not used. Instead, use the *nihōjiro* two-sectioned style [as shown above]. Thus, those helmets which have *kumogata* rim decorations and *shinadare* embossed sword-like features are known as *nihōjiro* – a helmet with gold or silver in two directions. This helmet should always be worn with *hiodoshi* armour – armour with red lacing.

大星之甲之事

Ōboshi no kabuto no koto

GREATER STUDDED HELMET

These helmets have raised studs [on the bowl]. Those with studs hammered over on the inside to secure them are called *shimekaeshi* (シメ返).

Commentator two

This is the same as a standard studded helmet but in addition it has raised bases for each stud. One type is known as chrysanthemum-patterned with spacers below each stud. Helmets that do not have such bases are known as *koboshi no kabuto* [see below].

小星之事

Koboshi no koto

LESSER STUDDED HELMET

Those [helmets] that have no base under the studs are normally called simply *hoshikabuto* – studded helmets. The number of studs is not definite; however, there are normally sixty-two ridges [running vertically along the bowl of the helmet]. There is also a type called the *igabachi* (伊賀鉢) – helmet bowl of chestnut spikes.

Commentator two

This name of *igabachi* does not come from the province of Iga (伊賀), but refers to a helmet shaped like a spiked chestnut shell (毬) [which is pronounced the same way].

毛鍪之事

Mōbō no koto

HELMETS WITH HAIR

There are four kinds of helmet with hair:

1. *shaguma* 赤熊 – red bear
2. *koguma* 黒熊 – black bear

3. *haguma* 白熊 – white bear
4. *torige* 鳥毛 – bird feathers

Having hair of two different colours has been avoided since ancient times.

Commentator two

Nige – hair in two colours – is disliked because the pronunciation is so similar to *nigeru*, which means 'to flee'.

頼政頭巾之事
Yorimasa zukin no koto
THE HEADGEAR OF YORIMASA[220]

This is worn by older people and *samurai*-monks.[221]

Commentator one

There are three types of headgear in this category:

1. *choppei* 直平 – cowl with a flat horizontal top
2. *daikokuzukin* 大黒頭巾 – multi-pleated cap
3. *chōhanzutsumi* 長範包 – cowl with covered face

Commentator two

These three styles are unusual and not used by younger warriors. Other than these, there are a lot of different kinds of helmet as listed below.

For the *yorimasa zukin* style of head gear [which is the subject of this article], the differences are determined by the number of pleats at the front and the rear. There should be eight pleats at the front, which represent the eight petals of the chrysanthemum, and twelve at the rear, which represent the Twelve Nidānas doctrine – the twelve links of causality in Buddhism.[222]

---

220 A *samurai*-monk from the Heian period who belonged to the Minamoto clan.
221 *Hōshi-musha* (法師武者).
222 Twelve connecting links that form throughout birth and rebirth, causing human suffering and the cycle of reincarnation.

TYPES OF HELMET

頭成
Zunari

Commentator one

Those that have no peaks are called *tominagabachi* (富永鉢), the helmet of Tominaga. The shape is taken from masterpieces from old times.

作成
Sakunari

雑賀鉢
Saikabachi

Commentator one

Saikabachi helmets were first worn in the battle of Saika, in the domain of Kishū. There are three places where blacksmiths[223] [construct these helmets]:

1. Tengūmae
2. Nichizengū waki
3. Uji Tatamiyachō Enoki no Shita

椎成
Shiinari

唐冠
Tōkamuri

鳶頭
Tobigashira

---

223 *Kaji* (鍛冶).

桃成
Momonari

烏帽子
Eboshi

無逢成
Mubōnari

Commentator one

The *mubō* style does not use fixing rivets (釘) or thread (糸).

鹿児皮成
Kanikawanari

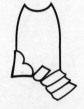

Commentator one
The *kanoko kawanari* style has a fine grain finish.

高麗笠
Kōraigasa

雲形
Kumogata

貝息
Kainoiki

火焔
Kaen

頓拝
Toppai

魚形
Uonari

廻甲

Meguri kabuto

緝甲[224]

Tatami kabuto

---

224 The ideogram 畳 is used in the Koga transcription.

一谷

Ichinotani

十王頭

Jūōgashira[225]

ナシ打

Nashiuchi

---

225 This helmet actually has three panels, but the image appears to show two. This is a mistake in the original artwork.

錐形

Kirinari

カタ白ノ兜

Katajiro no kabuto[226]

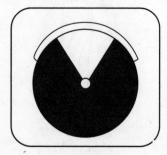

Commentator one

The sons of Nasu no Tarō Sukemune appear in volume forty-three of the war chronicle *Genpei Seisuiki* (源平盛衰記). It should be known that the eldest son, Jūrō, wore this *katajiro*-style helmet, while the youngest, Yoichi, wore a *takazuno*-style helmet.

Issui-sensei says

There are various other types of helmet, the names of many of which are not known. Also, there are many sub-types of the *kōraibachi* style, which are Korean-inspired helmets. In Japan we construct them according to our own preferences. Also, those that are made in the form of clams and fish are named after the creatures they resemble.

---

226 A helmet with a single gold or silver section on the helmet bowl rim.

Commentator two

Examples of helmets that are modelled on sea creatures include:

* *namazuo* 鯰尾 – catfish tail
* *shachihoko* 鯱 – a mythical fish with a dragon's scales and lion's head
* *sazae* 栄螺 – turban shell

立物之事
Tatemono no koto

CRESTS

[The three types of crest:]
1. *maedate* 前立 – crest fitted to the front
2. *wakidate* 脇立 – crest fitted to the sides
3. *ushiro-tatemono* 後立物 – crest fitted to the rear

Commentator two

Ushiro-tatemono rear crests should be large and have larger base mounts, for if they are small they cannot be seen above the helmet.

鍬形
Kuwagata
HOE-SHAPED CREST

It is said that a *kuwagata*-style crest with a dragon's head upon it should go on the front of the helmet and is only to be used by *taishō* lords. I am still not certain that the *kuwagata*-style crest with dragon head is only for the *taishō*. [I presume] this came about because of the assumption that other people should avoid using anything identical to the *taishō*'s gear. Also, because *kuwagata*-style crests are exceptionally exquisite objects [people may have thought that] both *samurai* and soldiers[227] should refrain from using them as they seem to be fit for lords only.

Commentator two

Dragons are said to hibernate in winter and wait for spring (*yō*) so they can ascend to heaven. Furthermore, the *I Ching* says that dragons represent the virtues of superiors. As the *taishō* has the virtues of a dragon, a dragon's head is used for his crest.

A *kuwa* [the first part of the name] is a hoe. As a tool for moving soil, the hoe symbolizes the Earth element, which represents the centre in Five Elements [theory].[228]

半月

Hangetsu

CREST OF THE CRESCENT MOON

天付

Tentsuki

CREST THAT PIERCES THE HEAVENS

---

227 *Shisotsu* (士卒).

228 This makes the hoe an appropriate symbol for a leader in total command at the centre of his troops.

When using one of the previous three styles of crest, it is advised that you add extra details as required. Also, know that someone once said that crests should be made to represent the horns of quadrupeds, such as deer and cattle.

The following are all names of crests:

藪潛
Yabukuguri
CREST THAT SWEEPS BACKWARDS

向掛
Mukōgakari
CREST THAT ADVANCES DIRECTLY FORWARDS

抱角
Kakaezuno
CREST THAT CURVES OUTWARDS AND FORWARDS

Commentator two

Crests with animal horn shapes are used as they represent the element of *yō*.

For the *kuwagata* hoe style, the size varies and there may be either two or three prongs. There are [variations, such as the] *ryūzu* dragon's head and the *takazuno* – high and sharp-pointed version. Furthermore, there are crests in the shape of statues of the Four Heavenly Kings (四天) and the Eight Dragons [kings] (八竜形).

From ancient times, helmet crests have symbolized the element of *yō* and are strong and high-spirited.

Issui-sensei says

Tradition says that crests serve as the identifying mark of the clan and in most cases there should be a standard one for all warriors and soldiers (*shisotsu*). However, captains may choose their own design within the set rules given. If there are no rules covering these matters, then lay down specific ways for your own clan.

Commentator two

The *hangetsu* crescent-style crest represents the *chi* of autumn which is comprised of mist or any chill air.[229] [Know that mist works against your enemies.]

The *samurai* Hara Mino no kami Nyūdō created a variation on the *hangetsu* style that had a thin gold crescent with an extended horn on one side. He was a retainer to Hōjō Ujiyasu of the area of Odawara.

---

229 An archaic ideogram comprising radicals that represent certain types of weather.

頬當之事
Hōate no koto

FACEGUARDS

Faceguards with a nose piece are called *menpō* (面頬) and those without a nose piece are called *sarubō* (猿頬). Smaller faceguards that cover only the lower jaw are called *etchūbō* (越中頬). Those with a removable nose piece are called *tsubakurabō* (ツハクラ頬).

Commentator one
Both *sakatsura-* and *yodaregake*-style face protectors were invented in the Kan'nō era (1350–1352) by Abō Hizen no kami. These were the first modern faceguards (*hōate*).

The following are types of face and neck protection:
- *sakatsura* 逆頬
- *udabō* 宇田頬
- *odabō* 織田頬
- *tsubakurobō* 燕頬
- *shiwabō* 皺頬
- *etchūbō* 越中頬
- *harimabō* 播磨頬
- *ubabō* 祖母頬[230]

Commentator two
In our school the *etchūbō*-style jaw protector should be used because it allows you to breathe freely.

The *sakatsura*-style face protector is no longer in use, but was invented

---

230 This final example appears only in the Koga transcription.

in the Kan'nō era (1350–52) and was first used by the warrior Bizen no kami Tadanuki.

It is desirable to make the faceguard easy to attach and detach, otherwise it may press too much [against the face] and breathing may be difficult. It is also beneficial to remove the nose part when you are under a boiling sun.

面頬

Mempō

FACEGUARD: FRONT VIEW

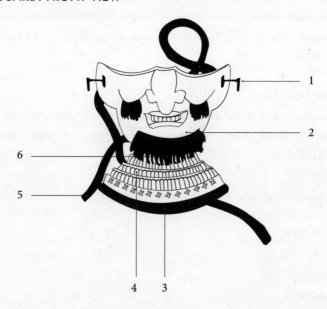

1

緒便金

Odayori no kane

Lead for the cord

Commentator two

It is also called the *odome no kugi* (緒留釘) cord bracket.

2

緒便金

Odayori no kane

Lead for the cord

Some [face protectors] have an *odayori no kane* lead for the cord at this point as well.

3

胸摺之板

Munesuri no ita

Bottom plate of the neck protector

4

涎懸

Yodarekake

Neck protector

Commentator one

This is also called the *shitagake* (下懸). The type called the *gosagari* (五サカリ) five layers is a method from old times.

5

甲掛

Kōkake

Connecting cord

6

ツユオトシノ穴

Tsuyuotoshi no ana

Saliva vent

Commentator two

This is also called the *asenagashi no ana* (汗流穴) sweat vent.

CHAPTER TWENTY-SIX

ARMOUR: FRONT VIEW

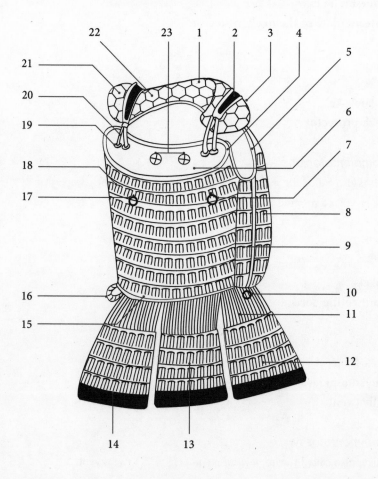

1

肩當

Kataate

Neck and shoulder padding

The clasp at the shoulder cords is called the *gyōyō* (杏葉) and the metal fittings are called *gyōyō no kane* (杏葉ノカネ).[231]

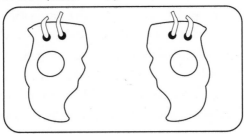

Commentator two

The honeycomb-patterned stitches [on the neck and shoulder padding] are called *hawase no ito* (這之糸).

2

障子ノ板

Shōji no ita

Vertical plate on the shoulder pad

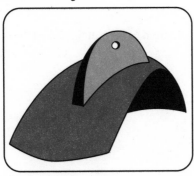

---

231 These are small protective plates, which sit over the cords at the top of the shoulder.

3

小手カクシ

Kotekakushi

Upper sleeve cover

[Only the position is shown in the main image.]

[The following section was on a sheet attached to commentator one's annotation.]

One theory states that the *kotekakushi* [which is a very small shoulder guard] is also sometimes called the *kobire*, meaning 'small fish fin', but this is a mistake. [The small shoulder guard] is different from the *shōji no ita* [which is the small standing plate between the shoulder and the neck].[232] This plate [between the neck and the shoulder] has a part which stands vertically and is named the *shōji* – door. These two small standing plates have holes through them, which are used to attach and carry things on the back (*wassoku*). Do not pass the *aibiki no o* shoulder connecting cords through the holes – to do this is wrong.

4

矢留ノヒネリカヘシ

Yadomari no hinerigaeshi

Folded hem at the top of the plate

Commentator one

The folded hem [at the bottom of the plate] is called the *omeri* (ヲメリ).

Commentator two

This is also known as the *obimawashi* (帯周).

---

232 The commentator is saying that these two parts are very close to each other and people have mixed them up. One is a form of 'fin' that sticks up vertically between the shoulder and the neck, the other is a small padded area. The small vertical fin can be seen in the modern image in Section 2.

5

爪

Tsuma

Shoulder hems

These are also called *hinerigaeshi* (ヒネリカヘシ), *hinerigaeshi no ita* (捻返板) or *kanemawashi* (金周) – these are hems made from an extension of the lining of the armour.

6

胸板

Munaita

Chest plate

一ノ板	ICHI NO ITA
二ノ板	NI NO ITA
三ノ板	SAN NO ITA
胴ノ板	DŌ NO ITA
一ノ革	ICHI NO KAWA
二ノ革	NI NO KAWA
三ノ革	SAN NO KAWA
ホッテ	HOTTE

[Each band of Japanese armour is numbered from top to bottom, the *munaita* plate being the very top with the rest in the following order:]

- *ichi no ita* 一ノ板 – first plate
- *ni no ita* 二ノ板 – second plate
- *san no ita* 三ノ板 – third plate

- *dōnoita* 胴ノ板 – body plate
- *ichi no kawa* 一ノ革 – first leather plate
- *ninokawa* 二ノ革 – second leather plate
- *san no kawa* 三ノ革 – third leather plate
- *hotte* ホツテ – lowest plate with an upward curve

7

手拭付之鐶

Tenugui tsuke no kan

Ring for the *tenugui* cloth

8

後射向

Ushiro imuke

Rear left protection panel

9

前射向

Mae imuke

Front left protection panel

Commentator two

[Parts 8 and 9 together are] called *imuke no ita* (射向板) – protection panels.

10

繰締鐶

Kurijime no kan

Cord ring

11

揺ノ糸

Yurugi no ito

Tasset cords

12

射向先

Imukesaki

Left side of the armour[233]

13

玉睪蔵

Kinkakushi

Centre tasset

Commentator two

The whole tasset set can be known as the *kusazuri* (草摺), grass-touching plates, or also the *gesan* (毛散), the lower section that spreads.

14

大胴先

Ōdōsaki

Joint of armour at the right side[234]

15

發傳

Hotte

Lowest plate with an upward curve [to defend against a thrust]

16

根緒

Neo

Cord loop

---

233 We have given the literal translation of the Japanese. However, strictly speaking, this is the left tasset.

234 This term normally refers to the joint on the right side of the armour. However, here and in other scrolls such as the *Kinetsushū*, this word points directly to the right tasset of the armour, so it means either the whole right side at the joint or the right tasset.

17

再拝附

Saihaitsuke

Ring for the *saihai* war baton

18

千旦板

Sendan no ita

Second plate of body armour

19

相引ノ金物

Aibiki no kanamono

Metal clasp for the shoulder connecting cord

20

相引ノ緒

Aibiki no o

Shoulder connecting cord

Commentator one

One theory states that the *aibiki no o* [the cord at the shoulder] is called the *takahimo* cord. However, I think that in ancient times when the archaic *haramaki*-style armour was prevalent, they used the *sehikiai-ito* – the cord that joins at the rear – and therefore the *takahimo* cord [which ties at the side] would not have been required. This makes me think that there was no such cord in those days. Thus, the only cord at this higher [shoulder] position in those days was the *aibiki* cord. The present-day *takahimo* cord [which is the cord tied on the right side of the body armour] is also called the *hikiawase no o*.[235]

---

235 The commentator is saying that problems have started to arise during his time, and that cord names are starting to change. Today the *takahimo* cord is at the shoulder. However, in earlier times it was positioned at the side of the body armour.

21

綿噯

Watagami

Shoulder pad area

22

襟巻ノ亀甲

Erimaki no kikkō

Turtle patterning [on the neck padding]

This is also called *hawase no ito* (ハヽセノ糸) – narrow threading. These are the names for the hexagonal patterning on the padded neck section.

Commentator two

There is a style of patterning called *hawase no ito*, which is used on lashes for armour tassets or in the construction of chain mail. The name may come from the verb *hawase* – to crawl.

23

矢留金物

Yadomari no kanamono

Rivets for the upper chest plate

ARMOUR: REAR VIEW

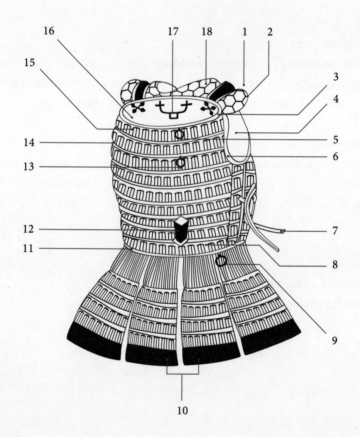

1

杏葉

Gyōyō

Shoulder-cord clasp

The parts connected with clasps are called *gyōyō*. The metal part is called *gyōyō no kane*.

[A small clasp to protect the cords at the shoulder.[236] Only the position is shown in the image.]

2

小鰭

Kobire

Extra shoulder padding

This is also called the *kugikakushi* (釘蔵) rivet cover.

3

襟巻之縁

Erimaki no fuchi

Back plate hem

4

浮張

Ukebari

Lining

This is the lining of the body armour.

5

母羅付鐶

Horotsuke no kan

Ring for the *horo* cape

6

金周

Kanemawashi

Armpit hem

---

236 While this component is positioned on the front, older ways had it high on the shoulder and it is therefore labelled on the rear view.

7

高紐

Takahimo

Side securing cords

8

發傳

Hotte

Lowest plate

Commentator two

This is also called the *dōjiri* (胴尻) – the bottom plate of the torso.

9

繰締鐶

Kurijime no kan

Ring for the securing cords

10

引敷

Hisshiki

Rear tassets

11

根緒

Neo[237]

Foundation cord

This is also called the *mizuhiki* (水引).

---

[237] This name appears twice. The front view of the armour has it as a small loop, whereas here it refers to a base cord that runs around the armour.

12

待請

Machiuke

Banner pole housing

There is a part called the *ukezutsu* (請筒), which fits into the *machiuke*. The base plate for the *machiuke* housing is called the *nezumi* (根直敷).[238]

Commentator one

Concerning the *nezumi* base for the banner pole: one theory is that it should not be pronounced *nezumi* but should instead be said as *nesumi*, but know that this is wrong.

13

総角付鐶

Agemakitsuke no kan

Ring to attach the *agemaki* cord

14

佐加板

Sakaita

Plate that overlaps in reverse

This plate has a ring for attaching the *horo* cape.

Commentator one

The *sakaita* plate is a secret thing. Every plate is joined to the one above and below it with lashes and the lower plate normally overlaps on the outside of the plate above. However, the *sakaita* plate overlaps the opposite way from the others and that is why its name contains the word *saka*, which means 'reversed'.

---

238 The *machiuke* is at the bottom of the housing, near the base of the spine, and is fixed to the armour by means of the *nezumi* base plate. The *machiuke* supports the *ukezutsu*, which is a long housing section that takes the banner pole.

15

押着板

Oshitsuke no ita

Pressing plate

16

望光之板

Bōkō no ita

Upper back plate

17

クモデ

Kumode

Guiding frame for the banner pole

When the armour does not have an integrated long housing section down the back of the body armour,[239] you insert a separate housing part through here. Those made of wood are called *kumode* and metal ones are called *gattari* (合當離).

Commentator one

The name *gattari* [used for metal versions of this part] comes from the sound of iron striking something[240] – do not believe any other theories about this name.

18

エリ

Eri

Collar

---

239 This is referring to the *ukezutsu*.
240 Meaning that it is onomatopoeic.

CHAPTER TWENTY-SEVEN

A BREAKDOWN OF THE BODY ARMOUR AND PLATE NAMES

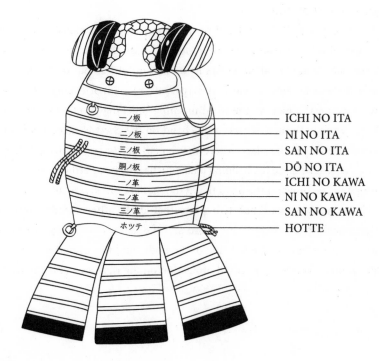

一ノ板 ——————— ICHI NO ITA
二ノ板 ——————— NI NO ITA
三ノ板 ——————— SAN NO ITA
胴ノ板 ——————— DŌ NO ITA
一ノ革 ——————— ICHI NO KAWA
二ノ革 ——————— NI NO KAWA
三ノ革 ——————— SAN NO KAWA
ホツテ ——————— HOTTE

一ノ板

Ichi no ita

First plate

This is also called *tsurubashiri no ita* – the plate where the bowstring scrapes.

Commentator one

It is so called because when you shoot an arrow, the bowstring scrapes along this part.

Archers have this plate covered with leather.

二ノ板

Ni no ita

Second plate

This is also called the *sendan no ita* (栴檀之板).

Commentator one

One theory says that this band on the body armour is called *sendan no ita* because this is the plate of good aroma, but I say that this is wrong. Another theory says that it is called *sendan no ita* because the colour of the thread here is of the *nioiito* style,[241] which is a type of gradational dyeing, and that the word *nioiito* is a play on the word meaning 'smelling good', but I believe this is *also* wrong. The actual reason this band on the chest is called *sendan no ita* is because this is the place where the *sendan no ita* [right] armpit protector hangs down. Because the hanging plate touches the body armour here, both the armpit protection and the band that it touches are called *sendan no ita*.

Take note, armour has two parts that derive their names from other components that touch them. These are: the *kotewa* (小手輪), which is the armpit protection on the left side of the body; and the *sendan no ita* [archaic ideograms], which is the armpit protection on the right side of the body.[242]

---

241 See the image on page 341.

242 The places where the two armpit protectors touch are named after the respective names of the hanging plates.

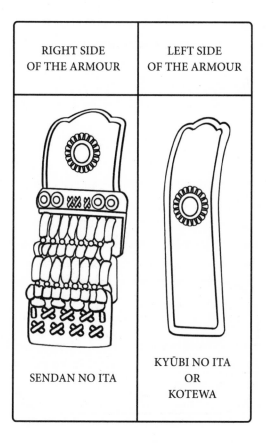

RIGHT SIDE OF THE ARMOUR	LEFT SIDE OF THE ARMOUR
SENDAN NO ITA	KYŪBI NO ITA OR KOTEWA

三ノ板

San no ita

Third plate

This is also called the *kyūbi no ita* (鳩尾之板), the band of the stomach [and is the position where a small plate covers the left armpit area].

Commentator one

Regarding the *ichi no kawa*, *ni no kawa* and *san no kawa* – the first, second and third leather plates – know that these were originally called *ichi no kiri*, *ni no kiri* and *san no kiri*. The word *kiri* was changed to *kawa*.[243]

---

243 The word *kiri* means 'to cut', which is something you would not want to do to your own armour. To avoid this negative connotation, the names were changed.

Avoid using the name *shi no ita* for the fourth plate, as the word *shi* sounds the same as the word for death. Use *dōita* instead.

Commentator two

The *kyūbi no ita* is so called because it touches the stomach area, which is called the *kyūbi*.

Issui-sensei says

In the area around the vertical joint of the body armour (*hikiawase*) on the right-hand side [there are names for the parts of armour that overlap each other]. The section that overlaps is known as the *ōdōsaki* (大胴先), while the section below it is called the *shōdōsaki* (小胴先). Also, there is a securing hinge (銓) on the left [which holds the armour together]. This style is called *omowaki* (表脇).

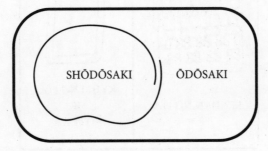

毛散
Gesan
Tassets
[The following points explain the parts called *gesan*, which are the tassets of the armour. See the image below.]

射向
Imuke no gesan
Left tasset

This is called the *imuke no gesan* (射向之毛散) – the tasset at the front when shooting.

メテノケサン
Mete no gesan
Right tasset

This is called the *mete no gesan* (馬手之毛散), the tasset of the right, but may also be called the *ōdōsaki no gesan* (大胴先之毛散).

睾丸隠
Kinkakushi
Testicle-covering tasset

Issui-sensei says

The term *kusazuri* (草摺) grass-touching plate is used to refer to the bottom band of the tasset plates, but remember that the general name for the tassets is *gesan*.[244]

It is desirable to line and stitch the back of the tassets with leather or cotton. If you wish, you can line only the bottom band. There are oral traditions here.

Commentator two

If tassets are not lined, [the sound they make] when they hit the saddle may startle the horse, or they may become cumbersome when walking. [The sound] will be especially disadvantageous during night raids, so tassets should be lined and stitched.

---

244 In modern terminology these terms are interchangeable. The writer is making it clear that the *kusazuri* is the lowest band of the *gesan*, which are the tassets.

發傳

Hotte

Lowest band on the armour

The *hotte* is the lowest plate of the body armour and it should be curved outwards. This curve is called the *yaridomari* – spear stopper. It is best if it is a steep curve.

Commentator two

A steep curve is good as it will deflect an enemy spear thrust that might otherwise pierce [your armour]. Such a blow is called a *nagare-yari* – glancing spear. If the bottom of the armour has a steep curve, know that it will be effective. The distance between you and an enemy is normally greater than you think. Know that seven or eight out of ten spear strikes delivered in a half-hearted way will glance off. Multiple thrusts that glance off, be it by yourself or the enemy, will simply continue on their path [if done half-heartedly]. If such a glancing strike happens to move towards the groin area, be warned it may go through and beneath where the quiver is secured (*neo-shita*). Therefore, [to avoid glancing blows stabbing into your groin,] this part has a steep curve called the *yaridomari* spear stopper. Make sure to have this in place.

Lining

The leather lining inside the body armour is called the *ukebari* (浮張). It is best to apply gold leaf on the inside [of the armour] below the lining; this will help protect from sunlight.

Commentator two

As for applying gold leaf, it is the same as described in the chapter on helmets. Gold will resist the heat and will help prevent arrows or bullets from penetrating too easily.

Thongs and fastenings

The *kotetsuke no kohaze* thongs and fastenings for the armoured sleeves need to be as robust as possible. They should be made from hemp or tanned dog hide or you can use a *sageo* sword cord instead.

Commentator one

Monkey leather is stronger than dog hide.

Commentator two

All cords should be strong, but armoured sleeve fastenings are especially important. If these break, your armoured sleeves (*kote*) will sag, which can be harmful. You should consider this.

Sliding rivets

There are plates on the body armour [that are secured differently]. These are the top pair of bands on the chest (胸二段) and the *hotte* – the lowest band. Bind these in the *agake* (アガケ) style, which uses rivets that can slide within a slot [to allow freedom of movement].

Commentator one

This [extra movement given by the sliding rivets] helps when engaged in *kumiuchi* grappling.

Commentator two

The primary benefit of this is for *kumiuchi* grappling. [However, details] are transmitted in another scroll. Also, these sliding rivets are good for movement when riding.[245]

Carry bags

It is best to keep your *hanagami bukuro* cloth carry bags underneath your tasset.

Commentator one

Such bags should be positioned to each side or could even go under all three tassets.

---

245 The translation of this last sentence is hypothetical. The sentence contains the word *kuradama* (鞍玉), meaning 'saddle and ball', which we believe may refer to the rotational motion of horse-riding.

Commentator two

These carry bags should be positioned underneath your tasset. This is done for the same reason as lining the tassets, as mentioned above [i.e. to muffle the sound of the tassets clanking when you move].

Tasset cords

Since ancient times the cords that connect the tassets to each other[246] have been 1 *sun* 5 *bu* long. However, these days the length has changed.

Commentator two

Whereas the length was about 1 *sun* 5 *bu* in olden days, today it should be between 2 *sun* 5 *bu* and 3 *sun*. In ancient times warriors used to secure their armour with their outer sash. Present-day armour is secured with *kurijime* cords and therefore longer tasset cords are required.

Shoulder cord covers

The *gyōyō* (杏葉) is a small clasp placed over the fasteners for the *aibiki* cords [which connect the two halves of the armour over the shoulders]. This is to protect the cords and the fastener at the shoulders.

Commentator one

In ancient times this was made in the shape of plum leaves or the leaves of the *karamomo* plant.[247] Its function is to cover the cord of the *aibiki* connecting sections [at the shoulder]. It is still made in this way today; the name comes from the leaf of the plum tree – *gyōyō*.

高紐

Takahimo
Side securing cords

There is nothing of note to record about the *takahimo* cords [beyond what has been said].

---

246 *Yurugi no ito* (揺糸).
247 *Mycga Zingiber mioga* (Japanese ginger).

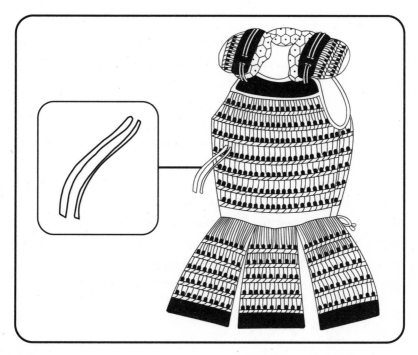

真之圖

Sane no zu

Different types of *sane* plates

[The following are the various patterns formed by Japanese armour lacing:]

ケビキ

Kebiki

Complete lacings with no gaps[248]

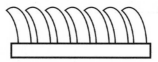

---

248 Other versions of this lacing style may allow some plates to show through.

ヒシトヂ
Hishitoji
Lacing with cross stitching

ムナメトヂ
Munametoji
Lacing with horizontal straight stitching

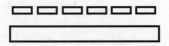

Commentator three

The above three are types of lacing, whereas the following are ways to form the *sane* plate itself.

小サ子
Kozane
Small plates

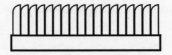

中サ子
Chūzane
Middle-sized plates

矢筈頭
Yahazugashira
Arrow-nock-shaped plates

山道
Yamamichi
Mountainous-path-shaped plates

碁石頭
Goishigashira
***Go*-stone-shaped plates**

Commentator one

Larger versions of the above *goishigashira*-style (碁石頭) plates are called *hiroshimagashira* (廣嶋頭) today.

金比中真

Kanai-chūzane[249]

Notched middle-sized plates

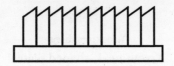

Commentator two

The term *odoshige* (威毛) is used to describe the lacing in armour. [The ideograms used imply a powerful, intimidating presence.] This word and its ideograms conjure the image of animal hair – think of the way a boar's hair bristles when the boar is in a state of anger. People wear these lacings to stir dauntless courage within themselves and to intimidate the enemy, just as an animal does with its bristling hair.

Back plate

The name for the entire back plate of the body armour is the *oshitsuke* (押付). The plate curves inwards, which is called *semizo* (セミソ) the grooved back; it is recommended that you wear a back plate with a deep groove.

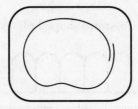

---

249 This final version appears only in the Koga transcription.

Commentator two

The name of the *oshitsuke* back plate implies that a warrior pushes forcefully forward when advancing. Ones with a deeply curved back are more comfortable to wear.

Hidden bag

Beneath the *kotekakushi* shoulder cover you should attach a small bag called the *shinobi-bukuro* (忍袋) the hidden bag[250] – this is an oral tradition.

Commentator two

In our school, we put the *kaginawa* grappling iron in a hidden bag under this part of the armour. It is beneficial to have the *kaginawa* grappling iron at this higher position [instead of at the waist], especially when pinning an enemy.

Commentator three

The hidden bag is the place to keep your *hayanawa* quick-rope and *kaginawa* grappling iron.

Correct armour size

Generally, armour should be at the smaller end [of your size] and the length should be short – this is an oral tradition.

Commentator two

The teaching for this is that you should wear tighter armour, because armour that fits well at the beginning of a campaign will stretch and become loose after hard fighting. Therefore, armour that feels tight to begin with will fit better over time. There is also a teaching about *kisenaga* (着長) armour for lord-commanders.

Hayagusoku quick armour is to wear the long and short swords on top of the *shitagi* undershirt and then to put on the *dō* body armour on top of these. This is an oral tradition.[251]

---

250 The Odawara transcription calls this the *shinobi-nawa* – hidden rope.
251 Normally swords go on the outside of armour.

Commentator three

On a long campaign people normally lose weight. Therefore, looser-fitting armour is not desirable.

Banners

Concerning the banner housing (請筒): there is nothing special about this to record. However, know that the *hikae no o* supporting cord is used to secure the banner on the back. This is an oral tradition.

Commentator one

It is best to use bamboo for banner poles, as this will allow you to move them in and out of position freely. When waiting [for the enemy] do not remove the banner without proper consideration and furthermore there is a specific way to remove it – each soldier should be aware of this.

Commentator two

This should be orally transmitted when putting on armour. Use a longer pole when on foot and a shorter one when mounted.

CHAPTER TWENTY-EIGHT

具足之惣名之事
Gusoku no sōmyō no koto

NAMING ARMOUR

Commentator one

Generally armour without lacing on the body armour is called *susogane no gusoku* (スソ金ノ具足).

Commentator two

Gusoku (具足) is the modern form [of armour], but in ancient times there was *yoroi* (鎧) and *kogusoku* (小具足). *Kogusoku* means 'reduced armour' and is not fully sufficient [for protection], while *yoroi* is oversized. *Gusoku* (具足) – modern compact armour – took elements of both of the older styles. The following text explains the kinds [and names] of *yoroi* – archaic styles. Although *yoroi* is not in use any more, these terms are now also used for *gusoku*.

著長[252]

Kisenaga

Great armour for the *taishō* commander

This has gold plates and cord lashings of purple. It is the name for the armour used by the *taishō*.

Commentator one

The [lacing on this armour] is called *murasaki odoshi* purple lashings, while

---

252 The ideograms 着長 are used in the Koga transcription.

the plates are gold. However, the name varies according to the colour of the thread. For example, it may be called *asagi-odoshi* – threads of pale blue. In ancient times [purple and gold] was not used by anyone below the third rank of the court.

[Terms for the armour of nobility]
The term to describe the back of armour for noble people is the *kisei* (著背) – this does not represent full armour but only the rear. The front of the armour for nobles is called the *makkō* (真向). The left side of the armour for the nobility is called the *imuke* (射向), while the right side is called the *katte* (勝手).

[Terms for the armour of normal soldiers]
The front of armour for normal soldiers is also called the *hamukō* (羽向), the left is called the *yunde* (弓手) and the right is called the *mete* (馬手).

Issui-sensei says

Armour with purple lacing and gold plates is called *goten'iro yoroi* (御天色鎧) – palace armour. Furthermore, armour with gold plates and pale-blue, purple or red threads are worn by generals, including those above the position of *jijū* chamberlain – it was forbidden for normal *samurai* to wear [this armour]. As recorded in the historical traditions of both Japan and China, to be given permission to wear purple and red is an honour. However, [Confucius says]:

悪紫奪朱
Purple is not appropriate to be used instead of red.[253]

Commentator two

Gold plates are respected because gold is yellow in colour and therefore [according to the Five Elements theory] it belongs to the element of Earth, which governs the four directions. Purple is a neutral colour as it is a mixture of red and black[254]

---

253 The five proper colours of China are, in alphabetical order: black (黒), blue (青), red (赤), white (白) and yellow (黄).

254 Although this seems counter-intuitive, as red and blue, not red and black, are mixed to make purple, we have left this text the way it appears in the original. Note also that these

and is therefore a combination of the elements of *in* and *yō*. In China, purple is disliked because it steals from red, but in Japan it is regarded as a distinguished colour. In both *yoroi* archaic armour and *gusoku* compact armour, the name *kisenaga* (著長) is given to the armour of the *taishō* commander. This is because the second ideogram, 長, is also read as *osa*, which means 'a leader of people'. The term *kisenaga* comes from [two ideograms in] the phrase:

衆長嘆美

A leader of people should admire beauty.

The term used for connecting [armour together] with lacing is *kebiki* (ケヒキ). Furthermore, the style of armour known as *tatenashi* – armour of full protection[255] – was used by the warrior Shinra Saburō Yoshimitsu.

甲州成
Kōshūnari
Kōshū-style armour
This style is larger around the chest.

Commentator one

Kōshūnari means armour in the style used in the area of Kōshū. It is so named because it was invented by Kōshū *samurai*.

Commentator two

Kōshūnari – the armour of the Kōshū area – was used mainly in the Takeda clan. This is a form of *yoroi* archaic armour called *tatenashi*, which was handed down through the Takeda clan. This single type is broader around the chest and allows for better breathing.

Tatenashi was one of the eight [great] armours of the Genji clan. Here is the full list [followed by explanations of each one]:[256]

---

colours relate to Five Element theory.

255 The ideograms mean 'armour that does not need a shield'.

256 The *Genji-hachiryō* (源氏八領) eight sets of armour are considered as treasures of the Takeda clan.

1. *tsukikazu* 月数
2. *hikazu* 日数
3. *genta ga ubuginu* 源太が産着
4. *hachiryō* 八竜
5. *omodaka* 沢瀉
6. *hizamaru* 膝丸
7. *usukane* 薄金
8. *tatenashi* 楯無

月数
Tsukikazu

This armour originally had thirteen metal panels (金物), but these were reduced to just twelve. There are no loose small plates (*sane*) in this style, as all sections are fixed together firmly. This is what is called *hotoke no dō* Buddha-style armour or *okegawa* barrel-style armour.

日数
Hikazu

Hikazu armour has sixty panels (間) and 300 studs (星).

源太が産着
Genta ga ubuginu

[*Genta ga ubuginu* armour was given by the court to Hachiman Tarō Yoshiie (1039–1106) when he was born and is named thus because Yoshiie's name as an adolescent was Genta.]

八竜
Hachiryō

[*Hachiryō* armour, literally 'eight dragons', is so called because it has three golden dragons on the front and five golden dragons on the rear.]

沢瀉
Omodaka
[No details about this armour are known.]

膝丸
Hizamaru
[*Hizamaru* armour is made of leather plates laced together. The leather came from the knees of cattle.]

薄金
Usukane
[*Usukane* is made of very thin iron plates, but has good defensive strength.]

楯無
Tatenashi
Tatenashi armour was transmitted by Shinra Saburō Yoshimitsu [who was the third son of Minamoto no Yoriyoshi]. Later [the armour] was idolized as a representation of an incomparable god of war and the shape of the armour was copied thereafter.

[This is the end of the description of the eight great armours of the Genji clan].

胴丸
Dōmaru
Rounded body armour
This is similar to *okegawa* bucket armour, which opens at the side.

Commentator two
Since ancient times [such armour] was made with rivets and the rivet heads were flattened [to make the body flush]. This way of riveting is associated with the *haramaki* style of armour.[257]

---

257 The position of this commentary is unclear in the original manual, but we believe it might belong here.

四枚金胴

Shimaikanadō

Body armour of four iron plates

This type has four vertical iron plates joined with hinges.

小具足

Kogusoku

Reduced armour

This existed in ancient times and was worn below [other sections of] armour. The body section is flexible, while below the waist is chain mail. The gauntlets (*kote*) should reach up to the elbow and the tassets should be divided into three front sections.

Commentator one

Kogusoku reduced armour used to exist in ancient times but has now faded from use. There is a part of armour called an *omodakaodoshi* (沢瀉威), which is an iron fitting [but this is also a form of lacing in a triangular pattern]. *Kirinodai* – the foxglove leaf base plate – is the name of another iron fitting.

小真

Kozane

Small plates

These should be joined together using the method called *aigasane kebiki* (逢重毛引) – overlapping lacing.[258] Furthermore, the way of flexible binding is called *yurugizane* (揺真), and the style known as *kanai* (金ヒ) is to have single plates with notches at the top [to imitate multiple plates laced together].[259]

---

258 This is the common way to lace together individual small plates to make up classical Japanese armour.

259 The first method is to fully lace the plates of the armour so that they are bound tight; the second is to lace only the bottom parts of each plate so that they are more flexible; while the third is to have fewer and larger individual plates, but with cut outs at the top of each plate to give the illusion of a greater number of smaller sections.

Commentator one

To work out whether plates have been fastened together with two, three or five layers of thread in the style of *yurugi* flexible armour, simply try to manipulate them with your fingers.

Concerning *dōmaru* – rounded body armour of individual horizontal bands: this has nine bands of iron that are hammered out and bound together with lashings or pegs.

Concerning *kanai* (金比) – single plates that look like multiple plates laced together: know that each section of these plates is hammered out. [When constructing armour,] these should not overlap each other. Both the upper and the lower sections should be rounded. This is an old type of armour.

Commentator two

When manipulated with the fingers, *yurugizane* flexible construction will move, whereas *kanai* single-plate construction will not. In our school we use *yurugizane*.

矢筈頭
Yahazugashira
Arrow-nock-shaped plates

This is a type of plate that has cut outs along the top in the shape of arrow nocks. These plates need to be bound together with a method called *nuinobe* (縫延).

裳濃[260]
Susogo
Lacing with the darkest colour at the bottom

This pertains to the colours used on the *koshisandan*, which is the bottom band on the body armour, and also on the bottom plates of the tassets. These plates are joined together with indigo-blue thread. If the *koshinidan* on the body armour is bound with indigo-blue thread, know that this should still be considered as *susogo* lacing.

---

260 The Koga text uses the ideograms 裾濃.

Commentator one

The reason why indigo blue is used is because of a man called Tamate no Minema from the area of Shinobugun in Ōshū, who presented armour of this *susogo* style to the court.

Commentator two

Susogo lacing is indigo thread in three bands from the waist upwards [and also the same system is used] on the bottom bands of the tassets. There are various theories as to why this lacing style is followed, but we believe it is because it is associated with the element of *in*.

腹巻

Haramaki

Ancient armour which fastens at the rear

This is an older form of armour, which opens at the rear. This style has strings to pull and secure at the shoulders and at the waist.

Commentator one

This has a *kōhei no ita* rear protection plate [which covers the rear fastening]. This is also called the *tamadare no ita*, the plate of the hanging pearl, but craftsmen call it *okubyō ita* – the coward's plate. This plate covers the joint at the rear of the armour.

Commentator two

The plate used to cover the joint at the rear of the armour is called the *kōhei* (甲塗)[261] or the *tamadare no ita* (玉垂ノ板), the plate of the hanging pearl, but it is also commonly known as *okubyō no ita* – the coward's plate.

火威

Hiodoshi

Orange armour with red lacing

These are red threads for *shugusoku* (朱具足) red armour.

---

261 *Kōhei* is not a common reading for these ideograms.

Commentator one

One theory says that *hiodoshi* means to lash [armour] with pale-blue threads because water connects with fire [in the Cycle of Destruction]. However, [thinking that this type of armour has pale-blue threads] is a drastic error to make. In ancient times the warrior Hatakeyama gave a complete set of [red] armour to Nakamura Shinbei, and since then red armour has been regarded as the mark of a brave warrior. Nakamura Shinbei was called Yari Nakamura – Nakamura of the spear.

There is also another type of armour [with the similar-sounding name] *hiuoodoshi* (氷魚威)[262] and this is made of silver plates lashed together with red lacings [giving it a red-and-white effect].

During the battle of Ujigawa, the warrior Minamoto no Yorimasa saw three enemy warriors being carried away in the flow of the river Ujigawa. At this, his son Izu no kami Nakatsuna wrote the following poem:

伊勢武者ハ皆火威ノ鎧キテ宇治ノ網代ニ懸リケルカナ
The warriors from Ise who were in armour of the hiodoshi style
were caught in the fishing nets of the river Uji.[263]

This poem means that they looked like *ayu* fish caught in wickerwork traps in the river. Based on this episode, I think the style of *hiodoshi* [which is normally pure red armour has variations comprising] gold or silver plates with red

---

262 There is a further reading; however, the ideograms do not exist in modern Japanese.

263 This issue is complex. The main text lists a type of orange-red armour with red lacing known as fire lacing (火威). This armour is called *hiodoshi* (ひおどし). However, *both* commentators mention a slightly different-sounding version called *hiuoodoshi* (ひうおおどし) – fish lacing. This is a type of armour with gold or silver plates and red lacing, like the silver-and-red *ayu* fish (*Plecoglossus altivelis*). Commentator one guesses from the poem that the warriors were wearing a type of armour that made them look like *ayu* fish. From this he appears to surmise that the *hiodoshi* style did not have to involve orange armour with red lacing, but that it could include other colour combinations, such as, in this case, silver or gold armour with red lacing. In short, samurai themselves were often confused between *hiodoshi* and *hiuoodoshi* armour as the two words sound almost the same. Simply understand that lacing of different colours has different meanings and that some types have, over time, become confused. The main text *and* the Natori-Ryū encyclopedia both define *hiodoshi* as armour with orange plates and red lacing, but the commentators here give an alternative version based on classical poetry.

lacings. Know that the stitches should be *muname* (ムナメ) straight stiches or *hishitoji* (ヒシトヂ) cross stiches and that the hem should have a *takuboku* (啄木) dappled pattern. The word *hiuo* or *hio* [which makes up a part of the name of the armour] is the name of a small fish that lives in the river Ujigawa and that is caught with wickerwork traps. The *Genpei Seisuiki* document mentions this type of wickerwork in a tale about the Heike clan forces being surrounded and finding it difficult to escape.

Commentator two

There is a theory that the colour of this armour is actually silver and red, or red with white threads, and that it is called *hiuoodoshi* (氷魚威), meaning 'lacings like a young *ayu* fish'. Around the period of Jishō (1178–1181), the warrior Minamoto no Yorimasa served Prince Takakura at the battle of Ujigawa where he destroyed a bridge. Then, looking at the drowning *samurai* of the Heiji clan [more commonly known as Heike], Yorimasa's son, the warrior Nakatsuna, composed a poem about fishing for young *ayu* fish in the river Ujigawa:

伊勢武者ハ皆氷魚威ノ鎧キテ宇治ノ網代ニカカリコソスレ
The warriors from Ise in armour of the hiodoshi style
were caught in the fishing nets of the river Uji.

It is said that 'the warriors in the river were wearing *hiodoshi* (火威) armour' [which is red], but it should be read as 'the warriors in the river were wearing *hiuo* (氷魚) armour' [which is red and white]. Therefore, it seems many warriors of Ise were wearing *hiuoodoshi* (氷魚威) armour, which is red and white. The name *hiuo* (氷魚) refers to the young *ayu* fish, which comes from the river Ujigawa and can look like a goldfish. The site [where the warriors drowned] was in Uji and their armour was red and white [just like the fish], which inspired Nakatsuna to write this excellent poem.

卯花威

Unohana odoshi

Threads of the flowers of the Deutzia plant[264]

This is the custom of wearing white threads with silver armour. Armour with light-yellow threads mixed here and there also comes under this style.

Commentator two

This style has light-yellow thread like the flowers of this plant.

小櫻威

Kozakura odoshi

Cherry blossom threads

This armour has white threads on the top two layers, pink threads on the three middle layers and *asagi* pale-yellow threads on the bottom two plates of the shoulder guard. Armour with gold plates and a mixture of red and white lacing is also called by this name.

Commentator one

The style of *kozakura* (小櫻), small cherry blossoms, has plates that are connected with threads of different colours. A variation called *go'on-odoshi* (五音威) is inspired by the five Chinese musical notes. It uses five different coloured threads, one for each layer. Then there is also *momiji gasane* (紅葉重), threads of the maple leaf, which has red threads on the top rows and white threads on the bottom rows. This may also have pale-blue flashings here and there in some cases.

Commentator two

There are various theories about *kozakura odoshi* – cherry blossom threads. Across all types of armour there are thirteen kinds of metal fittings and [one theory is] that armour having cherry-blossom-shaped rivets is known by this name. Another theory states that this armour has metal fittings with fine engravings of cherry blossoms on them.

---

264 *Deutzia crenata.*

裙縄目

Fushinawame

Diagonal lacing

This [armour] has gold [or simply metal] plates bound with *takuboku no ito* – dappled threads.

Commentator one

The term *takuboku* (啄木) used in the description above means woodpecker. The thread is named thus because it is dappled, like the holes pecked into a tree by a woodpecker.

Commentator two

This was named after the woodpecker, which makes scars on trees that look just like this pattern.

黒火威

Kurohi odoshi

Black armour with red lacings

This has black plates and red threads.

黒糸威

Kuroito odoshi

Black lacing

This has gold (金) plates with black threads.

黒革威

Kurokawa odoshi

Black leather thongs

This is black armour with black lacing. Sometimes it has dark- or light-yellow threads instead.

大荒目

Ōarame

Larger plates and lacings

This style comes under the *dōmaru* classification, which is rounded body armour. It is used with *nuinobe* (縫延) plate connections.

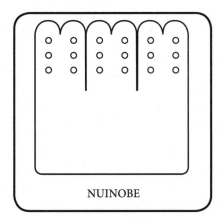

NUINOBE

Commentator one

[The plates of this armour] are wrapped with leather finished with a crushed effect. This *dōmaru* rounded body armour is made in a form called *nuikugumi* (縫クヽミ).

Commentator two

Ōarame is a style [of binding thread with] *nuinobe* (縫延) plates and has a crushed leather finish (絞皮). The shape of the armour comes under the *dōmaru* rounded-body classification. The effect on the armour looks like *arame* seaweed.

赤革威

Akagawa odoshi

Red armour with pale-yellow lacings

This armour has red plates with *asagi* (絧) lacing [which is yellow].

佛之胴

Hotoke no dō

Buddha's body

This has a [smooth] rust-coloured body bound together with rivets (鋲).

Commentator one

Sometimes armour in the *hotoke no dō* Buddha's body style has diagonally stitched bindings.

Commentator two

It is said by some that the *hotoke no dō* Buddha's body style is the same as the *tatenashi* style.

胸目威

Muname odoshi

Horizontal lacings

Leather thongs are used for this. This is the same as *hishitoji* (菱綴) cross-stitch binding.

絞革包

Shibokawa zutsumi

Armour plates with a crushed leather finish

[These plates are] have a covering of crushed leather.

Commentator one

There are two types of finish for this:

1. *ōshibo* 大シホ – rough textured
2. *koshibo* 小シホ – fine textured

Commentator two

These [are plates] covered with crushed leather.

洗革威

Araikawa odoshi

Tanned deer leather thongs

This armour has rust-coloured plates bound in *orame* larger stitches with pale-blue[265] lacing (薄浅黄).

Commentator one

The document *Musha Monogatari*[266] says that this form is bound with pale-pink lacings (薄紅梅).

Commentator two

Araikawa processed leather resembles seaweed that has been washed ashore. It also carries connotations of gracefulness and purification by water.

肩白威

Katajiro odoshi

White lacings on the top two bands of the body armour

This is to have white lacing on the *katanidan* (肩二段), the two highest bands of the body armour, but to have red lacings on the lower bands.

Commentator two

This is considered as *yō no gusoku* – armour of the element of *yō*. According to one theory, this style has diagonal lacing as shown in the image below.

The word *katanidan* used previously refers to the top two bands of the body armour, but this excludes the *kobire* [which is a small pad around the shoulder area].

---

265 The colour of this lacing is debated and confusion was evident in the medieval period. The Natori-Ryū encyclopedia shows almost white lacing.

266 Published in English as *Samurai War Stories* by the authors.

烈鳥威

Kashidori odoshi

Lacings of the colour of the Japanese jay[267]

This [armour] has black plates bound with pale blue lacing (*asagi*).

Commentator two

This is so named because its colour is similar to that of the Japanese jay.

山吹威

Yamabuki odoshi

Japanese-rose-coloured lacings[268]

This [armour] has black plates bound with yellow lacings.

Commentator one[269]

According to the *I Ching*, yellow [or gold] is the colour of peace and is at the centre [in Five Element theory]. This is because the colour gold represents the Earth element, which gives birth to all trees and plants. Another theory states that yellow is the colour of impartiality and a gentle nature. Therefore, lords should wear yellow clothes as it is considered to be an important and honourable colour. The *Original Record of Sui* mentioned this in connection with Emperor Wen of Sui. According to the *Taiheiki* war chronicle, Emperor Gomurakami wore armour with yellow lacings when he fought with Ashikaga Yoshiakira in Hachiman.[270] Both in Japan and China gold is the colour of honour because gold represents the Earth element and governs the centre.

Commentator two

One theory says that this *yamabuki* flower grows along watersides and, because the colour associated with the element of Water is black and the colour yellow is

---

267 *Garrulus glandarius.*

268 *Kerria japonica.*

269 In this section the commentator switches between yellow (黄) and gold (金).

270 Although normally the name of a deity, in this case Hachiman appears to be referring to a place, probably Kyōto.

associated with gold and gold belongs to metal, this mixture creates a situation of generation in the Cycle of Creation.[271]

[The type of lacing] called *kuchiba* is to have red vertical threads and yellow horizontal threads.

緗菫威[272]

Shōkin odoshi

Armour with light yellow threads

This is black armour with pale-yellow lacing. Two layers of the shoulder guard have white lacing and the rest graduates to a darker-yellow colour.

[シナ]皮威[273]

Shinagawa odoshi

Threads of reddish tree bark

This is reddish-orange (橙) and has a leather covering with a crushed finish and also has diagonal lacings (縄目) of whitish-yellow. It is said that this form originated in the area of Obata, in Bushū, during the reign of the fifty-first emperor, Emperor Heijō.

Commentator one

The colour is that of the bark of trees called *shina*, which is reddish.

Commentator two

This tree is also called *shinakaki* (シナカキ).[274]

---

271 According to the commentator, the reasoning for this colour combination is based on the Cycle of Creation. Water, which is represented by the colour black, nourishes Earth, which is represented by the colour yellow/gold. Thus, the black plates are in a creative relationship with the yellow threads. This is an example of *samurai* armour drawing on *yin–yang* theory.

272 Possibly uses the ideogram 菫 but uses 緗匂威 in the Koga transcription.

273 The meaning of the first ideogram is not known, and therefore just the phonetic marker has been placed here.

274 We believe that the 'reddish tree' referred to in the original scroll and by the two commentators is a small species of persimmon (*Diospyros japonica Siebold et Zucc.*).

唐錦威

Karanishiki odoshi

Chinese brocade lacing

This form can be bound with lacing made of *gomengawa* (御免革) leather and has gold plates. Alternatively, it has iron plates with red lacings.

Commentator two

Gomengawa (御免皮) mentioned above[275] is purple-dyed leather with a fine pattern, while *shōheigawa* (承平皮) is light-yellow/beige leather with a fine pattern.

天狗具足

Tengu gusoku

Goblin armour

This has layered [scale-like] plates in the shape of feather [tips] that have been stitched to cloth.[276]

Commentator one

Tengu gusoku goblin armour originated in the Negoro-ji temple. It is round in shape and is on the whole like a bucket.[277]

Commentator two

This [armour] is made of leather or iron [semi-]oval-shaped pieces sewn onto cloth [creating a scale or feather effect]. The image below shows what each plate looks like:

---

275 Albeit with slightly different ideograms (the reason for the difference is not known).

276 This is what Western people term lamellar armour or, more colloquially, scale armour. However, it is meant to represent feathers as the *tengu* goblin can take the form of a crow.

277 Not literally a bucket, but this is simply implying the shape of the cross section.

桶カワ[278]

Okegawa

Barrel-like armour

This is made with [thin iron sheets] hammered out. There are various points on how to construct this.

Commentator two

This [armour] consists of vertical iron plates constructed like a barrel.

It is called *okegawa* barrel style because it consists of thin plates jointed in an overlapping way.

Issui-sensei says

The above points are concerned with the different colours for the lacing of armour and this knowledge has been transmitted from ancient times. Modern lacings are designed for their aesthetic appeal [and according to personal taste] and derive their names from the main colours used.

Commentator two

The above points are traditional principles that have been transmitted from ancient times. In our modern times there are no set principles in place any more and as a result things are in a state of flux and variation. Such modern colour schemes should be named based on the major colours used.

[The different variations of armour:]

- For helmets (*kabuto*) there are more than eighty variations.
- For armour (*gusoku*) there are forty-eight variations.
- For faceguards (*hōate*) there are six variations.
- For gauntlets (*kote*) there are twelve variations.
- For greaves (*suneate*) there are three variations.

---

278 The ideograms in the Koga transcription are 桶側.

CHAPTER TWENTY-NINE

鎧之事
Yoroi no koto

ARCHAIC ARMOUR

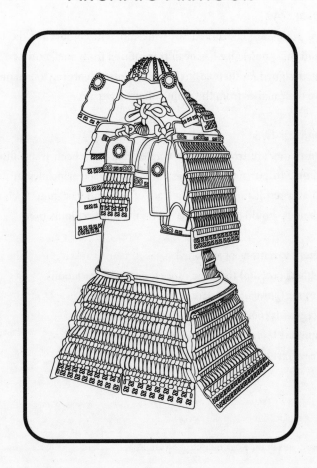

This is larger than normal [compact] armour (*gusoku*) and was the armour worn by *taishō* commanders in ancient times. In the present day this armour is not actually worn but instead is displayed as part of the *taishō*'s war gear in the 'inner chamber'[279] during a campaign. One theory says that this should be displayed together with a mirror as an offering to the gods and that the *taishō* should celebrate the gods of war there.

Yoroi archaic armour has a ring on the back which is used to attach an *agemaki* cord. It has four tasset sections, which cover all four sides, just like normal armour (*tsune no gusoku*).

The four tassets of *yoroi* armour:[280]
1. *yurugi no ita* 揺之板 – the plate of flexibility [front tasset]
2. *hisshiki* 引敷 – the rear covering
3. *yunde no waidate* 弓手之脇楯 – the left shield
4. *mete no kusazuri* 馬手之草摺 – the right grass-touching plate

Commentator one
The *agemaki* [cord attached to the rear of armour] is actually named after an [ancient] hair style for children where the hair is parted in the middle and has a loop on each side of the head.

Commentator two
These ways are ancient; even the methods of correct lacing have been lost [to many] now. In our school the tradition has remained and it is transmitted using a model.

Yoroi archaic armour is tremendously grand, takes extreme effort and requires a vast amount of attention, which is why it is not so common these days.

---

279 *Jōdan no ma* (上段ノ間), a raised floor space in a *shoin*-style room – the position where the person of the highest rank sits.

280 In all transcriptions this list of four is given in the *ōsode* – larger shoulder section, however it most likely concerns the four tassets and has been moved to this position.

Issui-sensei says

Ōsode larger shoulder guards should be held in place by tying them to the *agemaki* cord at the rear [of the armour], but know that there are formal and informal ways to tie them. The names [for these parts of *yoroi* armour] are [generally] the same as for *gusoku* armour.

Also, the shape [of *yoroi* armour] is similar to that of *gusoku* armour. [*Yoroi* armour] has a ring called the *agemaki no kan*, which is for the *agemaki* cord. This is positioned centrally on the back, on the second plate from the top (二之板). The base where the ring [for the cord] is installed is called the *uraita*, the rear base plate, or alternatively it is called the *daiza no kane*, the metal base plate.

Commentator two

The *ōsode* larger shoulder guards should be held with the *agemaki* cord, by attaching them with a knot called the *tombo musubi* (蜻蛉結) – the dragonfly knot. The informal way spoken of above is the normal dragonfly knot (常ノトンホウ), while the formal way is the *sutra* dragonfly knot (シュタラ蜻蛉結).

The *agemaki* cord represents fire, so it should always be red for its association to the *myōō* (明王), who are the wisdom kings. [Another reason it is red] is because the *agemaki* cord was originally called the *tōhō musubi* – the eastern knot. East is the direction of sunrise and the sun looks like fire when it is rising, so the colour is defined [as red].

The *ōsode* were used in ancient times, but these larger shoulder guards fell out of use during the reigns of Lord Nobunaga, Lord Hideyoshi and Lord [Takeda] Shingen, because they restrict movement. [Earlier,] in the reigns of Lord [Minamoto no] Yoritomo and Lord [Ashikaga] Takauji, the intricacies of such matters were not investigated.

Issui-sensei says

[Two] small metal protective plates of a similar size to the *yodarekane* (ヨダレ金) neck protector should be hung at the front and held in position [at armpit level] from the *aibiki* shoulder cords. These small [armpit] protectors help to prevent the *aibiki* cords from being cut off and are meant to cover the openings on the sides [around the armpit area]. The one on the left is called the *kotewa* (小手輪)[281] and the one on the right is called the *sendan no ita* (栴檀之板).

Commentator two

The above is transmitted with a model [in our school]. Such matters are passed down secretly within warrior families.

大袖之事
Ōsode no koto

LARGER SHOULDER GUARDS

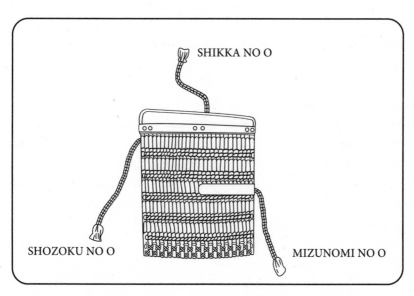

SHIKKA NO O

SHOZOKU NO O

MIZUNOMI NO O

These shoulder guards should be 1 *shaku* 2 *sun* long and 1 *shaku* wide.

[The cords of the *ōsode* larger shoulder guard are named as follows:][282]

---

281 This is more commonly known as the *kyūbi no ita*.
282 Only three names have been given, whereas other Natori-Ryū scrolls show four cords.

- [The cord at the top centre inside of the shoulder guard that connects the guard to the shoulder itself is called the] *shikka no o* (志加之緒). This should be 1 *shaku* 2 *sun* long. How to tie the knot and connect it is an orally transmitted tradition.
- [The cord on the front that connects to the chest area is called the] *shōzoku no o* (装束之緒). This should be 1 *shaku* 2 *sun* long. How to tie the knot and connect it is an orally transmitted tradition.
- [The cord to connect the shoulder guard to the *agemaki* cord on the back plate is called the] *mizunomi no o* (水呑之緒). [This is found on the rear edge of the shoulder guard and] should be 1 *shaku* 2 *sun* long. How to tie the knot and connect it is also an orally transmitted tradition.

This style of shoulder guard is not used with *gusoku* armour and how to tie these cords are passed down in secret within military families.

Commentator one

[The attachable and removable] version of this shoulder guard is called the *okisode* (置袖).

Commentator two

This way is now out of use in modern times, because it offers too little manoeuvrability. Therefore, *kisenaga* commander's display armour and *ōsode* larger shoulder guards are now worn only on ceremonial occasions. These older styles were used because of their capacity to defend against arrows and projectiles.[283]

The fourth cord not named here is commonly known as the *kakeo* (懸緒).

283 This is commonly understood as a bullet. However, this style of armour was fashionable before muskets arrived in Japan. Therefore, it is not known whether 'projectile' refers to something shot from an archaic firearm, or some other form of missile, such as a stone.

小手之事
Kote no koto

GAUNTLETS

Gauntlets with *kosode* lesser shoulder guards attached are called *bishamon kote*, the gauntlets of the god Bishamon, while those without attached shoulder guards are called *oda-gote*, the gauntlets of Oda.

PARTS OF THE ARMOURED SLEEVE AND SHOULDER GUARD

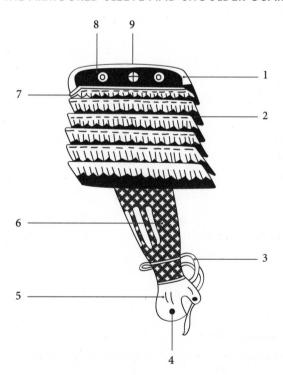

1

冠ノ板

Kamuri no ita

Crown plate

2

志加之鐶

Shikka no kan

Ring for the *shikka* cord

[The *shikka* cord is shown in the previous image.]

3

手首ノ紐

Tekubi no himo

Wrist cord

4

ツマミ

Tsumami

Finger loop

5

手カウ

Tekō

Armoured hand covering

6

ムキハラ

Mugiwara

Thin reinforcement plates

[These are not shown in the image, but the position is given.]

7

経如之板

Keshō no ita

Band below the comb-shaped upper plate

8

櫛形

Kushigata

Comb-shaped upper plate

9

小手付ノコハセ

Kotetsuke no kohaze

Toggle for attaching the sleeves

[This is not shown in the image, but its position behind the shoulder plate is indicated.]

PARTS OF THE ARMOURED SLEEVE

Commentator one

The name for the entire arm is the *ieude no kusari* (家腕之鎖).[284]

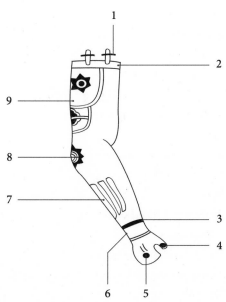

---

284 Possibly a reference to the full chain-armoured sleeve or the base cloth.

1
小手付ノコハセ
Kotetsuke no kohaze
Toggle for attaching the sleeves

2
カムリノ板
Kamuri no ita
Crown plate

3
標緒
Shirushi no o
Marking cord

4
ツマミ
Tsumami
Finger loops

Commentator two
These allow you to slip your finger and thumb in and are found on the back of the armoured hand guard. They can also be called *sashinuki* (指貫).

5
手カウ
Tekō
Armoured hand covering

6
手首
Tekubi
Cuff

7
桴
Ikada
Floating plates
The section below the *kamuri no ita* crown plate is called the *ikada* (イカタ).

8
臂金
Hijigane
Metal elbow protector

9
額之板
Gaku no ita
Reinforcement plates on the sleeve
[These include plates in the following styles:]
- *fukube* フクヘ – gourd style
- *keshi* ケシ – poppy-seed style
- *botan* ホタン – button style[285]

Commentator one
[The different types of *kote* gauntlets:][286]
- A *nagato-gote* type sleeve is thinner [than most armoured sleeves] towards the top part (*kamuri*).
- A *kizō-gote* type sleeve has a shoulder guard (*sode*) that is divided into three sections.
- An *okuda-gote* type sleeve [has full plates] that form an armoured cylinder [around the arm]. This was invented by Okuda Saburōzaemon from Yamato.
- An *etchū-gote* style sleeve [is made of chain with metal plates attached].

---

285 According to the Natori-Ryū encyclopedia, these are alternative names for the same thing – gourd-shaped protection panels.
286 All of these types are illustrated in a later volume in the series.

- A *namazu-gote* style sleeve has round *tekō* armoured hand coverings in a catfish shape.
- A *tominaga-gote* style sleeve has both shoulder parts bound together [to create a combined single pair of sleeves] and is similar to the *ubu-gote* style.

The area above the elbow is called the *takate* upper arm, while the area below the elbow is called the *kote* gauntlet.

The writing *Teikinōrai* (庭訓往来) mentions the term *tebuta haidate* (手蓋ハイタテ). This is [an earlier] version of the term *kote* – gauntlet. The standard term *kote* has existed since the time of the Heiji rebellion and it was after this period that the name began to be employed by the warrior Minamoto no Sanetomo, who was the Minister of the Right under the Kamakura shōgunate.

A poem [by Minamoto no Sanetomo] states:

武士ノ矢並繕ラフ小手ノ上ニ霰たばしる那須の篠原

Mononofu *warriors align their arrows within their quivers as hail falls upon their gauntlets in the bamboo fields of Nasu.*

Commentator two

Apart from the above, there is also a style called *okisode*, which can be easily attached and detached.

The *etchū-gote* style sleeve is made completely out of chain mail.

The *oda-gote* style has metal fittings called *hyōtan* gourds or *ikada* floating aids. This is the most widely used type of gauntlet today, because it allows greater mobility [than the others].

Issui-sensei says

The [previous image of the armoured sleeve] is called *inari-gote* – which means it is constructed with an angle [sewn into the] sleeve. There are no special instructions to be given for this. However, some versions have detachable *tekō* armoured hand coverings.

Commentator one

Concerning *inari-gote* gauntlets: these are the best type and there are traditions for this.

Commentator two

In our school we use *inari-gote* style sleeves, which have no parts that rub against anything [but allow free movement].

弓小手之事
Yugote no koto

ARCHER'S GAUNTLETS

The length of these depends on the wearer. They should be wrapped around [the arm] and tied up with lace. Some have connected shoulder sections sewn onto them [so that they make a connected pair of sleeves. These types are called:]

- *gusoku no shitazashi* 具足ノ下指
- *ubu-gote* 産小手
- *tominaga-gote* 富永小手

The cloth used should be satin damask or fabric made of bleached ramie. Also there may be a flower-like frill attached to the end of the wrist section.

PARTS OF THE ARCHER'S GAUNTLET

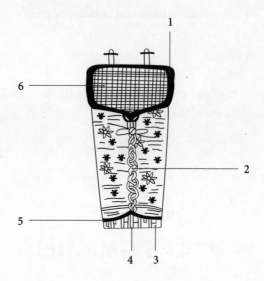

1

冠板

Kamuri no ita

Upper sleeve plate

[This is not shown in the image, but the position is given.]

2

双経

Morokagari

Lacing

3

菊トチ

Kikutoji

Ruffle

The ideograms for *kikutoji* can also be 菊綴.

4
芥子
Keshi
Tack and fold at the cuff

5
手首
Tekubi
Cuff

6
家裡
Ieura
Inner lining

Commentator two
The base cloth is called the *ieji* (家地).

CHAPTER THIRTY

胸掛
Munegake

CHEST PROTECTOR

The entire part should be made of chain mail[287] and tied up at the back of the neck.

---

287 The image does not show chain.

喉輪
Nodowa

NECK PROTECTOR

Commentator one

The *nodowa* neck protector is modern and was not found as an item of military gear in ancient times.

Commentator two

[Alternative design]

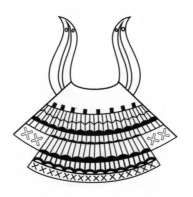

腋當之事
Wakiate no koto

SIDE PROTECTORS

Those that are joined by tying cords together are called *tsuriwakibiki* (釣脇引); those that are attached with toggles are called *wakiate* (腋當); and those that are integrated with the *kote* gauntlet sleeves are called *shitsuke wakiate* (仕付脇當).

Commentator two

The image below shows the *wakiate* style, which is also called *yarifusegi* (鑓防) – the protector against spears.

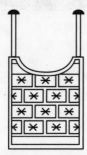

The image below shows the *tsuriwakibiki* style, which means suspended side protectors.

佩楯之事
Haidate no koto

THIGH PROTECTORS

- Thigh protectors made of chain are called *etchū haidate* (越中佩楯) – the thigh protectors of Etchū.
- Those that fasten around the back of the thigh are called *fungomi* [*haidate*] (踏込) – trouser-style [thigh protectors].
- Those with metal plates 1 *sun* square bound alongside the chain are called *iyo haidate* (伊予佩楯) – the thigh protectors of Iyo.

PARTS OF THE *HAIDATE* THIGH PROTECTORS

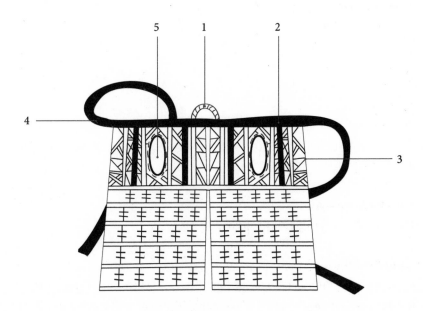

1

コサルヲ

Kozaru-o

Lesser monkey loop

Commentator two

This can also be called the *maejime* (前締) tying to the front or the *tsubo no o* (壷ノ緒) container cord.

2

力革

Chikaragawa

Strengthening leather

3

ハイタテノ家

Haidate no ie[288]

Foundation cloth

4

腰帯

Koshiobi

Waist sash

5

ムチサシノ穴

Muchisashi no ana

Hole for the rod to pass through

Commentator one

There is one type of thigh protector called the *hōdō haidate* (膀胴佩楯), which is the same as the *kusari bakama* – armoured [half-length] *hakama* pants. These

---

288 *Ieji koshitsuke no* [illegible ideogram] in the Koga version.

were invented around the period of Genō (1319–1321). The modern *haidate* is of the *fungomi* style, which has leg straps [that go around the rear of the leg].

Commentator two

Our school transmits the [correct] protocol to be followed for [*haidate* thigh protectors] before spear battles, but this is mentioned in another scroll.[289] Furthermore, there is one type called the *hōdō haidate* (ホウトウ佩楯), which is the same as the *kusari bakama* (クサリ袴) – chain-armoured pants. These were invented around the period of Genō (元應) (1319–1321).

[*Haidate* thigh protectors] are also called *suneyoroi* (脛甲).

臑當[290]
Suneate

GREAVES

十王頭

Jūōgashira

GREAVES WITH JŪŌ 'CROWN OF HELL' KNEE COVERS[291]

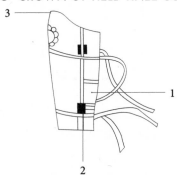

---

289 The teaching is to take them off before entering into a spear battle.

290 The Koga transcription uses the ideograms 脚當.

291 Literally 'the crown of hell', the three part shape represents the crown of Enma, the Japanese Devil.

1

鉸具摺

Kakuzuri

Rubbing pad

2

蝶番

Chōtsugai

Hinges

The hinges shown here [were invented] in the Tenshō era (1573–1593).

3

十王頭

Jūōgashira

'Crown of hell'

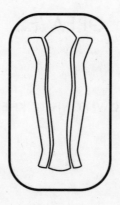

Commentator one

These are also called *jūōsuneate* (十王スネアテ) – 'crown of hell' leg protectors.

Commentator two

Those greaves with lining are called *shitsuke suneate* (仕付脛当) – lined greaves.

篠臑當
Shino suneate
GREAVES WITH VERTICAL REINFORCEMENT STRIPS

Commentator one

These are also called *mategara* (マテガラ) – razor-clam-shaped protectors.

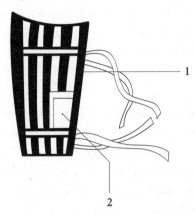

1
篠竪
Shinodate
Protective bars

2
鐙摺
Abumizuri
Rubbing pad

Commentator two

This is also called the *kakuzuri* (カクスリ) – rubbing pad for the stirrup.

Issui-sensei says

Jūōgashira greaves are good for mounted warriors, while the *shino* style is used by footed warriors. [The *shino* style] is also called *mategara* (蟶殼), the razor-clam-shaped protector. The *kakuzuri* part [the leather rubbing patch] should be of horse leather.

Commentator one

In the *Taiheiki* war chronicle it says that you should wear *ōdateage no suneate* (大タテアケノ臑當) greaves with large knee covers and also *hiza yoroi* (ヒサヨロイ) knee armour. The word *ōdateage* means the same as *jūōgashira* – the 'crown of hell' – but the term *hiza yoroi* actually means *haidate* thigh protectors [even though its literal translation is 'knee protectors'].

Commentator two

There are variations of *shinosuneate*-style greaves, such as the *mategarawara* (マテガラワラ) razor-clam style. There is another variation that can fold into three sections, which is called *okesuneate* (桶スネアテ) barrel greaves.

Jūōgashira greaves are good for riding because they cover your kneecaps when you are on horseback, but they are not good for walking because they hinder movement. *Shino* greaves with reinforcements are good for foot soldiers, because they do not hinder the movement of the knees.

沓之事
Kutsu no koto

HEAVY-DUTY FOOTWEAR

Some footwear is made of tanned leather, while other footwear is lacquered. However, the latter is worn only by *taishō* commanders. In ancient times, aristocratic *samurai* (公家侍) wore footwear in accordance with their imperial positions, which differed from what modern soldiers wear. Also, there are *momitabi* (モミ足袋), which are made of bear fur or are of coloured fur. In addition to this there are also *waranjigake*. If [normal soldiers] want to wear such heavy-duty boots, there are rules to follow relating to imperial positions.

For this they should ask a *shokugen* (職原) – a person proficient in court rituals, practices and customs.

Commentator one
According to the *Shokugenshō* document, the types of footwear appropriate for official ranks are:

- *asakutsu* 沓 – wooden footwear
- *kanokutsu* 靴 – footwear to be worn at official seasonal court events
- *fukagutsu* 深履 – long leather boots to be worn in muddy ground
- *hōka* 半靴 – half-boots for horse-riding and to be worn by people ranked between aristocrat and *samurai*

Commentator two
Such heavy-duty footwear is made of bear fur and is worn for full assembly (セイ揃之場) and official events. Know that when noble people are present, it is considered disrespectful and improper to wear *waranji* straw sandals. In such cases, fur ankle boots should be worn. These have hobnail soles.[292] Furthermore, they should be decorated with twilled cloth. The sole should be of double *itamegawa* leather [which is leather treated with glue and hardened] and the cords should be of black leather measuring 6 *bu* in width and 2 *shaku* in length. [The fur] should be tucked [up] for a length of 5 *bu* at the toes. These tucks should be fastened with silver fittings with a metal hem. The securing fittings for the cord should be of silver and have heart-shaped openings. The metal base and the silver fittings should have lines [engraved/embossed] at 3 *bu* intervals. The reinforcement section should be approximately 7 *sun* long.

---

292 This is a speculation; the original states 'metal soles'.

CHAPTER THIRTY-ONE

具足六具之事
Gusoku rokugu no koto

THE SIX PARTS OF ARMOUR

1. *kabuto* 冑 – helmet
2. *hōate* 頬當 – faceguard
3. *dō* 胴 – body armour
4. *kote* 小手 – gauntlets
5. *haidate* 佩楯 – thigh protectors
6. *suneate* 臑當 – greaves[293]

[The following is a list of the *rokugu* – the set of six tools used by warriors.]

Commentator two
The word *roku* means 'six' and the term *rokugu* refers to the six sections of:

1. left arm
2. right arm
3. left leg
4. right leg
5. head
6. torso

The *gu* part of *rokugu* means 'prepared and equipped', and therefore the term *rokugu* represents universality, 'a complete set of equipment'. It is based on the word *rokkon* (六根), which refers to the six sense organs.

---

293 The Koga transcription uses the ideograms 脚當.

In Buddhism the term *rokugu* consists of two parts:

法報應

Sanjin

Trikaya **doctrine**

- *dhammakāya* 法 – the body of the ultimate law and truth
- *sambhogakaya* 報 – the body of bliss and reward
- *nirmanakaya* 應 – the manifested body

身口意

Sangō

Karma **doctrine**

- *shin* 身 – actions done by the body
- *ku* 口 – actions done by speech
- *i* 意 – actions done by the mind

With these [above six points] combined, the concept of *rokugu* comes to represent completeness.

In *bumon* – the affairs of military families – the term *rokugu* also consists of two parts:

三徳

Santoku

The three virtues

1. *chi* 智 – wisdom
2. *jin* 仁 – benevolence
3. *yū* 勇 – courage

三法

Sanpō

The three principles

1. *sei* 成 – achievement
2. *gon* 権 – authority
3. *hai* 敗 – failure

Combined, the [six phases] above are considered as the complete concept of *rokugu*.

[This philosophical concept is carried through all the following examples of the six tools.]

一締六具之事
Isshuku no rokugu no koto

THE SIX TYPES OF CORDS

1. *hachimaki* 鉢巻 – headband
2. *shinobi no o* 忍緒 – helmet strap
3. *kurijiime no o* 繰締緒 – cord to secure the body armour
4. *uwaobi* 上帯 – outer sash
5. *koshiate no o* 腰富緒 – sword clasp
6. *hikae no o* 扣之緒 – support strap for the banner

Commentator two
These are the six cords of securing. The headband should be worn *over* the helmet as it represents a state of bravery when advancing.

TOOL ONE
It is said that in China a headband is called a *mattō* (抹頭) and is made of red silk. Use the standard width for bleached cloth[294] in the *takabakari* (鷹秤) measuring system.[295] There are three ways of tying [the headband] but that is an oral tradition.

---

294 34 centimetres.
295 A bamboo cane cut to a standard length and used for measuring cloth.

Commentator two

This is concerned with the making of headbands. *Taka* from the *takabakari* measurement system mentioned above means 'hawk', which is of course a form of raptor. When parent hawks feed young hawks, [the chicks] try to peck at their parents' eyes and so the parent hawks through fear of such a hooked beak gashing their eyes, feed food to their chicks from above. A measurement of 1 *shaku* [in the *takabakari* system] is longer than 1 *shaku* on the carpenter's (金尺) scale but shorter than 1 *shaku* in the *kujirajaku* scale (鯨尺).[296] There are oral traditions for this.

[The headband] should be tied in one of the following knot styles:
- *benkei-musubi* 弁慶結 – knot of the warrior Benkei
- *hana-musubi* 花結 – rosette knot
- *eboshi-musubi* 烏帽子結 – *eboshi* knot

Details should be transmitted when donning [armour].

The formal headband worn by a *taishō* commander should be made of white patterned silk (綾).
- The *benkei-musubi* knot of the warrior Benkei should be tied at the front.
- The *hana-musubi* rosette-style knot should be tied at the left and allowed to hang down. One end should be a little longer than the other.
- The *eboshi-musubi* knot should be tied at the back with the ends trailing.

It is said that [the commander Uesugi] Kenshin had his headband tied in a *katsura-musubi* (カツラ結) knot during battle. This is the same as the *hana-musubi* rosette-style knot mentioned above.

TOOL TWO

The *shinobi no o* helmet strap is made from half of the width of a roll of bleached cloth.[297] If you are fixing it to four rings [inside a helmet], it should be 7 *shaku* 8 *sun* long on the carpenter's scale (曲尺). If you are fixing it to three rings, it

---

296 A measurement system used for *kimono* making, etc.

297 In the *kujirajaku* measurement system, the standard width is 9 *sun* 5 *bu* (approximately 36 centimetres).

should be 7 *shaku* and 3 *sun* long [on the same scale]. There are various ways of tying this cord, but they are oral traditions.

TOOL THREE

For the *kurijime no o* cords for securing body armour, the length is the same as for the helmet strap, but [the width is only] half that of the helmet strap. The ways of tying the cords are also an oral tradition.

Commentator two

The ways of tying are to be transmitted when donning the armour.

TOOL FOUR

The *uwaobi* outer sash is made of bleached cloth. This should be wrapped double around the waist and tied at the front. One end should be longer by the length of one hand grip. If needs be, it is acceptable to wrap it around three times.

TOOL FIVE

The *koshiate no o* sword belt should be made of unbleached cloth. It is two-thirds the width [of a standard roll]. The length should be 8 *shaku* 2 *sun* for bigger men and 8 *shaku* for smaller men.

Commentator two

The *koshiate* sword belt is used with the *uwaobi* outer sash when in armour and is used for wearing swords. However, in ancient times, it was said that you should have a *tachigake* (太刀掛) great sword belt instead of a *koshiate* (腰當) sword belt. This made it easier to wear swords, but it was harder to take off.

TOOL SIX

The *hikae no o* banner support cord should be made of bleached ramie cloth. The method of securing it is to be orally transmitted and information is to be found in the *Kōketsu* scroll. The width should be one-third of a standard roll. [Given that the] *koshiate no o* sword belt [uses two-thirds of a roll,] you can use the remaining third for this cord.

Chapter Thirty-one

Commentator one

This is also called the *wassoku* (ワツソク).[298] Tie this cord around the banner pole in the *shirushizuke* style (印付) and secure it to the front [of your armour]. Make sure to twist it [and secure it] onto the *uwaobi* outer sash.

Commentator two

In other schools this cord is called the *wassoku no o*. Traditions [about this] are mentioned later. Details should be transmitted when donning [the armour itself].

Issui-sensei says

According to tradition, the above six tools require one roll (反) of bleached ramie cloth. When making these cords, face the direction of *gyokujo* (玉女) and [start cutting the cloth by] pushing forward three times with a small knife (小刀) – one with a handle of Chinese sumac – then after that pull back [slightly]. Next, cut the cloth by pressing forward again with the main part of the knife. When cutting with your knife, the assistant should hold [the cloth] by forming their hands into a diamond shape (イノ目) [and you should] cut the cloth by pushing forward with the part of the blade nearest the handle (裁留) until you have cut all the way through. Know that when cutting and stitching each cord, there is a certain width for folding [the cloth over]. How to wear and how to tie the above cords are oral traditions.[299]

Commentator one

The direction of *gyokujo* is the ninth zodiac sign [counting clockwise from and including] the sign for that day. The concept of *gyokujo* is [connected to the deity] Inseijin (陰生神) [which contains the element of *in*. You should also understand that the direction opposite to *gyokujo* is called] *kikigami*, which is the third direction from the zodiac sign of that day. This is found to

---

298 This term commonly refers to tying something over your back. Here it is used to mean securing a pole to your back.

299 The 'cords' are created by cutting cloth, rolling it and stitching it together. Here the *samurai* and his assistant face the ritual direction on an auspicious day and cut the cloth in a symbolic gesture of victory.

your rear when you face the direction of *gyokujo*. The direction of *kikigami* is [connected to the deity] Yōseijin (陽生神) [which contains the element of *yō*]. Therefore, [when you face the direction of *gyokujo*] you face a direction associated with the element of *in*, but you have the element of *yō* to the rear [meaning that you face the element of defeat with the support of the element of victory].

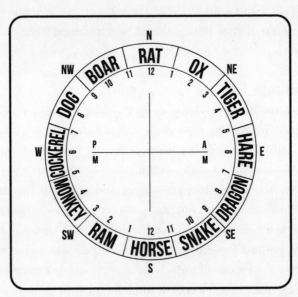

Chinese sumac [which is the wood from which the knife handle is made] has the name *kachinoki* (勝軍木) which means 'the tree of victory in battle'. Remember, when Prince Shōtoku defeated his enemy Moriya, he used this wood to make statues of the Four Devas. Also, this wood is burned in Buddhist rites to invoke divine assistance.

Commentator two

Regarding the concept of *gyokujo*, this is also used to choose an appropriate time. The concepts of *gyokujo* and *kikigami* were used solely by military families.

Chinese sumac is also called *kachinoki* (勝軍木), the tree of victory in battle. You 'push forward three times', because this represents the three virtues of:

1. *chi* 智 – wisdom
2. *jin* 仁 – benevolence
3. *yū* 勇 – bravery

To pull represents the element of *in*, which is linked with retreat, and to push represents the element of *yō*, which is linked with advancing. [The main text also says] 'cut the cloth by pushing forward … until you have cut all the way through.' This represents the will to advance.

[When making] cords that go above the waist, hold the cloth with your hands in a diamond shape (猪之目); but for those cords below the waist, hold the cloth with your hands in the shape of a boar hoof (猪之爪).

Chinese sumac, also called *kamaegi* (構木) or *enbushi* (塩麩), is a useful tree for various reasons. According to the *Chronicles of Japan*, Prince Shōtoku made statues of the Four Devas from this wood and wore them on his head [as was the ritual fashion]. He then swore that if the gods would let him defeat his enemy, he would build a temple to celebrate the Four Devas. Later, [after his victory] he founded the temple in Tamatsukuri in the province of Sesshū and renamed this tree *kachinoki*, which means 'the tree of victory in battle'.

歩立六具之事
Kachidachi rokugu no koto

THE SIX TOOLS FOR *SAMURAI* ON FOOT

1. *ōgi* 扇 – fan
2. *tachi* 太刀 – great sword
3. *sashimono* 指物 – banner
4. *kasajirushi* 笠効[300] – helmet marker (also called *kobata* 小旗 – small 'flag')
5. *yari* 鑓 – spear
6. *yugake* 指懸 – archer's glove[301]

---

300 The Koga transcription uses the ideograms 笠印.
301 The Koga transcription uses the ideograms 決拾. *Yugake* normally reads as 'archer's

When *samurai* on foot carry bows, they have to have arrows in a basic quiver (尻籠), and in this case they do not also carry a spear. The same applies for *samurai* who carry a musket [i.e. the spear is replaced by a musket].

Commentator two

The spear should be removed from the list when a bow is carried, because they are of equal worth.

軍奉行六具之事
Ikusa-bugyō rokugu no koto

THE SIX TOOLS FOR WAR COMMANDERS

1. *horo* 武羅 – arrow cape
2. *ebira* 箙 – quiver
3. *yumi* 弓 – bow
4. *muchi* 鞭 – riding crop
5. *uchiwa* 團扇 – war fan
6. *yugake* 決拾 – archer's glove

Various commanders (奉行) and captains (頭) should have these six tools. However, if the *horo* cape is not used, [the commander] wears his own banner. Furthermore, if they do not carry a bow and quiver, they instead use a war baton (*saihai*) and battle jacket (*haori*).

Commentator two

The *ikusa-bugyō* minister of war is one of the six commanders. Sometimes two *musha-bugyō* warrior commanders are used instead of having two *ikusa-bugyō*

---

glove'; however, there is no bow on the list. The ideograms used in the Tōkyō transcription mean 'finger covers' and the ideograms used in the Koga transcription have no obvious meaning. Other manuals list these as the archer's glove.

and these normally command the army. The six commanders also include the *hata-bugyō* flag commanders and the *yari-bugyō* commander of the spears.

大将六具之事
Taishō rokugu no koto

THE SIX TOOLS FOR A COMMANDER-IN-CHIEF

1. *katchū* 甲冑 – armour and helmet
2. *tachi* 太刀 – great sword
3. *muchi* 鞭 – riding crop
4. *uchiwa* 團扇 – war fan
5. *yugake* 決拾 – archer's glove
6. *kutsu* 沓 – boots

When the *taishō* goes out to war, his riding crop (*muchi*), war fan (*uchiwa*) or war baton (*saihai*) should be carried by another person, but in the actual battle he should hold them himself. On such occasions, list the war baton (*saihai*) instead of *katchū* armour in the six tools.[302]

大将戦場ニテ堅ムル六具之事
Taishō senjō nite katamuru rokugu no koto

THE SIX TOOLS THAT GUARD THE COMMANDER-IN-CHIEF DURING BATTLE

---

302 This means that the commander should consider the war fan as more important than armour, not that he should not wear armour.

1. *katchū* 甲冑 – [the *taishō*] should be in helmet and armour
2. *tachi* 太刀 – [the *taishō*] should wear the great sword and sit on a *kyokuroku* (曲彔) stool[303] with a war fan in hand
3. *hatadate* 籏立 – the banner in its stand
4. *yari* 鑓 – the spear should be stood erect[304]
5. *yumi* 弓 – there should be bows in line on both sides
6. *teppō* 鉄砲 – muskets should be in line on both sides

The last two should be positioned and aligned on both sides of the commander. For these six tools the word *katamuru* (堅ムル), meaning 'to guard', or *sonaeru* (備ル), meaning 'to be equipped with', can be used.

戦場ノ備六具之事
Senjō no sonae rokugu no koto

THE SIX TOOLS USED WHEN TAKING UP A FORMATION ON A BATTLEFIELD

1. *hata* 籏 – standards
2. *maku* 幕 – war curtains
3. *shōgi* 将机[305] – folding stool
4. *tate* 楯 – shields
5. *taiko* 太鼓 – drums
6. *hora* 螺 – conch shells

The above six tools are standard items used within the rules laid down for the army.

---

303 A folding chair with back rest.

304 All transcriptions list only five tools here. However, the spear was mentioned at the end of point three and so we have moved it down to become the fourth tool of defence in its own right.

305 The Koga transcription uses the ideograms 床机.

一己六具之事
Ikko rokugu no koto

THE SIX TOOLS FOR EACH INDEPENDENT WARRIOR

1. *gusoku* 具足 – armour
2. *ōgi* 扇 – fan
3. *sashimono* 指物 – banner
4. *yugake* 決拾 – archer's glove
5. *yari* 鑓 – spear
6. *tachi* 太刀 – great sword

The above are used by mounted *samurai*.

軍中馬之六具之事
Gunchūba no rokugu no koto

THE SIX TOOLS FOR WARHORSES

1. *bamen* 馬面 – armoured horse mask
2. *munagai* 胸懸 – breast collar
3. *umayoroi* 馬鎧 – horse armour
4. *habaki* 脛半 – leg protectors
5. *muchi* 鞭 – riding crop
6. *kanegutsu* 金履 – metal horse shoes

The above are also called *umayoroi* – horse armour.

番所六具之事
Bansho rokugu no koto

THE SIX TOOLS FOR GUARD DUTY [OR PATROL]

1. *hayanawa* 早縄 – quick rope for binding
2. *kumade* 熊手 – bear-claw staff
3. *tsukubō* 突棒 – spiked T-bar staff
4. *hyōshigi* 拍子木 – wooden warning clappers
5. *bō* 棒 – quarterstaff
6. *sasumata* 指胯 – U-shaped pronged staff

Concerning the above, for active guard service there is also a tool called the *mojiri* (モジリ), which is a staff with a multi-pronged barbed head. This should be added to the list instead of the wooden warning clappers to make up the six tools.

Commentator one

Concerning the *hayanawa* quick rope: there is also the *hananeji* horse-nose twister and the *chigiriki* staff with a ball and chain. The *chigiriki* staff should measure up to your chest level. This is why it is named *chi* (乳).[306] It should come to about 3 *shaku* 5 *sun* in length and if it has a chain it is also called by this name. This is an oral tradition.

---

306 Literally, 'reaching chest height'.

忍者六具之事
Shinobi-mono rokugu no koto

THE SIX TOOLS FOR A *SHINOBI-MONO*[307]

1. *jishaku* 磁石 – compass[308]
2. *amigasa* 網笠 – straw hat
3. *hiuchi* 火打 – fire striker (this includes the *tsuketake* thin wooden splint)
4. *kaginawa* 鍵縄 – hook and rope
5. *hanagami* 鼻紙 – thin paper
6. *tenugui* 手拭 – cloth

平世士心掛ノ六具之事
Heizei samurai kokorogake no rokugu no koto

THE SIX TOOLS THAT *SAMURAI* SHOULD BE PREPARED WITH IN TIMES OF PEACE

1. *jishaku* 磁石 – compass[309]
2. *ken'nawa* 間縄 – measuring rope
3. *hayanawa* 早縄 – quick rope
4. *sekihitsu* 石筆 – stone pencil
5. *hiuchi* 火打 – fire striker
6. *kusuri* 薬 – medicine

---

307 This list differs slightly from the one given in the *Shōninki* manual, which appears to combine elements from this list and the one directly after it. However, as seen in other lists, it is acceptable to swap items out for others. The real meaning of 'six tools' is a combination of: (1) defensive equipment held by the Four Heavenly Kings when they protected the Buddha on Vulture Peak; (2) the six elements of Buddhism and *samurai* ways; and (3) two arms, two legs, head and body, which represent completeness.

308 This may also be read as 'magnet'.

309 As above.

相圖六具之事
Aizu rokugu no koto

THE SIX TOOLS FOR SIGNALLING

1. *noroshi* 狼煙 – smoke signal
2. *aizubata* 相圖旗 – signal flag
3. *hora* 螺 – conch shell
4. *ryūsei* 流星 – signal rocket
5. *taimatsu* 明松 – torch
6. *teppō* 鉄砲 – musket

These [signals] are used during battle.

狩場六具之事
Kariba rokugu no koto

THE SIX TOOLS FOR HUNTING

1. *hata* 旗 – flag
2. *yumi* 弓 – bow
3. *yugake* 指懸 – archer's glove[310]
4. *yakago* 矢籠 – arrow quiver[311]
5. *habaki* 行纏 – gaiters
6. *kutsu* 履 – boots

---

310 The Koga transcription uses the ideogram 弽.
311 The Koga transcription uses the ideograms 矢籠.

犬追物六具之事
Inuoumono rokugu no koto

THE SIX TOOLS FOR DOG SHOOTING³¹²

1. *ebira* 箙 – quiver
2. *shigetō yumi* 滋籘弓 – laminated bow³¹³
3. *hikime* 蟇目 – whistling arrow
4. *yugake* 決拾 – archer's glove
5. *habaki* 行纏 – gaiters
6. *kutsu* 沓 – boots

Know that the last two articles above do not directly concern warfare.

There are various sets of 'six tools' depending on each family tradition. However, the above sets are from ancient ways. When at war, it is desirable to use any tools that offer advantages over standard versions. Therefore, know that it is not inappropriate to discard some items from these sets and replace them with more advantageous tools.

Commentator two

A *sodetōyu* (袖唐油) raincoat should be oiled and have holes under [the sleeve] so that rain water will not collect inside.

Some manoeuvres in hunting, such as advancing and retreating, are similar to those undertaken in warfare, which is why these last two lists of tools have been included.

---

312 *Inuoumono* dog shooting was a popular sport during the Kamakura and Muromachi periods (1185–1573). It involved mounted archers shooting at dogs with padded or blunted arrows to prevent the arrows from killing the dogs. *Inuoumono* was eventually banned during the reign of Tokugawa Iemochi (1858–1866).

313 Layered bow bound with rattan.

CHAPTER THIRTY-TWO

着籠之事
Kikomi no koto

CHAIN MAIL

This is to be worn under armour and should be made to measure your body. In older days it covered all parts and the mesh of the chain was larger[314] around the back and the waist.

Tradition says that it is desirable to construct this with lightweight rings and with metal reinforcements (筋金) attached. Also, leather or sharkskin can be added to the chain mail in parts to make it lighter. Imported steel from Europe (南蛮鐵) is sometimes used. Chain mail, even when made from imported metal, is not good as protection against a spear.

There is a tradition for *hayakusari* temporary and fast mail, but it is secret.

Commentator two

Hayakusari temporary and fast mail is a secret matter and should be transmitted orally. This is something akin to satin damask cloth that has been soaked in water for one day to strengthen it.

When on campaign, you should wear [chain mail] under your armour (*gusoku*). It can compensate for gaps in your armour's defences, but mostly it is worn for capturing [criminals].

Nanban no tetsu imported steel is of high quality. The best in Japan is *shisōkane* metal of Shinshū province, but this cannot compete with imported steel.

---

314 The term is based on the adjective *arai* (荒い), meaning 'coarser', 'rougher' or 'larger'.

膚着之事
Hadagi no koto

UNDERSHIRT

This is made of bleached ramie cloth or silk crepe. It is also possible to use dyed material. However, persimmon (柿色) [tannin] dying should be avoided. The main body [of the shirt] is constructed in *hangiri* (半切), which means 'half-cut' fashion, and the sleeves should be narrow and reach down only to the upper arm area. Strings should also be attached [at the chest to tie it together]. The collar should be a high collar like that on a rain cape (カツハ). There is nothing else to be recorded on this matter.

Commentator one

From ancient times it is said [that in war you should use] *hidari karamushi* left-laid cloth of the ramie plant, because right-laid cloth of the ramie plant is used for normal purposes.[315] [To cover] dead bodies, use cloth that is woven from strands that are left laid and know that the same [preparation for death] applies to military gear.

Military ways should not be followed in normal life and domestic styles should not be followed in warfare. This is a quote taken from the *Methods of the Sima* (司馬法).

Commentator two

Persimmon [tannin] dying is to be avoided, as it promotes blood flow. Dying cloth using the plum tree and the like is recommended instead.[316] The colour pale blue (浅黄) is also desirable.

---

315 Thread and rope is laid either to the left or the right during construction. This ends up with the strands going either clockwise or anti-clockwise. Here it means that the threads spiral to the left, which represents death and is thus used in battle.

316 This produces the colour *umezome* (梅染).

The length of the shirt should be 2 *shaku* 8 *sun*. To make a *hayajitate no shitagi* temporary undershirt, cut off the sleeves of your usual clothes and wear it by folding it up [from the bottom] into a shorter shirt. When infiltrating, wrap the tassets of your armour with this [undershirt]. To do this, turn up the longer shirt and wrap it over the tassets of the armour and secure it above [to your sash so that you can move in stealth].

股引之事
Momohiki no koto

LIGHTWEIGHT TROUSERS

Wear *sarumomohiki* shorter lightweight trousers. Also, *tōmomohiki* Chinese-style trousers are desirable and there are traditions on how to make them. The cloth used should be satin-damask or linen and there should be no pleats in them.

Commentator two

In our school *tōmomohiki* Chinese-style trousers should be worn. This is actually the normal style for these *momohiki* trousers, but they have extra space around the crotch so that it gives a loose fitting and causes no problems.

脚絆之事
Kyahan no koto

CLOTH GAITERS

Wear the type of gaiters called *gama-kyahan*[317] or *yama-kyahan* mountain gaiters. The material can be of any type. [Both styles] have cords attached; the cords at the top should be normal ones and those at the bottom should have clasps.

Commentator two

The style of gaiters called *gama-kyahan* are made by weaving the *gama* plant and are mostly found in the Shinano area. They have cords at the top and bottom. However, normal gaiters usually have buttons. Gaiters are good for wearing below greaves.

Commentator three

Mountain gaiters have cords at the top and bottom.

膚帯之事
Hadaobi no koto

LOINCLOTH

The style from Etchū is desirable, but there is a specific way to make it. Strings should be attached to the top waist band, which should be tied around the neck. The cloth to be used should be bleached. For a larger man it should measure 5 *shaku* 3 *sun* and for a smaller man it should measure 5 *shaku* 2 *sun*. The split should be 2 *shaku* 1 *sun* long and the cloth [does not come to a V-shape but] is squared off [as shown in the drawing below]. Cross the ends over at the rear

---

317 *Gama* (蒲脚絆) is a type of plant, *Typha latifolia L.*

and tie them to the front. There are move oral traditions. Generally, cords on military equipment should be tied at the front.

Commentator two

Military styles should not be worn in normal life and domestic styles should not be worn in warfare, but ease of use should be valued.

草鞋掛之事
Waranjigake no koto

FOOT COVERINGS

These should be made more durable on the bottom but constructed as normal. Avoid attaching cords to them and instead fasten them with 'buttons'. Only stitch them at various places [and not all the way around]. This is called *chidorinui* – cross stitches.

Commentator two

This [*chidorinui* stitching] is used for convenience as it allows pebbles to be removed, which is not normally possible when footwear has been fully stitched. Cords are not desirable, because they are not convenient to handle.

草鞋之事
Waranji no koto

STRAW SANDALS

The straw used to make these should be soaked in flowing water at the coldest time of the year.[318] Take them out after this period has ended. Footwear made like this is called *tsuyogutsu* – sturdy footwear. Furthermore, if you harvest and use the parts required of the *myōga* (茗荷)[319] plant when the frost is upon it, then the resulting footwear will be strong. Alternatively, the *gama* (蒲)[320] plant can be used. Another way to make stout sandals is to use plant fibre (麻) and cloth (布) together. If they are made of the grass called *shōjō* (猩々),[321] then, again, they will be strong. However, this type does not withstand water. Sandals made of thin whale baleen are considered to be robust.

There is another type of footwear that is secretly transmitted in our clan. These are called *shinobi-gutsu* (忍沓) – *shinobi* footwear. This is an oral tradition.

These points also apply to *ashinaka* (足中) half sandals and straw horseshoes.

Commentator two
Concerning *shinobi* footwear: this tradition is secret and is transmitted in our *shinobi* scrolls.

Commentator three
Concerning *shinobi* footwear: these are sandals made of human hair.[322]

Issui-sensei says
The above selection of garments are the basic items to be worn.

---

318 *Kanchū* (寒中). This is from the period of *shōkan* to the period of *daikan* – thirty days in total.
319 Japanese ginger.
320 *Typha latifolia L.*
321 The Koga transcription uses the ideograms 狗菰.
322 A form of silent sandal for infiltration.

CHAPTER THIRTY-THREE

大小之事
Daishō no koto

LONG AND SHORT SWORDS

A long sword (大) is best at a length of 2 *shaku* 5 *sun*, while a short sword (小) should be 1 *shaku* 5 *sun* in length.

According to ancient ways there was a type [of dagger] called the *yoroidōshi* armour-piecing dagger, which was 9 *sun* 5 *bu* long, and another called the *kubikirigatana* head-cutting blade, but the length for this is not known. The *ko-wakizashi* lesser short sword should be for used for the task [of beheading].

There are traditions for how to wear these:
- *in-tai* 陰帯 – wearing a sword in the sash in the element of *in*
- *yō-tai* 陽帯 – wearing a sword in the sash in the element of *yō*
- *shinobi-zashi* 忍指 – concealed sidearm

There are oral traditions for these points.

Commentator one

The length of the *sageo* cord is 3 *shaku* for a longer sword and 1 *shaku* 5 *sun* for a shorter sword.

Here the term *dai* [from the word *daishō*] does not refer to the *katana* long sword but actually refers to the *tachi* great sword. There is a type of *tachi* great sword that is worn with a *katana-obi* (刀帯) and this is called the *efu no tachi* (衛府太刀). The *efu no tachi* was so named because it was worn by those within the six sections of *e* (衛) and the six sections of *fu* (府) – these were military officials in the imperial court.[323] You should know that there are a variety of styles of *tachi* great sword. Furthermore, understand that the word *sayamaki* (鞘巻) is a subtle way to refer to a *tachi* great sword.

There are two main kinds of *tachi* great sword:
- *hosodachi* 細太刀 – ceremonial great sword
- *nodachi* 野太刀 – practical great sword[324]

The *hosodachi* ceremonial great sword is worn with traditional formal court dress, while the *nodachi* practical great sword is worn when you think there is a chance you will need to use it.

[The following list comprises the different types of *tachi* great sword.]

飾太刀
Kazaritachi
[Highly ornamental great sword for official rituals at court]

木地螺鈿太刀
Kiji raden no tachi
[Great sword with an exposed wooden-grain scabbard inlaid with mother of pearl]

蒔絵螺鈿太刀
Makie raden tachi
[Great sword with a scabbard inlaid with mother of pearl and using gold powder to create a pattern or drawing]

---

323 Originally there were two divisions within the imperial court called *e* and *fu*, which comprised military guards for aristocratic families. It was these warriors who wore this type of *tachi* great sword.

324 This sword type is often translated as 'field great sword'. However, while the ideogram 野 does mean 'field', its secondary meanings are: 'simple', 'unadorned', 'rustic', etc. These carry the connotation of practicality, and therefore we have translated the term here as 'practical great sword'. However, while the blade is valued above all for its usability, it may still have decorated mounts and fittings.

蒔絵細太刀

Makie no hosodachi

[Ceremonial great sword with a scabbard that uses gold powder to create a pattern or drawing]

樋螺鈿太刀

Hiraden no tachi

[Great sword with a scabbard that features a central groove inlaid with mother of pearl]

螺鈿野太刀

Raden no nodachi

[Practical great sword with a scabbard that has inlaid mother of pearl]

蒔絵野太刀

Makie no nodachi

[Practical great sword with a scabbard that uses gold powder to create a pattern or drawing]

活懸地太刀

Ikakejino tachi

[Great sword with a scabbard covered with a sprinkled pattern of gold or silver powder]

黒漆太刀

Kokushitsu no tachi

[Great sword with an all-black lacquered scabbard]

The swords listed above have been passed down from ancient times.

Aristocrats and ministers would use one of these great swords in accordance with their grade and official position and the type of official ceremony they were attending. This system does not exist any more, but the tradition may still be used in some families.

Generally, if you are not attentive concerning *tachi* great swords or *katana* long swords, it shows a lack of interest in *budō* military ways. However, even if you have one of the legendary Chinese swords known as the *kanshō bakuya*,[325] but you do not have enough courage in attacking, what good will it do you? Courage can make you defeat an enemy even with a dull sword. Remember the tale of [the courageous] Sasa Saizō and his accomplishments? Even though he was not modest about his achievements, he was correct [in his action].

In ancient times, when Minamoto no Yoritomo went to battle with Ōba Kagechika in the area of Ishibashiyama, the warrior Sanada Yoichi Yoshitada – despite having suffered with malaria – rode in upon a strong horse and engaged in combat with Okabe Yajirō, taking his head. However, the horse was startled by the noises made by some of the metal fittings of his armour and bolted out of control. Next Yoshitada fought with Matano Gorō, but, because he had not had time to wipe the blood from his sword after the previous fight (as the horse had been erratic), he had to sheath the bloody sword without cleaning it. As a result [it stuck in the scabbard and] he could not draw it in time when he was attacked by someone called Nagao Shinpachi, and so he was killed. Take note, because these are things you should be aware of.

Commentator two

Generally, on a battlefield shorter swords are preferable to longer swords. This is because it is not as easy to draw a longer sword when you are in armour, and also if you spend an extended time fighting you will get tired using a

---

325 This is the Japanese pronunciation of Gan Jiang (干将) and Mo Ye (莫耶), a swordsmith couple from Chinese legend. The tale involves a king who commissions a single sword from them, but instead they use the metal to form two swords of exquisite quality, one of which they keep. The outraged king executes Gan Jiang, for which their son swears to take revenge. To do this, he has his own head cut off and shown to the king by an agent. The king then boils the head in a cauldron but when taking a closer look, he in turn is decapitated by the agent. There are variations on this story that involve magic and animated heads. The reference in this text is meant to denote a sword of great renown.

longer sword. The [ideal sword] length is said to depend on a person's size and strength,[326] but this only applies in times of peace.

For a *kubikirigatana* head-removing blade, use the *aikuchi* dagger without guard, which measures between 7 *sun* 5 *bu* and 9 *sun* 5 *bu*. It is better to wear this under the tasset of your armour and to the side.[327]

There are teachings on how to wear both long and short (大小) swords:

- *in-tai* – wearing a sword in the sash in the element of *in*
- *yō-tai* – wearing a sword in the sash in the element of *yō*

When following the style of *in-tai*, wear your sword with the curve active (反), as this represents violent killing and is therefore of the element of *in*. The style of *yō-tai* involves wearing your sword in the conventional manner, as this represents peacetime, which is of the element of *yō*. Basically, the way of *in-tai* is for the *katana* long sword, while *yō-tai* is for the *wakizashi* short sword. Furthermore, know that the blade edge belongs to the element of *in*, while the back of the sword belongs to the element of *yō*.

The *shinobizashi* way of wearing a concealed sidearm is for the weapon known as the *yoroidōshi* (鎧通) armour-piercing dagger.[328] In our school, we use the *kubikirigatana* head-removing blade.

大小腕抜之事
Daishō udenuki no koto
WRIST CORD FOR LONG AND SHORT SWORDS

For a long sword this cord is 1 *shaku* 2 *sun* and for a short sword it is 8 *sun* 5 *bu*, but take note, these lengths are for when the cords are folded in half. That being said, sometimes the length is the same for both long and short swords. How to attach the cord is an oral tradition. Sometimes there is a hole in the hilt called the *udenuki no ana* – the hole for the wrist cord.

---

326 大小強弱.

327 The grammar is unclear here. However, it appears to mean that you should attach a dagger to the back of one of the side tassets on the armour.

328 A weapon used in close combat.

Commentator two
The wrist cord has three functions:
1. to stop you from dropping your *katana* long sword during a fight
2. to enhance your appearance as a warrior
3. to enable you to hold the strap in your mouth when mounting or dismounting

The way of attaching this cord is called *shirushizuke* (印付)[329] and it should be attached around the *fuchi* – the collar between the handle and the sword guard. Remember that this subject is mentioned in the article about the three virtues of the *udenuki* wrist cord found in the scroll *Heika Jōdan*. In our school, cords of the same length are preferred. Be warned that if it is attached through the hole in the hilt (ツバ), it may be cut off at times [which is why this method is not used here]. Generally, lack of attention to long and short swords shows an improper mindset.

太刀之名所之大事
Tachi no nadokoro no koto
PARTS OF THE GREAT SWORD

1
冑金
Kabutogane
Pommel

2
結金
Musubigane
Pommel ring

Commentator two
This is also called the *sarude* (猿手) – the monkey hand.

---

329 Most likely a lark's head hitch.

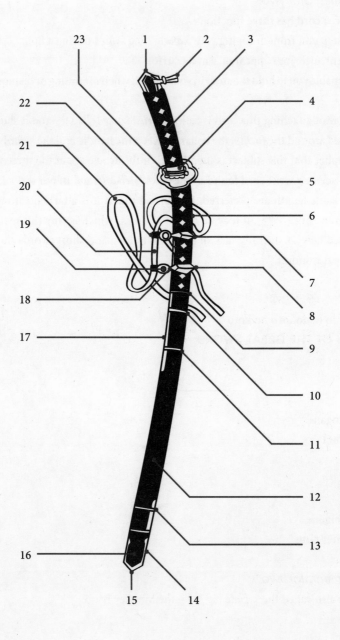

3

ツカナカ

Tsukanaka

Midpoint of the hilt

4

カツキ

Kazuki

Hilt collar

5

コヒロ

Koiguchi

Scabbard mouth

6

渡巻

Watarimaki

Scabbard wrappings

Commentator two

These are also called *kawasaki* (カハサキ).

7

一ノアシ

Ichi no ashi

First scabbard mounting

8

二ノアシ

Ni no ashi

Second scabbard mounting

Commentator one

The central point between the two scabbard mountings is called the *ashiai* (アシアイ) or *kamosaki* (カモサキ).

9

マキサシ

Makisashi

Scabbard wrapping stopper

10

一之責

Ichi no seme

First scabbard band

This is also called the *shibahiki* (芝引).

Commentator three

This can also be called the *shibahiki* (芝引) or *shibauchi* (芝打).

11

二之責

Ni no seme

Second scabbard band

12

渡

Watari

Unwrapped area of the scabbard

13

三之責

San no seme

Third scabbard band

14
雨ヲホヒ
Amaōi
Scabbard tip rain cap

15
石突
Ishizuki
Scabbard butt

16
イキノ緒
Iki no o
Scabbard end cord

17
雨覆
Amaōi
Rear-side rain protector

18
扣
Hikae
Mount support strap

19
皮之紋
Kawa no mon
Crest decoration

20

紐付

Himotsuke[330]

Mount connecting cord

21

帯紐

Obihimo

Belt cord

22

帯取

Obitori

Scabbard mount cords

23

切羽

Seppa

Hilt spacers

[These are metal fittings between the hilt, guard and blade:]

- *daiseppa* 大切羽 – large spacer
- *chūseppa* 中切羽 – medium-sized spacer
- *shōseppa* 小切羽 – small spacer

There are oral traditions on how to wear a *tachi* great sword. Senior counsellors should hold their *tachi* at the part called the *ni no seme*, those of a lower rank should hold it at the part called *ichi no seme*, and those even below that should hold it at the part called the *hikae* [all parts can be seen in the previous image].

---

330 *Hikotsuke* (ヒコツケ) in the Koga transcription.

Commentator two

The previous drawing shows a ceremonial *tachi*. Since *tachi* differ in design according to the [warrior's] official ranking, you should seek advice from a *shokugen* (職原) – a person well versed in the court and ceremonial customs.

The second type of great sword is a *nodachi* practical great sword, which is used by *bushi* warriors during times of war. It can be worn in whatever way is convenient, without regard for the rules [for court life]. The most important thing is to attach it in such a way that it will not fall out. Details for this should be transmitted when you are actually wearing the sword. When holding a *tachi* great sword for your lord, hold it at the bottom; the lower you hold the sword, the more respect you show to him.

There are two main kinds of *tachi* great sword:
1. *hosodachi* 細太刀 – ceremonial great sword
2. *nodachi* 野太刀 – practical great sword used for battle
The *hosodachi* ceremonial style is worn when in formal court dress. If you need to know how you should wear it, ask a *shokugen* expert in court practices. The *nodachi* practical type should worn by *bushi* warriors. It can be worn in any way, but needs to be secured so that it will not come off.

鎧巾着之事
Yoroi kinchaku no koto

POUCHES FOR USE WITH ARMOUR

These should be the same size as normal pouches. It is desirable to have a *netsuke*[331] toggle that can swivel just as *tochigane* (トチ金) rings do.

---

331 A *netsuke* is a small toggle attached to containers and pouches. It is pushed up under the belt and is pulled out to hang over the lip of the sash so that the container or pouch can hang on its cord.

Commentator two

The pouch should be able to move freely because it may become twisted when you are engaged in *kumiuchi* grappling or walking long distances.

馬上決拾之事
Bajō yugake no koto

HORSE-RIDING GLOVES

These should be made from *uzurafusube* (鶉薫) smoked leather, dappled with brown, black and white. Crests should be applied to the backs [of the gloves]. According to old traditions the length of the cord [on these gloves] should be 2 *shaku* 8 *sun* – by using the finger to measure with – and have a width of 1 *sun* and/or 8 *bu*.[332]

There is a detailed drawing in another scroll.

Commentator two

In ancient times the crest on the backs [of the gloves] used to represent *torii* gateways [as found at Shinto shrines], but family crests are used nowadays. *Uzurafusube* leather is good because it does not stretch and distort. For measurements, use the length of your middle finger folded over: [the length between the first and second knuckles is] the same as a 1 *sun* length. You can use your body to measure by using what is known as *hyōri* (表利); this is transmitted in the *Kōketsu* scroll. Details are mentioned in the scroll *Yugake no Maki*.

---

332 It is not clear if the measurement should be 1 *sun* 8 *bu* or either 1 *sun* or 8 *bu*.

胴肩衣之事
Dōkataginu no koto

SLEEVELESS TOP

Add any pattern you wish to the *dōkataginu*. It is sleeveless and crests should be put on the back. Secure the cords with toggles.

DOKATAGINU

Commentator one

This is similar to the normal *kataginu* jacket, but should be worn under the outer sash.

Commentator two

The *dōkataginu* has pleats at the shoulders, but there are a variety of styles. Details are in a scroll called *Setsuryaku*. These are not meant for ordinary *samurai* and are made of satin or other such materials.

陣羽織之事
Jinbaori no koto

BATTLE JACKET
[WORN OVER THE ARMOUR]

Details for this are given in another writing.

JINBAORI

Commentator one

One theory says that the *gusoku-baori* (具足羽織) jacket for armour is mentioned in the document *Genpuku no Ki* (元服之記) and that during the period of Daiei (1521–1528) the Shōgunal deputy called Hosokawa Takakuni [used it]. There is a wide range of varieties and colours, so they are not discussed here. However, there is one type called the *koromo haori* (裳羽ヲリ), which is similar to a monk's robe.

Commentator two

There is a variety of styles. Details are found in the scroll *Setsuryaku*.

陣引膚之事
Jinhikihada no koto

SWORD SCABBARD COVER FOR WAR

This should be made of a fabric called *sutamen* (スタメン)[333] or dyed leather when using a scabbard in normal times. When making a scabbard for war, do not decorate the scabbard cover.

In addition to this, understand that on a *tachi* great sword, use a metal *tsukagashira* pommel head and simplified versions of any metal fittings on the scabbard or other metal attachments.

Commentator two

In a military context, the term *oshihada* (押膚) is used, which means a scabbard cover to 'push forward with'.[334] Remember, if you use a normal scabbard then you should have a *hikihada* cover for it. However, a scabbard cover is not necessary for *jinkoshirae* (陣拵), which are swords with battlefield mounting. Remember that *jinkoshirae* is a style that does not have mountings such as those normally found on the pommel and scabbard.[335]

---

333 A fabric of wool and linen imported from Holland or made locally in imitation of the Dutch version.

334 *Oshi* (押), means 'to push forward', 'to advance'. In contrast, *hiki* (引) means 'to pull back' and thus should be avoided.

335 Most likely this means to use a simplified version in battle.

CHAPTER THIRTY-FOUR

指物之事
Sashimono no koto

BANNERS[336]

四半
Shihan
Square banner[337]
The shape is known as *shihō* (四方).

シナイ
Shinai
Single-pole flexible banner
The width of this is double the standard for cloth, but the length may vary.

折掛シナイ
Orikake-shinai
Banner with horizontal banner pole

Commentator one
This has a horizontal pole.

---

336 Not all the banner names are direct translations of the ideograms. Some translations derive from the shapes of the banners as they appear in later volumes of *The Book of Samurai* series. The original ideograms are here for reference.

337 This is not actually square, but shorter than other standards.

ツエツキ
Tsuetsuke
Triangular banner[338]

Commentator one
This is the same style as the *irokogata* (イロコガタ) fish-scale banner.

吹ヌキ
Fukinuki
Cylindrical flag

アンカウ
Ankō
Horizontal drawn-bow shape with streamers

ノフスマ
Nobusuma
Simple round streamer

Commentator one
This is similar to the *minote* (ミノテ) style.

エツル
Etsuru
Three splayed branches

シデ
Shide
Banner made with sacred paper

---

338 The original ideograms mean 'cane' and 'use', but the illustrations within Natori-Ryū show a triangular flag. Outside the Natori-Ryū context, this term can be used for any small flag.

キラキラ

Giragira

Crenellated flag

ハタ

Hata

Standard

ノホリ

Nobori

Slender banner[339]

ナヒキ

Nabiki

Curved banner

ヲンヘイ

Onbei

Draped sacred strips of paper

サイ

Zai[340]

War baton flag

ホンテン

Bonden

Shugendō prayer flag

---

339 Normally, the *nobori* is understood to be a long, slender banner. However, in the Natori-Ryū encyclopedia the name is changed to *shi* and the shape is short and square. We have followed the general understanding, which is also followed in the Tōkyō transcription, but know that another version exists.

340 Normally said as *sai*, but phonetics in other documents give the pronunciation *zai*.

白熊
Haguma
White bear flag

Commentator two
There is also the *shaguma* (赤熊) red bear flag and the *koguma* (黒熊) black bear flag.

カブロ
Kaburo
Bobbed hair of a youth flag

イロコ
Iroko
Fish-scale flag

Commentator two
The above banners are for normal use and there are set rules for constructing them. Measurements for large and small banners are transmitted in the scroll *Hata no Maki*, but only the names have been listed here.

御免之指物
Gomen no sashimono
Permitted banners
In addition to the banners listed above, there are fifteen other types and these are called *gomen no sashimono* (御免之指物) – permitted banners. They are as follows:[341]

磔
Haritsuke
Crucifixion banner

---

341 Illustrations of these are given in later volumes.

香車
Kyōsha
***Shōgi* chess piece banner**

Commentator two
The *shōgi* piece banner represents a determination not to yield an inch.

五輪
Gorin
Five-step *stupa* banner

塔婆
Tōba
Grave tablet banner

帘
Sakabayashi
Straw bundle banner

Commentator one
The *sakabayashi* style consists of straw bundles and represents *shishu* liquor stored in a large cup.[342] This flag represents a determination to die and an attitude of embracing each and every day of your life.

Commentator two
The *sakabayashi* banner is a mark of distinction.

位牌
Ihai
Buddhist memorial tablet banner

---

342 In Japanese culture, the *sakabayashi* represents the start of the season for alcohol.

猪
Inoshishi
Boar banner

Commentator one
There are upper and lower kinds of this flag, but the lower version is used by many.

Commentator two
The *inoshishi* banner demonstrates an intention to rush headlong into the enemy.

鐘
Tsurigane
Temple bell banner

Commentator two
The *tsurigane* banner is intended to be like a 'surprise to the ears of the enemy' and still works as a mark.[343]

一文字
Ichimonji
Ideogram 'one' banner

イロハ
Iroha
ABC banner

Commentator two
The *iroha* banner represents a model for people to follow.

---

343 This can be a flag with a bell image or a three-dimensional bell marker. The idea is that like a bell it shocks and surprises people.

天蓋
Tengai
Canopy banner

菖蒲
Shōbu
Shōbu **leaf banner**

Commentator two
The *shōbu* banner is a visual play on words: as well as being the name of a plant, the word *shōbu* also means 'victory in battle'. Therefore, carrying this banner represents an intention to gain victory that day.

打出
Uchidashi
Fringed banner

制札
Seisatsu
Prohibition board banner

Commentator two
The *seisatsu* banner rules over people with authority.

枯首
Sharekōbe
Skull banner

There is no definitive way to construct the banners listed above. All are described in another writing.

Commentator two

The fifteen banners above are higher ranking. [Among these fifteen,] the five banners below all represent a determination to die without fear:

1. *haritsuke* 磔 – crucifixion banner
2. *gorin* 五輪 – five-step stupa stone banner
3. *tōba* 塔婆 – grave tablet banner
4. *ihai* 位牌 – Buddhist memorial tablet banner
5. *tengai* 天蓋 – canopy banner

[The last banner can be swapped with the] *sharekobe* (枯首) skull banner.

The above list of [fifteen] banners show proud intentions and therefore they are to be given only by permission of the general (*shō*) and only to *samurai* who have achievements to their name. That is why they are named *gomen no sashimono* – permitted banners.

Another banner, called the *soboro* (ソボロ), is a vertical straw bundle, which represents the intention to attain 100 achievements.

There are also the following banners:

- *shugasa* 朱傘 – red parasol banner
- *noborigaki* 上り柿 – climbing persimmon banner
- *rokuji no myōgō* 六字ノ名号[344] – six-character Buddhist prayer banner

These can be worn if the general permits it. Take heed: if you do not have determination enough for the banner, you had better not wear it. However, this principle does not apply to banners that have been passed down for generations due to the achievements of a person's ancestors. During the invasion of Korea, the warrior Atobe Kii no kami, who was under the control of the warrior Asano Nagaakira, wore a banner depicting a straight spear.

Lastly, red military gear should be deemed as the [illegible ideograms] of the clan.

Tradition says that when writing ideograms on a banner, write them so that the [strokes in each] ideogram join together without a gap.

---

344 This refers to the six-character Buddhist prayer *namu ami dabutsu*.

Commentator two

When you write [on a banner], use the style of *kakariji* (カカリ字)[345] and fill the banner up to the edges. The style of *kakariji* is to write without spaces between strokes. If it happens that you do [or have to] write with gaps between the ideograms, then the ideograms have to be fully separated.

横手之金ノ事
Yokote no kane no koto
HORIZONTAL PARTS OF A BANNER POLE

柄杓
Hishaku
Ladle-handle-style horizontal part

Commentator three

[This horizontal bar] is metal and inserts into the bamboo.

折金
Oregane
Angled-metal horizontal part

---

345 A stylized, almost block-like form of writing, often used in modern Japan for events such as sumo and theatre. The actual text shifts between ideograms and strokes. So, most likely this means that all strokes and all ideograms should be joined up.

Commentator two
Both these horizontal parts should be made of iron so that they will not break.

竿留之クダノ事
Saodome no kuda no koto
TINY CYLINDERS TO PREVENT THE BANNER FROM FLYING UP IN THE WIND
There are multiple ways to construct this; however the version shown below is most desirable.

Commentator two
Make this by cutting thin bamboo and passing the strings through the cylinders. This will secure [the banner] so that it will not be blown up in the air by the wind.

指物竹之事
Sashimono-dake no koto
BAMBOO BANNER POLE
Use *uchitake* bamboo for this [which is strips of bamboo laminated together]. Also, in some cases you should have a *tsugitake* joint [which is made out of metal]. The type of [naturally tough] bamboo known as *ishihara* is desirable, but avoid using older plants. Ancient ways state that bamboo should be cut on the first day of the eighth month and that you must be facing *from* the direction of *kikigami* (聞神) *to* the direction of *gyokujo* (玉女) on that particular day.[346] There are other important ancient teachings to keep in mind about bamboo.

---

346 See pages 401–2.

Commentator one

The bamboo should not have its surface scraped off; this is disliked, because it is associated with the word *metsubushi*, which means to blind.[347]

The direction of *gyokujo* is the ninth direction from the zodiac sign for that day.

The direction *kikigami* is the third direction from the zodiac sign for that day.

Commentator two

The word *uchitake* used previously means bamboo that has been beaten as is done when creating a [laminated] bow. Furthermore, *uchitake* bamboo [when reconstructed from beaten bamboo into its final shape] can be pentagonal, octagonal or another such shape.

The word *tsugitake* used previously means that the pole has metal joints.

The word *ishihara* used previously refers to bamboo that is naturally tough.

The reason to avoid old bamboo is that it sometimes breaks because it has worms inside it. The secret traditions are transmitted below.

WHEN TO CUT BAMBOO

According to an old method, cut bamboo on the fifteenth day of the eighth month, facing the direction of *gyokujo* from the direction of *kikigami* after establishing [which of the Five Elements] the bamboo is. [You can discover the element by] looking for a knot [on the bamboo below] the first joint. Also, there is an important tradition about bamboo to be passed on.

Commentator two

Concerning the Five Elements in relation to bamboo: as is known, east is associated with Wood, south is associated with Fire, west is associated with Metal, north is associated with Water and the four corners are associated with Earth. [Therefore make sure to follow the Cycle of Creation when you take up a banner pole:]

---

347 The connecting sound here is *me*, which refers to the surface of the bamboo and its grain and is also a part of the word meaning 'to blind'.

- If the bamboo is of the element of Metal, the person should be of the element of Water.
- If the bamboo is of the element of Water, the person should be of the element of Wood.
- If the bamboo is of the element of Wood, the person should be of the element of Fire.
- If the bamboo is of the element of Earth, the person should be of the element of Metal.
- If the bamboo is of the element of Fire, the person should be of the element of Earth.

Cut bamboo of the appropriate direction [explained below] so that it [flows with the Cycle of Creation] for the element of the person it will be used with. [According to the Cycle of Destruction:]

- Water destroys Fire.
- Fire destroys Metal.
- Metal destroys Wood.
- Wood destroys Earth.
- Earth destroys Water.

[To discover the direction the bamboo is connected with,] observe the [lower part of the] bamboo. If it has an 'eye' or knot on the first joint from the ground, [then the direction that the knot is facing] is deemed to be the direction, and therefore the element, of that bamboo.

Any 'eyes' should *not* be shaved off due to a verbal association [with blindness].

The directions of *gyokujo* and *kikigami* were mentioned earlier. Also, the fifteenth day of the eighth month [which is the day you should make the banner pole] is in the middle of autumn, so is an excellent time to do this. One theory says that over the first fifteen days of a month [the energy of the period] increases, and over the last fifteen days of a month [the energy] decreases. The fifteenth day is in the middle [of the month], so the properties of that time are excellent.

- If the knot faces east, the bamboo is of the element of Wood.
- If the knot faces west, the bamboo is of the element of Metal.
- If the knot faces north, the bamboo is of the element of Water.
- If the knot faces south, the bamboo is of the element of Fire.

Consider this so that the bamboo fits with your own element [in the Cycle of Creation and Destruction].

A further tradition for bamboo banner poles is this: apply fire to straighten fresh bamboo so that it will not break. Take note, this is an important tradition.

腰桶之事
Koshioke no koto

CONTAINERS ATTACHED TO THE WAIST

- *ōgimentsū* 扇メンツウ – fan-shaped box
- *marumetsū* 丸メンツウ – round box
- *kori* コリ – rectangular box
- *uchigai* ウチカイ – waist bag[348]
- *waramentsū* ワラメンツウ – container made of straw

There are various types, but they all serve the same purpose and therefore there is nothing more to record on this matter.

Commentator one

Tradition says that they contain what you should not forget [to carry] when going to battle, but if they become too weighed down with food this can be detrimental. Therefore, use lightweight containers. Be aware that good lids will help you to be able to drink water or soup from them.

---

348 This item has been listed using phonetics rather than ideograms and therefore the meaning is lost. It may be a container to carry food.

Commentator two

The *waramentsū* straw container listed above should be made by weaving together *shibe* – the central stalks of dried rice plants [as shown below]. Rations are of primary importance in warfare. However, once the food has been eaten, you do not want the empty container still to be heavy [and therefore straw is useful because of its lightness].

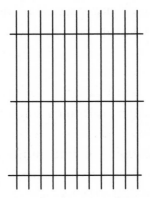

水呑之事

Mizunomi no koto

Water flask

Use a bamboo cylinder. However, a leather drawstring pouch will serve just as well. Sometimes water can be drawn using a folded paper container. There is no more to be recorded on this matter.

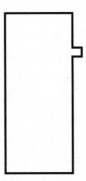

Commentator two

Bamboo containers are used to suck water from. Leather drawstring pouches should be stitched up tightly and folded paper containers should have the astringent juice of persimmons applied to them [to make them waterproof].

Bamboo flasks should have joints at the top and bottom and a hole in the middle [section] so that you can drink water from it. For emergency situations, soak water into floss in one of the above [containers].[349] The paper container has an oral tradition attached to it.

---

349 The cotton or linen floss can then be squeezed out whenever drinking water is required. This is a way to reduce evaporation and sloshing of water while travelling.

CHAPTER THIRTY-FIVE

鑓之事
Yari no koto

SPEARS

Any blade shorter than 7 *sun* is said not to pierce a person's armour right through to the back plate. The shape of the blade can be of any design – forms vary from school to school and therefore the subject is not discussed here. The length of the shaft will depend upon the person. Also, a ring to attach a marker should be fitted [to the spear shaft].

Commentator one
Marks should be attached to spears and should be treated as a form of *umajirushi* – a standard for ordinary *samurai*. Sometimes torches should be attached [to spears] to help attack *shinobi no mono* infiltrators at nighttime.

Commentator two
Concerning the measurement of 7 *sun* and a spear not being able to pierce through a body: there is a gap between the armour and the body measuring 1 *sun* 5 *bu*. [This is at the front and the back,] so it adds up to 3 *sun* in total. The torso itself measures 4 *sun* [from front to back].[350]

A spear marker should be attached to the *shirushitsuke no wa* ring for the identification marker.

---

350 The measurement of the torso plus the gaps at the front and back make a total of 7 *sun*, meaning that any spear head shorter than this will not pierce through to the other side of the body.

Sometimes, when trying to stab at *shinobi no mono* and so on, a torch should be attached.

HOLES IN THE BUTT OF THE SPEAR

It is desirable to have a hole in the butt of the spear.

Commentator one

The butt of a spear should have a hole through it. This is to make it easier to pull out a spear that has been thrust into the ground. Also, the hole will take a rope for use during a ship battle and wood can be inserted through it to help when crossing a marsh.

Commentator two

The hole in the butt of a spear is used for attaching a *tenawa* – 'rope to keep in hand'. This is useful for times such as in ship battle or when aiming to stab at people who are in a lower position than you are. Also, when in a marsh or other such place, put wood through the hole [so that you can use the spear as a support to cross the area].

Yarijirushi identification markers on spears are strips of cloth of various shapes and colours that have the family crest or writing upon them. This is a way from old times. Alternatively, secure a bird feather to your spear or use cut sections of paper. Do this to make identification marks.[351]

It is said that at the battle of Nagakute, the warrior Ōsuga Gorōzaemon acted as *shingari* rear guard when the army was in retreat. He defended against the enemy using a pike with a handle that was 3 ken long.

---

351 On the spear a small ring is positioned to attach an identification marker. These markers as described in the text are used when armies form up and march together so that the various allied clans can be identified.

袋鑓
Fukuroyari
SHORT-BLADED SPEARS
How to use a *fukuroyari* short-bladed spear[352] is an oral tradition.[353]

Commentator two
Fukuroyari spears have easily replaceable blades, which can be put on a new bamboo staff if the original handle breaks. If the broken part is long enough, shave and smooth it down to reuse it.

Commentator three
Fukuroyari spears are good because they can still be used if the handle is broken.

PARTS OF A SPEAR

1
ホ先
Hosaki
Tip

2
シヲ首
Shiokubi
Throat of the blade

Commentator one
This is also known as the *kerakubi* (ケラ首).

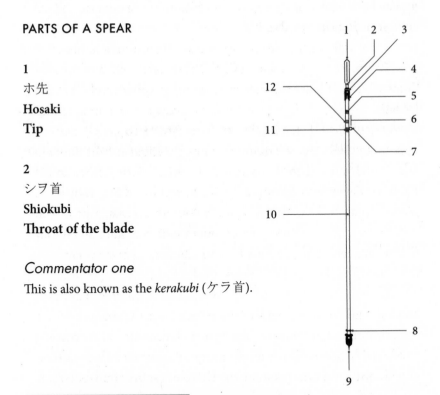

---

352 This is a spear that has a socketed and detachable blade.
353 This article is missing from the Tōkyō transcription.

3

クチ金

Kuchigane

Metal collar

4

サカハ

Sakawa

Metal sleeve

5

胴金

Dōgane

Metal securing ring on the shaft

6

太刀請

Tachiuke

Position where an [enemy] great sword is received

This is also called the *tachiuchi* (太刀討) – the section where a great sword strikes.

7

カギトメ

Kagitome

Fitted ring

Also known as the *shirushitsuke no kan* (印付ノ環) – the identification marker ring.

8

ミツカヘシ

Mizugaeshi

Water collar[354]

---

354 A metal collar that strengthens the lower part of the shaft, which is the area most

9

石付

Ishizuki

Metal spear butt

10

柄

E

Haft

11

血留胴金

Chidome dōgane

Blood-stopping band

Commentator two

This is also known as the *kaburamaki* (カフラ巻).[355]

12

中胴金

Naka-dōgane

Halfway metal ring

Turtleshell-patterned spears and white-handled halberds

From ancient times there have been:

- *taimai no yari* タイマイノ鑓 – the turtleshell-patterned spear
- *shirae no naginata* 白柄ノ長刀 – the white-handled halberd

The handle of the turtleshell-patterned spear should be of *nashiji*, which is 'pear skin' style [and has lacquering with extremely fine silver powder]. This kind of spear should be carried only by the *taishō* commander.

---

vulnerable to damp and rot.

355 Most likely this should read *kazuramaki* – rattan ring.

Commentator one

The *taimai no yari* turtleshell-patterned spear should be the *taishō* commander's own spear. There should be a marker (探り) to help identify the direction of the blade edge.

Issui-sensei says

Concerning the white-handled halberd:

The *shirae no chōtō* white-handled halberd should be 7 *shaku* 5 *sun* long and the blade should be 1 *shaku* 7 *sun* long.

The [*hamon* hardening line on the blade] should be of the *komidare* (小乱) style, which is to have a fine wave pattern. However, it should not use the style known as *yakidome* (焼留). Know that there are various ways of tempering [a blade].[356]

The point of the blade (*kissaki*) should have lines in *hakikake* (ハキカケ) style, which look like the marks left by a sweeping brush. This is sometimes also called *chiriharai* [which means dust traces of that which has been swept away].

The groove (大樋) [in the blade] should start from the *mitsugashira* (三ツ頭) section [which is below the tip of the spear blade] and the inside of the groove should be coloured in red.

The style of *saba no o* (鯖尾), the split tail fin of a mackerel, should be used for the end (*ishizuki*).

There should be something brave carved onto the *sakawa* sleeve [which is part 4 of the previous diagram]. Finally, the handle should also have a guiding mark to help identify the blade-edge side.

These ways are from *koryū* – old schools.

Commentator one

[Weapons] with silver-plated handles are described as *shirae* – white-handled. However, take care, as those with silver wrapping along the scabbard and the handle are known as *hirumaki* and are also described in the same way [as *shirae* – white-handled].

---

356 The text is not specific enough to know which part of the sword-making process this is referring to.

Taimai no yari turtleshell-patterned spears and spears with red handles are reserved for *samurai* who have achieved and the *taishō* commander.

Commentator two

While staying in Suruga province, the lord [Tokugawa Ieyasu] prohibited everyone from carrying a red spear. However, when the warrior Hosokawa Etchū no kami was assigned to the construction of the castle, one *bugyō* commander under him carried such a red spear and everyone who saw this reported it to the lord. However, the lord said that he was a warrior who had attained an excellent achievement the previous year at the battle of Nagakute. This warrior's name was Sawamura Daigaku. [The lord] said that he prohibited carrying red spears except by men of achievement, and so he ordered them to leave the warrior be.

鑓休之事
Yariyasume no koto
SPEAR RESTS

There are traditions [for spear rests] and their use with the outer *obi*. You can use the toggle (根付) of a pouch or a bent iron. These are attached to the waist [and connected to the spear so that a warrior can couch his lance].

There are oral traditions to be passed on for the above.

Commentator two

This is the *kinchaku no netsuke* – the toggle of a pouch [which can be used as a spear rest].

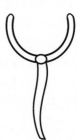

小荷駄ツゞラノ事
Konida tsuzura no koto

WICKER BASKETS FOR PACKHORSES

These are cylindrical baskets that have half-opening lids at each end. This type of basket is convenient for inspections. There is an oral tradition for this.

Commentator one
Points about inspecting these baskets are mentioned in detail in the scroll *Ippei Yōkō* [and involve checking for infiltrators who may be hiding in them].

Commentator two
Inspect inside these baskets, because a single person can hide within them. These inspections are also performed to prevent people from putting futons or bedclothes in the baskets. The half lid should be made like a door and the measurements should be similar to those of *yokotsuzura* side baskets; the diameter should be about 2 *shaku*.

ツゞラカゴ二入ル道具
Tsuzura kago ne ireru dōgu
TOOLS TO BE PUT IN PACKHORSE BASKETS
- *kama* 鎌 – sickle
- *nata* ナタ – hatchet
- *nokogiri* 鋸 – saw
- *kiri* 錐 – drill
- *tettsui* 鉄槌 – hammer
- *kugi* 釘 – nails
- *hasami* 鋏 – snippers
- *kaginawa* 鍵縄 – hook and rope

- *kumade* 熊手 – rake
- *kuwa* 鍬 – hoe
- *tōguwa* 唐鍬 – hoe with a square-edged blade
- *hosobiki* 細引 – thin rope

Any handles on the above tools should be short.

柿紙之事
Kakigami no koto

STRENGTHENED PAPER[357]

This is 1 *ken* 2 *shaku* long and 3 *shaku* 5 *sun* wide. Have loops 5 or 6 *sun* long at the four corners and also [in the middle] of both sides. Lastly, use hemp rope [to give it strength].

Commentator two

Strengthened paper can be used to enclose outside areas.

小屋柿紙
Koyakakigami
STRENGTHENED PAPER FOR HUTS
This is 2 *ken* long and 1.5 *ken* wide. Again, position the loops [at the corners and sides] and attach hemp rope [to give it strength].

Commentator two

This is to cover a roof.

---

357 Paper that has been treated to make it waterproof for use on campaign, e.g. to cover hut roofs, etc.

内カコイ

Uchikakoi

STRENGTHENED PAPER FOR INSIDE ENCLOSURES

This is 3 *ken* long and 3 *shaku* wide. It is used to keep servants (小者) separate [from others].

甲立之事
Kabutodate no koto

HELMET-CARRYING POLE

This is 6 *shaku* 5 *sun* long and has a hemisphere[358] of 7 *sun*. There is also a way to stand banners correctly, but this is in another writing.

Commentator two

Details for this are in the *Kabutodate no Maki* – 'The scroll of the helmet stand'.

It is not known when the *kabutodate* helmet-carrying pole came into use. The length is 6 *shaku* 5 *sun* and the circumference [of the hemisphere that holds the helmet is] 6 or 7 *sun*. There are no set rules, so it can be made in any form you wish. One that is triple forked at the top can also be used for crossing over walls or as a spear. There is also a type of static helmet stand for the display of a helmet. There is no extra information to be given on normal versions.

Kabutodate helmet poles are to be carried when marching.[359]

---

358 This is the part at the top of the pole that holds the helmet.
359 Helmets were carried on long stands alongside the *samurai*.

入子鍋之事
Irekonabe no koto

FITTED PAN SETS[360]

These are the same as regular pan sets. They should be kept in a wooden container with handles. There is another utensil called a *chōdo* (調度), which is made of copper. You can have your servant wear it as a helmet if need be. However, it is normally used for cooking, so it is best to have rings to hold it. The shape should be the same as a hat (笠).

Commentator one

One set should have seven or nine pans in total. The pans should be made of copper, but iron will do and the wooden container should have handles. Make sure to dry the wood fully in the sun before you construct the container [otherwise it will warp]. Iron rings should be fixed in various positions and the rest of the rings can be of bamboo. [The container] can also be used for drawing water in a battle camp. The item known as the *chōdo* should be made of thin copper or iron and be shaped like a helmet, although it does not have the *shikoro* neck plates attached. This is good for *komono* servants to wear. In the field, they should be used for cooking rice and boiling water, but can be used as helmets at other times. In one foreign country, it is said that attacks were orchestrated using signals made by beating drums and *chōdo*. The *chōdo* is the same tool as mentioned above.

---

360 A series of cooking pans that fit into each other.

物縫針之事
Mononuibari no koto

SEWING NEEDLES

Keep thread with these and carry three rolls of bleached ramie. There is an oral tradition for this.

Commentator one

This [equipment] can be used to repair any damage to the six important cords [of your armour]. It can also be useful if you lack thread or rope, and of course for a lot of other purposes.

笠之事
Kasa no koto

HEADGEAR

Create the form first and then paste multiple layers [of paper] and finally apply persimmon tannin juice [to make it waterproof]. There is also a version called the *mawarigasa* (廻り笠) rotating hat – there is nothing further to record here.

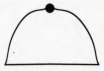

Commentator one

In the reign of the forty-fifth emperor, Shōmu, in Tenpyōshōhō 3 (749–757), a retainer of the general Tamura called Kasashige invented *kasa* headgear.

Commentator two

The *mawarigasa* rotating hat has a two-tiered structure with a [vertical] axle inside [to hold the tiers together], which is what allows it to rotate. This is convenient when you are in the woods or the like [because the rotation stops the hat catching on branches].

唐笠之事³⁶¹
Karakasa no koto

PARASOLS

The largest versions should be 8 *shaku* long; medium-sized ones should be 7 *shaku*; and the smallest should be 5 *shaku*. The length of the bag is 1 *jō* 2 *shaku* 5 *sun*. The *sagari* – a hanging string hem and fringe – is 1 *shaku* 5 *sun* [long]. It should be made of three [standard widths of] cloth. The cord should be made of black leather and should be tied with a dragonfly knot (蜻蛉結). The length of the leather cord should be 1 *shaku* 5 *sun* or alternatively 9 *sun* 2 *bu* and [the ends] should be cut like a sword tip.

Commentator one

The *sashigasa* (指カサ)³⁶² parasol was introduced during the reign of the seventh emperor, Kōrei.

Commentator two

It is hard to understand exactly what parasols should be like only from this text. This subject is a secret tradition among *shokugen*, who are those well versed in court and military practices – so you should study with them. Also, the drawings are in the *Setsuryaku* manual.

---

361 長柄傘 in the Koga transcription.
362 An alternative name for the *karakasa* parasol.

OTHER MILITARY TOOLS

The following items are described in other scrolls:

- *ōgi* 扇 – fan
- *uchiwa* 團 – war fan
- *taiko* 太鼓 – drums
- *maku* 幕 – war curtains
- *saihai* 采拝 – war baton

Commentator two

Details on these are in the thirteen scrolls.[363]

Uchiwa war fans are not for combating the heat but are a part of military equipment. It is said that this equipment will protect you from arrows and bullets. These should be carried by senior military officers (軍監). When the warrior Minamoto no Yoriyoshi attacked Abe Sadatō, it suddenly began to rain and visibility became poor, so he used his war fan to command his men and won. The war fan has been used ever since.

Drums came into use in [military command] some time around the period of Minamoto no Yoshitsune.

Saihai war batons originated from rods (鞭) or sacred staffs (御幣) that were offered at shrines. The *saihai* war baton was used for the first time by Prince Shōtoku when he subjugated Moriya. According to one document (宋朝會), there were three colours of the *saihai* war baton:

1. 黄 – yellow for the emperor (天子)
2. 朱 – red for kings (諸王)
3. 纁 – dark red for ministers (吏士)

---

363 Possibly an error, most likely the twelve scrolls of the Natori-Ryū encyclopedia.

Warriors of 2,000 *koku*[364] [or more] should use dark red.

FIRE TOOLS

Details on the following are also in other scrolls:

- *taimatsu* 炬 – torches
- *hinawa* 火縄 – fuses
- *dōnohi* 胴ノ火 – ember-carrying cylinder
- *noroshi* 狼煙 – fire signals
- *hiya* 火矢 – fire arrows
- *kagari* 篝焼 – battle camp basket fire
- *tōyu* 湯油 – tung oil

Commentator two

Details on these are in the *Gunyaku Yōhō* scroll.

Large and small *noroshidai* – bases for launching signals – should be built in accordance with the geography.

Put fuel such as grasses in the base to start the fire.

---

364 A *koku* is a unit of rice, enough to feed one person for a year. It was used as a form of salary to be shared out among a *samurai*'s family and servants. A warrior of 2,000 *koku* would have been a high-ranking *samurai*.

具足櫃之事
Kusokubitsu no koto

ARMOUR CONTAINERS

These are made of *kiri* wood[365] with good quality lacquer applied. Construct them so that they can also be used as water buckets. The *kabutobako* helmet box can be used as a bucket for a well and horses can be fed porridge from the lid.

There are no set rules for these subjects; it is just a matter of putting things to good use.

Commentator two
There is a type of armour container called the *tōgogata*, which is used in the Kantō region, but any type can be used. However, the above points should be considered.

馬具之事
Bagu no koto

TOOLS FOR HORSES

馬屋幕
Umayamaku
STABLE CURTAINS
Umayamaku (馬屋幕)[366] are curtains for the stable. They should be higher than a human and need to be 5 to 6 *shaku* wide.

---

365 *Paulownia tomentosa.*
366 The Koga transcription uses the ideograms 厩幕.

Commentator two

The *Ippei Yōkō* scroll explains how to install *umayamaku* stable curtains. The main reason for the curtains is to stop horses being able to see a long way, because this tends to make them go wild. They also help to stop the horses becoming irritated by noise made by lots of people passing by.

鞍之事

Kura no koto

SADDLES

Those saddles without the *umi* (海) curved part at the front and rear [which can be held on to] should be avoided, as saddles that are easy to grip should be used. It is desirable to secure and tie [the saddle] firmly. There are oral traditions for this.

Commentator two

The front and rear parts are made of naturally curved wood with grains [that flow along the same lines].

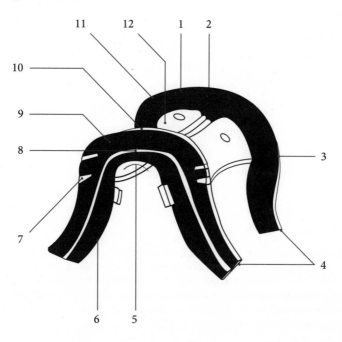

1

後輪

Shizuwa

Cantle (the hind raised support)

2

磯

Iso

Rear raised mound[367]

[This is not shown in the image, as it is located at the rear.]

3

切組

Kirigumi

Joint between the main saddle seat base and the saddle board

4

つま先

Tsumasaki

Saddle edges[368]

5

洲濱

Suhama

Gullet

This is also known as the *waniguchi* (鰐口).[369]

---

367 The front and rear boards of the saddle, which hold the rider in place, have both a flat panel and a raised support area. These are known as the 'beach' and the 'sea', because, viewed from the side, they resemble the mound of the beach as it meets the sea.

368 The lowest edge of the ends of the curved panels at the front and rear of the saddle.

369 This is a reference to the shape. It can mean either a form of bell used in temples and shrines or a crocodile's mouth.

6

鞍通

Kuradōshi

Slot for the stirrup leathers[370]

7

手形

Tegata

Hand grips[371]

These are also known as *tegake* (手掛).

8

前輪

Maewa

The complete front saddle board

9

海

Umi

Upper saddle board

10

山

Yama

Mountain[372]

---

370 The name is not an exact match for the current recorded name. However, the similarity between the terms makes it highly probable that this is what is meant.

371 Small cut outs in the main front saddle board to hold on to.

372 The highest point on both the front and rear saddle boards.

11

折目

Orime

Mound ridge

12

居木間

Igiai

Saddle seat

COUNTING AND VOCABULARY CONNECTED WITH SADDLES[373]

- To count one saddle use the term *hito-kuchi* (一口).
- To count one pair of stirrups use the term *hito-kake* (一懸).
- To count one *kittsuke* saddle pad use the term *hito-se* (一背) or *ippiki* (一匹).
- To count one *wake* (分) [unknown] use the term *hito-kukuri* (一括).
- To count one *migaki* (三垣) [unknown] use the term *hito-hikibun* (一匹分).
- To count reins use the term *hito-suji* (一筋).
- To count *kuchiwa* horse bits use the term *hito-kuchi* (一口).
- To count one *shōzoku* set of clothes use the term *mina* (皆).
- To count one *gu* set of military gear use the term *hito-yoso'oi* (一装).

For saddling a horse use the term *shibaru* (縛) – to tie.

For unsaddling a horse use the terms:

- *orosu* 卸 – to lower
- *toku* 解 – to untie
- *menzuru* 免 – to release

Commentator one

Tegata handholds were invented during the Heiji rebellion (1160) when

---

373 The Japanese counting system is complex and uses different terms depending on the object being counted. The following list only gives examples of one of each item; a *samurai* would then understand the correct terminology to continue counting within each system. This section is extremely vague in the original text. It originally appears as a memory hook and therefore we have had to add some words to make it comprehensible.

[Minamoto no] Yoshitomo was defeated and fled to the eastern area. It was early in the first month, with cold temperatures and snow. [Minamoto no] Tomonaga was frozen through and found it hard to mount his horse. When the warrior Akugenta Yoshihira saw this, he told him to create a handhold so that he could mount more easily. At this point the warrior Kamata Masakiyo made a handhold with his sword [for the warrior Tomonaga to mount].

Concerning the *aori* saddle skirt: during the period of Genryaku (1184–1185) the warrior Yoshitsune crossed over the mountain path called Hiyodori to attack the castle of Ichinodani. It was the sixth day of the second month, the valley was filled with snow and the horses were frozen up to their bellies and unable to move. This is what prompted the warrior Yoshitsune to instruct people to make these *aori* saddle skirts for the first time. The episode was recorded in the *Taiheiki Taizen* (太平記大全) document. I think that the saddle skirt had been square shaped until the reign of the Taikō Hideyoshi, but then the lord Hideyoshi called over [his famous tea master] Sen no Rikyū when he was viewing the riding horses and told him to improve the form [of the saddle skirt]. Consequently, the type we use now was designed by Rikyū based on his tastes and style. This information came from Sen no Sōsa Zuiryū [who was a disciple of the tea master].

The form of saddle skirt invented by Yoshitsune is now called a *numauke* (沼請), which means 'to receive the mud'. It is said that at some point this form was divided into two sections. The ideograms used for *aori* are 'mud' (泥) and 'to prevent' (障), making it the skirt that 'prevents mud'. However, I consider [the origin story concerning Yoshitsune to be] implausible.

Commentator two

For saddles during a military campaign, use *nerigura* (ネリクラ) hardened leather saddles. They should have higher saddlebows than normal saddles and should generally be larger.

The warrior Kamata Hyōe Masakiyo was having difficulty riding a horse because his hands were paralyzed with cold, so Akugenta Yoshihira suggested making handholds [on his saddle]. Masakiyo carved them out with his sword. That was the origin of handholds [of the saddlebow].[374]

---

374 While the essence of the story remains the same as the version in the main text, the

鐙之事
Abumi no koto
STIRRUPS
These should be made of metal. However, wood is preferable when you cross a river.

Commentator two

Wooden stirrups are good for river crossing, whereas stirrups made of iron are good for defending against arrows. In a battle camp [metal stirrups] are sometimes used as *kaketōdai* (カケ燈臺) hanging candle holders.

The word for stirrup, *abumi*, is a contraction of *ashibumi*, which means 'to tread on'. Stirrups were made of wood in ancient times but they were later replaced with iron versions. Know that wooden stirrups are called *kiabumi* (木鐙) and iron ones are called *kaneabumi* (金鐙).

力革之事
Chikaragawa no koto
STIRRUP LEATHERS
This is the leather that connects the stirrup [to the tack]. You should use a longer length for longer journeys.

Commentator two

One teaching on horse-riding says that the benefit of using longer leathers for longer distances is that it helps to prevent fatigue.

鞅鞦
Munagai
CHEST COLLARS
Know that extravagant chest collars are not beneficial.

---

characters' roles are different in this commentary.

Commentator two

Extravagant ones are not good. Above all else, ordinary *samurai* should avoid being flashy.

腹帯之事

Harubi no koto

SADDLE GIRTHS

These should be doubled up. Also, there is a way called *hishi harubi* (菱腹帯), the crossed saddle girth. There are metal fittings to put on the girth.

Commentator two

The metal fittings and style known as *hishi harubi* are hard to understand without demonstrating them in the flesh. Details are not mentioned here.

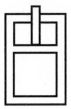

手綱之事

Tazuna no koto

REINS

Silk crepe is best, but bleached cloth can also be used. Insert chain inside them. Furthermore, reins should be black, as this is the colour of victory (勝色). Wrap both sides [around the hands]. When going to war wrap them outwards, and when returning wrap them inwards.[375]

Commentator two

Chains should be inserted inside [the reins] from the *mizutsuke* (水付) ring [which is the ring that the reins are attached to] and should continue for 3 *shaku* [up the reins].

---

375 i.e. when going out to war the reins extend to the horse on the outside of the rider's hand, and when returning from war they extend on the inside of the hand.

Black wins over all colours and for that reason it is called the colour of victory; this is an ancient way. During a campaign you should use *kiritazuna* (切手綱) separated reins. The reason for using two separate cords is so that one cord can be tied off to each hand. These separated reins should be tied loosely together [when not in use].

轡之事
Kutsuwa no koto
BITS
The *hami*, which is the mouthpiece of the bit, varies between different schools of horse-riding.

Commentator two
For *shinobi uma* horses moving in stealth, wrap the bits with paper. For this, thicker bits are desirable.

旅鼻革之事
Tabihanagawa no koto
TRAVELLING NOSEBANDS
These are the same as the normal version.

柄杓之事
Hishaku no koto
LADLES
Although some people say to avoid using metal ladles, they do have some advantages. Wooden ones are said to be preferable for river crossings [because of their lightness]. There is a tradition for the handle.

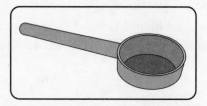

Commentator two

[Metal ladles] are good for giving horses medicine, as this can be done through the inside of the handle[376] and they are also good for decocting medicine. While metal ladles are heavier [and add to the overall weight to be carried], they should still be used for these reasons.

麻履之事

Asagutsu no koto

STRAW HORSESHOES

These should be worn for the same reason that humans wear *waranji* straw sandals.

馬鎧之事

Umayoroi no koto

ARMOUR FOR HORSES

This should generally be a lightweight form of armour. This also applies to the *hitaigake* forehead cover and the *habaki* gaiters.

雑鞭之事

Zōmuchi no koto

RIDING CROPS FOR LOWER-CLASS PEOPLE

This means *hananeji* nose twisters and you should be equipped with these. There are no extra notes for this article.

計曳之事

Kebiki no koto

PLIERS

Commentator two

This tool is used to remove objects like caltrops from a horse's hoof. It can also be used to repair armour.

---

376 A metal ladle with a hollow handle. The cup end can be used for mixing the medicine and then the medicine can be fed to the horse through the handle, which has a spout.

Commentator three

Attach pliers to the *shiode* saddle rings as shown in the drawing below.[377]

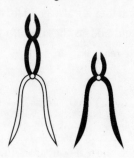

四益四加
Shieki shika

THE FOUR BENEFITS AND FOUR ADDITIONS

The above is a survey of military tools. However, you should use whichever tools are beneficial, whether they have been listed above or not. There is a teaching that should be applied to military gear called *shieki shika* (四益四加) – the four benefits and four additions.[378] Consult experienced and older men and do not carry tools that have no use. There is a tradition in military ways (兵法) where only eighty per cent [of tools] are used.

Commentator one

Concerning the skill of *shieki shika* – the four benefits and four additions.

---

377 In the drawing, the pliers on the left have a cloth or cord attached so that they can be secured to the saddle rings.

378 Although the two commentators give different examples to illustrate this teaching, the principle remains the same. It is a question of having four essential items and four that can be added but are not needed to carry out the function.

四益
Shieki

The four benefits are:

1. *tazuna* 手ヅナ – reins
2. *harubi* ハルビ – girth
3. *kutsuwa* クツハ – bit
4. *abumi* アブミ – stirrups

四加
Shika

The four additions are:

1. *shirigai* シリカイ – cruppers
2. *munagai* ムナカイ – martingales
3. *shiode* シヲテ – saddle horn
4. *chikaragawa* 力革 – stirrup leathers

The principle of *shieki shika* should not be limited to horse gear, but can relate to anything. Therefore, think carefully about each item, its uses and its benefits.

Overall, about eighty per cent of military gear (兵具) should be used. Know that the number eight is a number that has a minor element of *in*, but also remember that the element of *in* is disliked as it represents retreating. However, [this eight-out-of-ten principle] should be followed, because when something is pushed to the extreme it is transformed into an element of *yō*, which represents advancing.

[An explanation of the element of *in* within numbers][379]
- The number six is *daiin* (大陰) – the greater element of *in*.
- The number four is *shōin* (小陰) – the lesser element of *in*.
- The number eight is *rōin* (老陰) – an older element of *in*.

---

379 Additional information on the power of numbers and their relationship to the concept of *in* and *yō*. However, some of this differs from the latest research, so the commentator may have made some mistakes or this might be a variation or older system.

Commentator two

Shieki, the four benefits [of samurai armour], are:

1. *uwaobi* 上帯 – outer sash
2. *kurijime* クリシメ – armour-securing cords
3. *hachimaki* 鉢巻 – headband
4. *shinobi no o* 忍緒 – helmet cords

Shika, the four additions [of horse gear], are:

1. *tazuna* 手綱 – reins
2. *harubi* ハルビ – girth
3. *omogai* ヲモカヒ – headstall
4. *shirigai* 尻カヒ – crupper

These should be carried as additions, because they are easy to break when in use.

Normally, only eight out of ten parts of military gear are used. Remember that using a full set brings full benefit, but using only six or seven [out of ten parts] will not be satisfactory. Therefore, using eight out of ten parts [of military gear is considered best]. This concept of eight out of ten applies not only to military gear [but also to other elements]. This will make more sense when it is transmitted later.

This is the end of the scroll on *heigu* military gear. As there are no old men of achievement any more, you should rely instead on warrior families (軍家) to make sure that you will not be left vulnerable [in times of war].

GLOSSARY

asa 麻 – linen

bu 分 (i) – unit of length equivalent to approximately 3 millimetres

bu 武 (ii) – from *bushidō, bushi, budō*; pertaining to the military

budō 武道 – from its context and positioning within the original scrolls, generally translated as 'way of the *samurai*' in this book and not as 'martial arts'; it can also mean 'military rule'

bugei 武芸 – military arts and martial skills

bugyō 奉行 – commander or magistrate, a person of importance in both military and civilian life; the specific role may be further defined by a prefix, e.g. *yari-bugyō*, spear commander

buke 武家 – warrior families

bun 文 – literary arts and civilian life; see *bunbu*

bunbu 文武 – considered as the 'brush and the sword', meaning both military and academic study; warriors of Japan were taught military ways, but also the arts and literature; the concept can be broadly defined as elements needed for both war and civilian times

bushi 武士 – alternative name for *samurai*

chi 気 – the well-known Chinese concept of energy that flows through the body, most commonly understood as 'life force'; although often considered a mystical, metaphysical, atmospheric energy, *chi* can also refer to practical elements such as dust and clouds

chō 町 – unit of length equivalent to approximately 108 metres

chūgen 中間 – servants or people of lower rank

dō 道 – a path of life or a subject deeply studied, translated in the text as 'Way' or 'way'; the 'Way' is an overarching spiritual or moral path, whereas a 'way' is a practical set of techniques, e.g. 'the way of tea', 'the way of the sword', etc.

dōshin 同心 – a social level normally found at the lower end of the *samurai* class

Five Elements – see *gogyō*

gogyō 五行 – the Five Elements; the theory behind the foundation of all creation, in which five elements, namely Wood (木), Fire (火), Earth (土),

Metal (金) and Water (水), interact with each other in a creative or destructive way

gunbai 軍配 – esoteric side of warfare, including religious ritual, astrology, performance, etc.

gunbaisha 軍配者 – person who understands the esoteric aspects of military ways (*gunbai*), including assessing time, direction, stars and elements of luck and leading the worship of military deities

gundō 軍道 – the military way or path

gunjutsu 軍術 – military skills, practical warfare methods

gunpō 軍法 – 'military ways', the tactics of war

gunpōsha 軍法者 – person who understands the 'military ways' of *gunpō* and who is considered to be a high-level tactician

gunsha 軍者 – *samurai* of normal level who understands military ways and is considered to be part of the core military personnel

gusoku 具足 – military gear; this may also refer specifically to 'compact armour' to draw a distinction with *ōyoroi*, 'great armour'

haramaki 腹巻 – early Japanese armour; literally meaning 'belly wrapping', it was wrapped from the front and fastened at the rear

hei 兵 – pertaining to the military, e.g. soldier or weapon, or a military mindset

ikusa-bugyō 軍奉行 – minister of war; a position at the highest level of the army; two *ikusa-bugyō* generally make up one pair of the six members of the main command team; see *roku bugyō* (six *bugyō*)

in 陰 – originating in Taoist theory of the birth of the universe, this is one of two complementary forces that represents the dark, negative, female, moon, etc.; known as *yin* in Chinese; see also *yō*

ippei 一兵 – independent soldier, i.e. a retained soldier of warrior status and trained in the arts of warfare, who is in the service of a specific lord

ito 糸 – cords and lacing used to bind armour together

jikkan 十干 – the Ten Celestial Stems, a set of ten concepts from Chinese thought, consisting of five pairs that relate directly to the Five Elements, e.g. fire-larger, fire-lesser, water-larger, water-lesser, etc.; they also form the basis of a ten-day cycle and are often used in conjunction with the Twelve Earthly Branches (see *jūnishi*)

jō 丈 – unit of length equivalent to approximately 3 metres (or exactly 10 *shaku*)

jō-chū-ge 上中下 – ranking system of higher, middle and lower; often used in classifying achievements or skills

jō-shōgun 上将軍 – overall military commander of a force

jūnishi 十二支 – the Twelve Earthly Branches, understood as equivalent to the signs of the zodiac; the hours, days, months, years and directions are all divided into twelve and allocated one branch, each of which is represented by an animal; starting in the north and moving in order they are: rat, ox, tiger, hare, dragon, snake, horse, ram, monkey, cockerel, dog and boar; often used in conjunction with the Ten Celestial Stems (see *jikkan*)

kan 貫 – unit of weight equivalent to 3.75 kilograms; also a unit of currency

kashira 頭 – captain of men; often used as a general term to denote a leader

katana 刀 – long sword

ken 間 (i) – unit of length equivalent to approximately 1.8 metres

ken 権 (ii) – concept of responsive balance, according to which when one element outweighs an opposing element, the opposing element must adjust; e.g. if the enemy makes a movement to one area, the defending commander must respond to it

ki 気 – Japanese spelling of *chi*

Kōshū-Ryū 甲州流 – military school comprising teachings from retainers of the Takeda clan

kubō 公方 – term used for a *shōgun* in peace, or, in ancient times, the emperor

kumogata 雲形 – small decorative plates of gold or gold plate around the rim of a helmet that make an abstract cloud shape; they normally fit between the vertical ridges of a helmet

kun 君 – overall lord, main leader of an entire force; very similar to *shu*

kyojitsu 虚実 – concept of substantial and insubstantial

men 綿 – cotton

monomi 物見 – group of scouts

mononofu 武 – alternative reading of *samurai*

nuinobe 縫延 – method of connecting, or giving the appearance of connecting, small plates of armour; the two basic forms are *hon-nuinobe*, in which individual *sane* plates are laced together, and *nuinobe*, in which a single plate is made to look like multiple plates; see drawing on page 365

odoshi 威 – the concept of lacing armour together

ōmatoi 大纏 – larger battle standard

ōsō 王相 – concept that associates the energy of each season with a particular direction

ōyoroi 大鎧 – great armour; style of armour used in the first half of the *samurai* era, consisting of laminar style in the main and large shoulder guards known as *osōde*; sometimes the word is also used to refer to armour in general

roku bugyō 六奉行 – the 'six *bugyō*'; the lead command team, which regulates the army and is made up of three pairs: two *ikusa-bugyō* (ministers of war), two *hata-bugyō* (flag commanders) and two *yari-bugyō* (spear commanders)

rōnin 牢人 – *samurai* without a master, i.e. one who is not employed or retained

sakite 先手 – vanguard

sangun 三軍 – 'three armies'; a Chinese military concept to represent the full force of an army combined; the three forces are led by the upper *shōgun*, the *shōgun* of the left and the *shōgun* of the right

sarashi 曝布 – bleached cloth made of the ramie plant and later of cotton

seppuku 切腹 – ritual self-disembowelment with a dagger, normally assisted by a retainer

setsu (節) – timed judgement or to judge accordingly

shaku 尺 – unit of length equivalent to approximately 30 centimetres

shin 臣 – general of a troop or, in peace, a minister

shinadare シナダレ – decorative lines on a helmet; often in groups of three and gold in colour, they represent a Chinese-style sword

shinobi 忍 – secret agent, spy and commando-infiltrator; also known as a *shinobi no mono* and more commonly today as a *ninja*

shō 将 – general of a force

shōgun 将軍 – leader of a force; can also refer to a peacetime political leader, such as Tokugawa Ieyasu, but in these scrolls it refers to a military position

shu 主 – main military leader of a force, also known as *jō-shōgun*; very similar to *kun*

sun 寸 – unit of length equivalent to approximately 3 centimetres

tachi 太刀 – great sword; longer than a *katana*, a *tachi* is generally worn blade-edge down when in armour

taishō 大将 – main leader or lord; translated in the text as 'lord commander'; often used to simply mean leader

teaki 手明 – utility troops who have not been assigned a specific role and can be called upon to help in any situation

Ten Celestial Stems – see *jikkan*

tsubo 坪 – unit of area equivalent to either 1 *ken* square (1.8 square metres) or 3 *ken* square (5.4 square metres) depending on date and usage

Twelve Earthly Branches – see *jūnishi*

umajirushi 馬験 – 'horse marker', a standard or three-dimensional marker used to mark out a warrior's horse so that specific warriors can be identified on the battlefield

Way/way – see *dō*

yō 陽 – originating in Taoist theory of the birth of the universe, this is one of two complementary forces that represents the light, positive, male, sun, etc.; known as *yang* in Chinese; see also *in*

yon bugyō 四奉行 – the four commanders; leaders in a *samurai* army, they predominantly deal with the organization, maintenance and distribution of the army finances and logistics

yoriki 与力 – a form of support warrior added to squads of men; they are distributed among the army and assist captains where needed

zōhyō 雑兵 – lower-level soldiers and aides

INDEX

WATKINS
Sharing Wisdom Since 1893

The story of Watkins began in 1893, when scholar of esotericism John Watkins founded our bookshop, inspired by the lament of his friend and teacher Madame Blavatsky that there was nowhere in London to buy books on mysticism, occultism or metaphysics. That moment marked the birth of Watkins, soon to become the publisher of many of the leading lights of spiritual literature, including Carl Jung, Rudolf Steiner, Alice Bailey and Chögyam Trungpa.

Today, the passion at Watkins Publishing for vigorous questioning is still resolute. Our stimulating and groundbreaking list ranges from ancient traditions and complementary medicine to the latest ideas about personal development, holistic wellbeing and consciousness exploration. We remain at the cutting edge, committed to publishing books that change lives.

DISCOVER MORE AT:
www.watkinspublishing.com

Read our blog

Watch and listen to
our authors in action

Sign up to
our mailing list

We celebrate conscious, passionate, wise and happy living.
Be part of that community by visiting

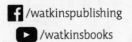 /watkinspublishing   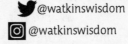 @watkinswisdom

/watkinsbooks   @watkinswisdom